FIVE CHAPTERS ON RHETORIC

FIVE CHAPTERS ON RHETORIC

CHARACTER, ACTION, THINGS, NOTHING, AND ART

Michael S. Kochin

The Pennsylvania State University Press
University Park, Pennsylvania

LIBRARY OF CONGRESS CATALOGING-IN-PUBLICATION DATA

Kochin, Michael Shalom, 1970–
Five chapters on rhetoric : character, action, things,
    nothing, and art / Michael S. Kochin.
            p.   cm.
Includes bibliographical references and index.
Summary: "Examines concepts for persuasive
communication. Explores the art of rhetoric and how
it aids in clarification when we speak to communicate,
but also helps to protect us from clarity when we speak
to maintain our connections to others"—Provided by
publisher.
ISBN 978-0-271-03455-3 (cloth : alk. paper)
1. Political oratory—United States.
2. Rhetoric—United States.
3. Persuasion (Rhetoric).
I. Title.

PN4193.P6K63 2009
808—dc22
2008036902

The Pennsylvania State University Press is a member of
the Association of American University Presses.

It is the policy of The Pennsylvania State University
Press to use acid-free paper. This book is printed on
Natures Natural, containing 50% post-consumer waste,
and meets the minimum requirements of American
National Standard for Information Sciences—Perma-
nence of Paper for Printed Library Material,
ANSI Z39.48–1992.

לזכרו של סרן משה טרנטו (הנדסה קרבית),
שנפל בפעולה מבצעית בציר פילדלפי, ט״ז כסלו תשס״ה.

In memory of Capt. Moshe Taranto (IDF), age 23,
killed in action 29 November 2004.

Combat engineers . . . have an unofficial, very
cynical and very ancient motto: "First we dig 'em,
then we die in 'em," to supplement their official
motto: "Can do!" Both mottoes are literal truth.

—ROBERT A. HEINLEIN

CONTENTS

ACKNOWLEDGMENTS

"The easiest way to guarantee failure with any perceptive audience," Wayne Booth reminds us, "is to be seen in advance as an expert in rhetoric." Whatever failings I have as a student of rhetoric are despite the efforts of the institutions, colleagues, and friends who have done so much to help me.

I first began thinking about the themes of this book as a Social Sciences and Humanities Research Council Postdoctoral Fellow at the University of Toronto and was supported at subsequent stages by an Alon Fellowship from Israel's Council for Higher Education, a Dan David Prize Research Scholarship from the Dan David Prize, and a Laurance S. Rockefeller Visiting Fellowship at Princeton University's Center for Human Values. I owe a great deal to the students who subjected these ideas to sometimes hostile but always serious and thoughtful critique in my courses on rhetoric at Tel Aviv and Yale, and I also benefited from the comments and questions of seminar audiences at Tel Aviv, Princeton, and Yale, and panel audiences at the 1998 and 2003 meetings of the Midwest Political Science Association. George Anastaplo, Norma Thompson, Joseph Macfarland, Katherine Philippakis, Alasdair McIntyre, Clifford Orwin, Alkis Kontos, Daniel Doneson, Alberto Spektorowski, Eyal Chowers, David Schaps, Tamar Meisels, Arlene Saxonhouse, Jerry Schneewind, Roslyn Weiss, Daniel Markovitz, Adam Kissel, Paul Perritore, Walter Nicgorski, Catherine Zuckert, and Levis Kochin helped with various parts of the story. Nathalie Moise served as my research assistant for a brief but vital period. Wade Gungoll, Yitzhak Harari, Zeev Emmerich, Charles Blattberg, Gad Barzilai, Ivan Donchenko, Meir Fenster, and Anna Kochin read drafts of *Five Chapters,* and M. J. Devaney, the copy editor for Penn State Press, did much at the eleventh hour to clarify both expressions and thoughts. I was encouraged at crucial moments by the three Steves: Steve Lenzner, Steve Elkin, and Steve Fuller. Were it not for the work of Irad Kimhi and of Josiah Ober the book could not have been conceived.

Some of the material in chapter 1 was previously published in "Individual Narrative and Political Character," *Review of Metaphysics* 55, no. 4 (June 2002): 691–709. Copyright © 2002 by *Review of Metaphysics*. Reprinted with permission. Material in chapter 2 was previously published in "Time and Judgment in Demosthenes' *De Corona*," *Philosophy and Rhetoric* 35, no. 2 (2002): 77–89. Copyright © 2002 by Pennsylvania State University Press.

INTRODUCTION

The fundamental elements of public persuasion might appear most clearly in a public speech that lays out the principles of public speaking. To find such a speech we would do well to look back to an age when public speaking and rhetorical education were more highly esteemed than they are today and sift through the speeches and writings of those who were considered by the educated taste of those times to be the most eloquent and persuasive speakers. Following these principles, we might light on the noted English advocate Lord Brougham's essay on Demosthenes or the youthful Winston Churchill's short sketch "The Scaffolding of Rhetoric."[1] But for a concise statement of the central truths of persuasion we can do no better than the address "Adams and Jefferson" by Daniel Webster or, as he was known to contemporaries enthralled by his oratory, "Godlike" Daniel Webster.

Webster, at that point a former New Hampshire congressman and leading member of the Boston bar, was chosen to eulogize John Adams and Thomas Jefferson at a memorial meeting in Faneuil Hall on 2 August 1826, less than a month after their deaths on the fiftieth anniversary of the Declaration of Independence, 4 July 1826. To present the life and public character of John Adams, Webster invented a speech Adams might have given in the debate on the question of independence in the Continental Congress.[2] Webster had to invent a speech to put in Adams's mouth, since even by Webster's time the great speeches of the revolutionary period, most of which had never been written down, had largely been lost to memory.[3] Jefferson's

1. Winston S. Churchill, "The Scaffolding of Rhetoric," in Randolph S. Churchill, companion volume, pt. 2, to *Youth: 1874–1900*, vol. 1 of *Winston S. Churchill* (London: Heinemann, 1967), 816–21; Henry Brougham, "A Critical Dissertation upon the Eloquence of the Ancients," in *Speeches of Henry, Lord Brougham*, 4 vols. (Edinburgh: A. and C. Black, 1838), 4:427–519.

2. Daniel Webster, "A Discourse in Commemoration of the Lives and Services of John Adams and Thomas Jefferson," in *Webster's Great Speeches* (Boston: Little, Brown, 1879), 156–78.

3. Barnet Baskerville, *The People's Voice: The Orator in American Society* (Lexington: University Press of Kentucky, 1979), chap. 1.

public character had less need of Webster's powers of invention, since Jefferson could claim the central political act of the Revolution, the Declaration of Independence—as Webster himself says in the speech, "the merit of this paper is Mr. Jefferson's."

By inventing a speech that Webster claims to be exemplary of Adams, Webster is effectively, and principally, praising himself. Webster shows Adams to be a master of true eloquence in a speech that displays, at its glittering surface, Webster's own eloquence.[4] But Webster's preface to his fictive Adamsian speech provides a theory of rhetoric in itself:

> The eloquence of Mr. Adams resembled his general character, and formed, indeed, a part of it. It was bold, manly, and energetic; and such the crisis required. When public bodies are to be addressed on momentous occasions, when great interests are at stake, and strong passions excited, nothing is valuable in speech farther than as it is connected with high intellectual and moral endowments. Clearness, force, and earnestness are the qualities which produce conviction. True eloquence, indeed, does not consist in speech. It cannot be brought from far. Labor and Learning may toil for it, but they will toil in vain. Words and phrases may be marshaled in every way, but they cannot compass it. It must exist in the man, in the subject, and in the occasion. Affected passion, intense expression, the pomp of declamation, all may aspire to it; they cannot reach it. It comes, if it comes at all, like the outbreaking of a fountain from the earth, or the bursting forth of volcanic fires, with spontaneous, original, native force. The graces taught in the schools, the costly ornaments and studied contrivances of speech, shock and disgust men, when their own lives, and the fate of their wives, their children, and their country, hang on the decision of the hour. Then words have lost their power, rhetoric is vain, and all elaborate oratory contemptible. Then patriotism is eloquent; then self-devotion is eloquent. The clear conception, outrunning the deductions of logic, the high purpose, the firm resolve, the dauntless spirit, speaking on the tongue, beaming from the eye, informing every feature and urging the whole man onward, right onward to his object—this, this is eloquence; or rather, it is something

---

4. See James M. Farrell, "The Speech Within: Trope and Performance in Daniel Webster's Eulogy to Adams and Jefferson," in *Rhetoric and Political Culture in Nineteenth-Century America,* ed. Thomas W. Benson (East Lansing: Michigan State University Press, 1997), 27.

greater and higher than all eloquence,—it is action, noble, sublime, godlike action.[5]

Webster shows how this true eloquence results not merely in words or speeches but in action. We judge a speech, Webster teaches, by the character of the speaker as displayed in the speech, when we perceive the speaker's "clear conception," "high purpose," "firm resolve," and "dauntless spirit." There is an art of rhetoric taught in the schools; this Adams had surely mastered in his years of formal education, but school rhetoric in itself yields only "vain oratory." Not all oratory is vain: in eulogizing Adams and praising himself, Webster aims to teach us the difference between vain oratory—mere human words—and true eloquence—godlike action.

True eloquence is rare because most human things are determined in their courses by preexisting relationships rather than by communicated information; as the sociologist of science Bruno Latour writes, it is only at certain moments that "the strength of a word may sway alliances and demonstrate something, where very, very rarely everything else being equal, someone speaks and persuades."[6] Yet through speech and writing, and through conscious reflection on the available means of persuasion, we can reweave community and thus reconfigure the world and our relations within it.[7] We talk to maintain a relation, and we talk to communicate something to those with whom we share a relation.

To sustain our social lives we frequently refuse to assess the statements made to us. "That's interesting," we reply to the crank at the cocktail party. A large part of my work in this study will be to determine the extent to which speech and writing are used to protect human relationships from the threat of ever-changing facts and circumstances. As Goethe wrote, "We politely misunderstand others so that they shall misunderstand us in

5. Webster, "John Adams and Thomas Jefferson," 167.

6. Bruno Latour, "Irreductions," 2.4.3, in *The Pasteurization of France*, trans. Alan Sheridan and John Law (Cambridge, Mass.: Harvard University Press, 1988), 183–84. That it is very difficult to change minds, much less behavior, through words is well known to both advertising professionals and parents, but this difficulty seems not to be taken seriously by communication scholars and psychologists studying persuasion experimentally; contrast Michael Schudson, *Advertising: The Uneasy Persuasion* (New York: Basic Books, 1986), and Herbert E. Krugman, "The Impact of Television Advertising: Learning Without Involvement," *Public Opinion Quarterly* 29, no. 3 (1965): 349–56, with Rebecca L. Collins, Shelley E. Taylor, Joanne V. Wood, and Suzanne C. Thompson, "The Vividness Effect: Elusive or Illusory?" *Journal of Experimental Social Psychology* 24, no. 1 (1988): 1–18.

7. See Steve Fuller, *Philosophy, Rhetoric, and the End of Knowledge: The Coming of Science and Technology Studies* (Madison: University of Wisconsin Press, 1993), 18.

return."[8] Human relations are complex, mutable, subject to decay over time, and therefore fragile. Goethe's point is that we preserve these complex relations by refusing to judge one another by the truth or significance of our statements.

The most extreme example of abstaining from judgment in order to mend the fraying bonds that connect us with each other can be found in the psychotherapeutic setting. In Haruki Murakami's novel *Norwegian Wood*, the main character visits the patients in a liberally administered mental hospital:

> "What do you people talk about?" I asked Reiko, who seemed not quite to get my meaning.
>
> "What do we talk about? Just ordinary things. What happened today, or books we've read, or tomorrow's weather, you know. Don't tell me you're wondering if people jump to their feet and shout stuff like 'It'll rain tomorrow if a polar bear eats the stars tonight!'"
>
> "No, no, of course not," I said. "I was just wondering what all these quiet conversations were about."
>
> "It's a quiet place, so people talk quietly," said Naoko. She made a neat pile of fish bones at the edge of her plate and dabbed at her mouth with a handkerchief. "There's no need to raise your voice here. You don't have to convince anybody of anything, and you don't have to attract anyone's attention."[9]

This is an example of conversation without any communicative interest whatsoever; the human interest in saying something of relevance to our quotidian concerns is dissipated by the rules and structure the asylum provides. But this complete suspension of interested motives for talking is only possible in an asylum cut off from the world, whose patients are not self-governing in their relation to the outside world. For those of us outside the asylum, in terms of our life lived in language, the way that the patients go on in Murakami's novel is a form of death, sometimes temporary, sometimes permanent. Max Horkheimer has suggested that we look to philosophy "to keep the course of humanity from resembling the meaningless round of the asylum inmates' recreation hour."[10] In this book, I look not to

---

8. Johann Wolfgang von Goethe, *Torquato Tasso* 5.5.3337–38, quoted in Nietzsche, "Richard Wagner in Bayreuth," in *Untimely Meditations*, ed. Daniel Breazeale, trans. R. J. Hollingdale (Cambridge: Cambridge University Press, 1997), 216.

9. Haruki Murakami, *Norwegian Wood*, trans. Jay Rubin (New York: Vintage, 2000), 106.

10. Max Horkheimer, *Eclipse of Reason* (1947; repr., New York: Continuum, 1974), 186.

philosophy as such, as Horkheimer suggests, but to our collective project of living together freely in the world. I look to politics and to the fundamental structures of persuasion that enable this project to be genuinely shared, that enable the project to be more than the manipulation of the many by the few or the one.

To understand the concept of communicative interest we must understand how something particular, some fact or proposal, emerges to prominence out of the mush of "information." How, as Walter Lippmann asked, can "news . . . separate itself from the ocean of possible truth"?[11] Our encounter with the facts, ordered and congealed out of the ocean of possible truth, is mediated. A genuinely disinterested party, one who had no interest in what use its audience made of the facts, would have to have no interest even in his or her own reputation as a reliable provider of relevant facts and so would be of no use to his or her audience. We therefore have no choice but to get our information from interested and thus biased sources, and we must endeavor to discount the interest motivating that mediation.[12]

A source can refuse to take a line openly; this is how the source lets the facts speak for themselves. Yet the information one presents should already be filtered by the interests of those to whom one is presenting it. Otherwise one will not merely be discounted, as happens to Lippmann's biased speaker—rather, as happens frequently to all speakers, one will be ignored.[13]

To explore the public sphere or the common, I focus on two fields of examples of the common: political rhetoric and scientific communication. Political rhetoric is illustrative because the public speaker lives "in the greatest fame and in the middle of the light of public things," as Quintilian wrote.[14] Both the scientific and the political communities are instantiations of the common—that is, structures through which speakers and writers persuade and are persuaded.[15] For our purposes in this book what

11. Walter Lippmann, *Public Opinion* (1922; repr., New York: The Free Press, 1965), 215.

12. Lippmann, *Public Opinion*, 158, 218–25; contrast Leo Strauss, *The City and Man* (Chicago: Rand McNally, 1964), 232–33, cited in Robert Howse, "Leo Strauss—Man of War? Straussianism, Iraq, and the Neocons" (unpublished MS, University of Michigan Law School, available at http://faculty.law.umich.edu/rhowse/Drafts_and_Publications/straussiraq.pdf, accessed April 2007).

13. Lippmann, *Public Opinion*, 241.

14. *In maxima celebritate et in media rei publicae luce vivendum est* (Quintilian, *Institutio oratoria* 1.2.18). All translations of extracts from *Institutio oratoria* are mine, except where otherwise noted.

15. "When done properly," Steve Fuller has written, "the philosophy of science is nothing other than the application of political philosophy to a segment of society" (*Social Epistemology* [Bloomington: Indiana University Press, 1988], 6).

is fundamental about political institutions is that in them we hold officials accountable for their official acts, in the paradigmatic case by constituting deliberative assemblies with legislative powers. What is fundamental about modern science as an example of the common is that it has been enormously successful not only in organizing communities of the human and the non-human, as Bruno Latour has emphasized throughout his work, but also in organizing communication about things among men and women.

The central institutions of modern science are the learned journal and the independent scientific association, both realized together in the Royal Society, founded in London in 1660. David Landes writes of Chinese science that what distinguishes its history more than anything else from that of Western science is that the scientific and technical results achieved in China in one place and time were not communicated or handed over in any organized fashion to contemporaneous or subsequent inquirers. The same results were repeatedly recreated; though some Chinese investigators were doubtless giants, in Newton's phrase, all stood on their own two feet.[16] It is this institutional network that we must understand, as Charles Peirce argues, if we are to see how the concrete life of both the scientist and the politician is lived within their respective institutions of communication: "But if I am asked to what the wonderful success of modern science is due, I shall suggest that to gain the secret of that, it is necessary to consider science as living, and therefore not as knowledge already acquired but as the concrete life of the men who are working to find out the truth. Given a body of men devoting the sum of their energies to refuting their present errors, doing away with their present ignorance, and that not so much for themselves as for future generations, and all other requisites for the ascertainment of truth are insured by that one."[17] Taking Peirce's remarks to heart, we can

---

16. David S. Landes, *The Wealth and Poverty of Nations* (New York: Norton, 1999), 51, 335–44. On the loss and reinvention of ideas, and on the way this cycle was overcome in the West by the widespread use of printing, see Elizabeth L. Eisenstein, *The Printing Press as an Agent of Change* (Cambridge: Cambridge University Press, 1980). That scientific progress depends on a succession of scientists having access to the results of the work of their predecessors, on which they then attempt to improve, is already noted by Francis Bacon (*The New Organon*, trans. Michael Silverthorne, ed. Lisa Jardine [Cambridge: Cambridge University Press, 2000], 13, 90). When David Hull claims that science is globally progressive while biological evolution is only locally progressive (*Science as a Process* [Chicago: University of Chicago Press, 1988], 464), he does not take account of the fact that the progressive character of modern science comes precisely from its having extended the web of science to cover the globe, making science local everywhere.

17. Charles Sanders Peirce, "Scientific Method," in *Science and Philosophy*, vol. 7 of *Collected Papers*, ed. Arthur Burks (Cambridge, Mass.: Harvard University Press, 1958), §50, cited in Jürgen Habermas, *Knowledge and Human Interests*, trans. Jeremy J. Shapiro (Boston: Beacon Press, 1971), 94.

then appreciate how facts and artifacts are produced in these institutions.[18] I offer the modern scientific community as an example of the common not out of any desire to debunk science but rather to put forward the institutions of modern science as structures of communication from whose very successes we have much to learn.

Rhetoric is systematic thought about how to move the audience to act or move it to refrain from acting. Within the institutions of public life and scientific research, I focus on what rhetoric can contribute to two different modes of organizing knowledge for action, the knowledge diffusion model and the knowledge mobilization model.

The knowledge diffusion model is expounded by the pioneer theorist of public relations, Edward Bernays, in his conception of propaganda or "public relations." Although Bernays's writings are not new, they have not been superseded: since Bernays had to argue for the use of new and controversial techniques of advertising, marketing, and public relations, his defense of these techniques is clearer than most of what has appeared in the subsequent literature teaching or criticizing the practices that Bernays had a key role in introducing.

In Bernays's story, there is knowledge among the few of facts and of interests—their own interests and the interests of others. "The politician understands the public. He knows what the public wants and what the public will accept." The public, however, is not initially equipped with self-knowledge, so the politician's understanding of facts and of interests has to be spread or propagated: one has to make the public understand both what it itself wants and what it itself can obtain. The principal obstacle to this propagation Bernays calls "social inertia," illustrated by Richard Steele's observation about Bernays's fellow progressive, Franklin Delano Roosevelt: "[Roosevelt] saw public attitudes not as a mandate for initiatives generated outside the White House, but as potential obstacles to courses he had already decided upon."[19] To minimize the inertia in the implementation of policy, the public

---

18. Arriving at an understanding of how facts and artifacts are produced both in public life and in scientific journals and organizations means replacing the Edinburgh "Strong Program" of explaining scientific knowledge and scientific error symmetrically with a more Fullerian or Paris School of Mines program of explaining knowledge in public life and knowledge in science symmetrically.

19. Edward L. Bernays, *Propaganda* (New York: Liveright, 1928), 96, 135; Bernays, *Public Relations* (Norman: University of Oklahoma Press, 1952), 123, 329, 330; Richard W. Steele, "The Pulse of the People: Franklin D. Roosevelt and the Gauging of American Public Opinion," *Journal of Contemporary History* 9, no. 4 (1974): 215, quoted in Samuel Kernell, *Going Public: New Strategies of Presidential Leadership*, 3rd ed. (Washington, D.C.: Congressional Quarterly Press, 1997), 23.

relations expert must be consulted in the formation of policy. Expert knowledge dictates the policy goals "in themselves," but these goals must be modified by public relations considerations. These public relations considerations are shaped by opinion polls. Using polls, the few that act can anticipate the effect of their actions. It is true that "in the interest of public relations, a client's policies and practices might have to be changed fundamentally" in order to "affect circumstances before they happen to make news." Bernays distinguishes his profession of public relations from the "zany world of press agentry" that preceded it by noting that "it is the public relations counselor's client's basic policy and practice that should be the determining factor in winning public understanding and support." The task of the public relations counsel is to advise the client on the proper manner of presenting the client's "basic policy and practices."[20]

On Bernays's account of public relations, the client's goals are formulated before the policy, and the policy is formulated before the public relations counsel is required to come up with a plan for presenting it. The role of the public relations expert is "engineering consent" to the policy. For Bernays, "objectives and goals are predicated on a coincidence of public and private interest," but his formulation assumes that interests are already formed and that this coincidence of public and private interest is perceived by the few whose peculiar interests are at stake rather than produced by the many acting on and with the few. Through the techniques of public relations, we can locate "opinion leaders," Bernays says, those whose opinions today determine the opinions of the public tomorrow.[21] Policy is then implemented by reaching out to the opinion leaders and through them to public at large. The intended audience for the propaganda, in Bernays's conception, has no role in formulating goals, in deciding on policies to achieve those goals, or in assessing achievements.

Bernays is thinking in terms of the example of the Catholic Church, which at one time, he claims, determined "all thinking," and of his uncle Sigmund Freud's program for the propagation of psychoanalysis.[22] But the central application for Bernays's understanding of public relations is marketing a product. Generally, the product is designed or invented and then must be marketed. Even if the product is designed at the same time that

---

20. Bernays, *Public Relations*, 86, 89, 94, 90; contrast Harry Reichenbach, *Phantom Fame: The Zany World of Press Agentry* (New York: Simon and Schuster, 1931).

21. Bernays, *Public Relations*, 73, 83, 254.

22. Bernays, *Public Relations*, 18.

the market for it is being investigated, the company's goal, making money from selling products, is nonetheless fixed.

Here we can see why Bernays's concept of propaganda cannot comprehend all of the possibilities for persuasion in politics. The concept of the public requires that there are no fixed goals of the sort that could be described as policy goals. The only determined goal of the public is to continue in existence through time, while goals and projects come and go.[23]

Yet Bernays's knowledge diffusion model can, notwithstanding its fundamental misunderstanding of the public or the common, successfully be imposed on a society. That is precisely why Ronald Reagan's old joke about the most frightening eleven words in the English language is so funny: "I am from the government and I am here to help," or as David Mamet glosses it: "I am going to suggest solutions to problems in which I'm not only uninvolved but to which I feel superior."[24] I am going to help my way, the way I have formulated before I propagate my plan to the public, with the assistance, as necessary, of public relations professionals. This preformulated policy I am going to propagate is, of course, what I take to be the right policy. Yet I am led to that policy not only by the case I have built for its merits but also because I "see like a state," to use James Scott's phrase.[25]

When the state learns to "see like a state," soon there is nothing to see except what can be seen from the state's perspective. Scott is concerned with conflict between state-imposed planning and "local knowledge," the wisdom, experience, and practical know-how that the targets of the state-imposed scheme have accumulated and to which they appeal in order to satisfy their needs. The fact that there is local knowledge contributes to our sense that something has been lost when we see a state-imposed "solution" that has

---

23. Michael Oakeshott's distinction between "civil associations" and "purposive associations" and F. G. Bailey's somewhat more resonant distinction between "communities" and "organizations" capture the idea of human associations whose only aim is their own continued existence versus those whose aim is to produce a separate product or carry forward a distinguishable purpose. See Oakeshott's *On Human Conduct* (Oxford: Oxford University Press, 1975) and F. G. Bailey's *Morality and Expediency: The Folklore of Academic Politics* (Oxford: Basil Blackwell, 1977).

24. David Mamet, *Three Uses of the Knife* (New York: Columbia University Press, 1997), 17.

25. James Scott, *Seeing Like a State: How Certain Schemes to Improve the Human Condition Have Failed* (New Haven: Yale University Press, 1999). See also Frantz Fanon on the postcolonial party-state under which the party is transformed from an instrument of mobilization into an "information service" ("The Pitfalls of National Consciousness," in *The Wretched of the Earth*, trans. Constance Farrington [London: MacGibbon and Kee, 1965], 145–46) and Ien Ang's discussion of "communication-as-transmission" ("In the Realm of Uncertainty: The Global Village and Capitalist Postmodernity," in *Communication Theory Today*, ed. David Crowley and David Mitchell [Stanford: Stanford University Press, 1994], 195–97).

failed to contribute to human betterment. There can be local knowledge, but there can also be the erosion of local knowledge. If the centralization of knowledge were simply an illusion, the Leviathan would be far less fearsome: the knowledge diffusion model indeed succeeds in making knowledge flow, in imposing knowledge developed at the center on the periphery. It is fitting that Bernays was so fond of the term "propaganda," because what is ominous about the Roman Catholic Congregation for the Propagation of the Faith—*Propaganda Fide*—is precisely the ability of the center to impose what it knows on the periphery, whether that knowledge is valid or useful under local conditions or not.

The knowledge diffusion model is just one way of organizing social knowledge, however. Bernays himself describes the knowledge diffusion model in terms of the "two-way street." On Bernays's account the public interest is but the distributed private knowledge of private interests, which the public relations expert can integrate. These private opinions of private interests are taken by the public relations expert as infallible in their sphere. The public relations expert simply integrates the private opinions of private interests with the private interest of his client, aiming to anticipate public reaction to the client's various possibilities of action. The expert thereby formulates the client's policy properly before selling that policy to the public, so that he or she can allow basic policy and practice to be the determining factor in winning public understanding and support. Bernays gives the prescription in simple language: "Finding out what people like and doing more of it, then finding out what people don't like and doing less of it." In following this prescription, one does not communicate with survey respondents but rather merely deals with their moods the way that a farmer would adjust his feed mix to minimize the complaints of a sick cow.[26]

But consider a knowledge mobilization model, instead of Bernays's knowledge diffusion model. Think of an audience as a mob that wishes to become an army: each must somehow contribute his own force to the collective, and the force must therefore be mobilized or directed in order to

---

26. Bernays, *Public Relations*, 5, 83, 86, 122, 90, 112. Leon Mayhew claims that Bernays and his predecessor Ivy Lee aspired "to represent the public to their client as well as transmitting the public to their client" (*The New Public: Professional Communication and the Means of Social Influence* [Cambridge: Cambridge University Press, 1997], 203–4), but Mayhew does not recognize that Bernays, at least, did not aspire to represent the public's beliefs faithfully in order to assess their truth but merely in order to weigh the extent to which they might drag down or boost the client's program. Contrary to Mayhew, therefore, the public relations counsel's inability to guide his client toward a "symmetrical version" of the two-way street is not a failure but an implementation of Bernays's understanding of the proper institutionalization of communication, namely, as knowledge diffusion.

effect change. Knowledge, in Bernays's account, is transmitted through a politics of issues rather than of personalities; in the mobilization model, on the other hand, knowledge is transmitted by mobilizing the knowers. The utopian limit of knowledge mobilization is set out by Hannah Arendt in her account of the council system in *On Revolution*, in which people move with their knowledge from the local to the regional to the national level. Through knowledge mobilization knowledge can be used collectively, not just for the collective, or in the interest of the collective, but by the collective. Through knowledge mobilization, knowing and doing, as Arendt says, remain united.[27]

On the knowledge mobilization model the politician seeks an understanding of policy through his or her operations within political institutions, just as the scientist seeks understanding through his or her operations within scientific institutions. This book makes use of sociology of science precisely because the social reality of science provides a well-studied model of a knowledge mobilization network and because science is a clear case where persons not only are put in the know and mobilized by the network but also are brought to labs, trained, and exported to other labs. Scientific knowledge is thus created and distributed throughout the network: it is not merely diffused through it from center to periphery. I appeal to this clear case to explain the unclear case of public life: because the social structure of science is well studied, the rhetorical concepts I want to explicate are more clearly visible in it. Yet at the same time we must remain aware of the ways in which the contemporary social structure of science fails to realize a knowledge mobilization model and thus fails to instantiate what Steve Fuller has called "a civic republican theory of knowledge management."[28]

The metaphor of mobilization is enlightening because to speak persuasively is "to effect social agreements that never before existed," just as the

27. Bernays, *Propaganda*, 101–2; Hannah Arendt, *On Revolution* (New York: Viking, 1963), 268. Arendt's paradigm wherein revolutionary councils serve as institutions for the mobilization of knowledge is, of course, the system of demes, council, and assembly that was the backbone of the Athenian democracy; for a brief and clear account of this historical instantiation of a knowledge mobilization model, see Josiah Ober, "Classical Athenian Democracy and Democracy Today," in *Athenian Legacies* (Princeton: Princeton University Press, 2005), 27–42. Walter Lippmann claims correctly that "the action of a group as a group is the mobilization of the force it possesses" (*The Phantom Public* [1925; repr., New Brunswick, N.J.: Transaction, 1993], 47). Where the knowledge mobilization model departs from Lippmann is in seeing this mobilization of force as a mobilization of *knowledge*. The public may not design the car, to use one of Lippmann's examples, but in choosing whether or not to buy the car it is acting on its opinion about the merits of the car, an opinion unlikely to be without reasonable grounds.

28. Steve Fuller, *Knowledge Management Foundations* (Woburn, Mass.: Butterworth-Heinemann, 2002), chap. 4.

citizen army emerges as a new thing out of the mob drilled to constitute it.[29] Insofar as things are socially constituted, that is to say, constituted by social agreement, to speak persuasively is to bring new things into existence. I explore how persuasive speech produces things, how persuasive speech reweaves our relations to others, and how a conscious art of persuasion contributes to that verbal productivity and reweaving in words. Bernays has given a clear and in many respects unsurpassed account of how a conscious art of persuasion can be put to work in diffusing knowledge. I aim to understand the role of an art of rhetoric in mobilizing knowledge.

Our quest for such an understanding of rhetoric as an aid to the mobilization of knowledge is built around five fundamental concepts that illuminate the possibilities and limitations of persuasive communication. The first chapter discusses character and what in Aristotelian rhetoric is called "ethical proof," or the argument for the truth of what is communicated based on the reliable character of the speaker. Insofar as most of what we know we learn from others, whether from their speech or from their writings, virtually all of our knowledge about actions and facts is mediated by our judgment of the character of those who communicate with us. Our judgment of those from whom we propose to learn depends on our judgment of their actions, which forms the subject of the second chapter. I explore the standards of judging action as they appear in the greatest surviving speech from the Athenian democracy, the speech *On the Crown* of Demosthenes. *On the Crown* not only defends Demosthenes' actions in counseling resistance to Philip of Macedon but sets out canons for assessing action, canons according to which Demosthenes demands that he himself be judged. In the third chapter, "Things," I explore the ways speakers persuade us of their knowledge of things by deploying concrete illustrations and making specific factual claims.

Chapters 1–3 explain how persuasive speech mobilizes audiences by making claims and presenting demands, but we also need to understand how speech is used to preserve the communities of trust necessary for claims to be presented, judged, and put into action. The fourth chapter, "Nothing," will illuminate how we speak sweet nothings, that is, how we talk so as to sustain human relations in the face of changes in our view of things. Thus we weave and reweave the web of human relations so that it will not be unraveled easily when we form new judgments and learn new facts.

---

29. Roderick P. Hart, *Verbal Style and the Presidency: A Computer-Based Analysis* (Orlando, Fla.: Academic Press, 1984), 6.

Finally, the last chapter, "Art," analyzes the central features of the conscious art of persuasion, the art of rhetoric, in the light of the preceding analyses of saying something (chapters 1–3) and saying nothing (chapter 4). The simplest possible way to understand the power of rhetoric is in terms of the notion that speech itself has power over thought and action distinct from the power of things or reasons. Rhetoric is then the art of applying this special power of speech consciously and therefore more effectively. Such an understanding was presented originally by the Greek rhetorical master Gorgias, who argues for the unique powers of his art by claiming that the effect of speech can be understood as the effect of a rarefied body emitted from the speaker that has an impact on the listener. In Plato's *Gorgias*, Socrates grants to the rhetorician an art sovereign over appearances and denies that public speech can show things as they are. Socrates thus accepts a fundamental premise of Gorgias's account: both Socrates and Gorgias contend that speech is some kind of thing, a kind of body for Gorgias, a kind of appearance for Socrates, and both therefore deny that speech is a mode of presenting or communicating things.

Only by rejecting both Gorgias's claim that rhetoric is sovereign over embodied speech and Socrates' reply that rhetoric may indeed be all powerful but only over appearances, can I clear the ground for an understanding of what rhetoric can and cannot do for us. Rhetoric, the conscious art of persuasion, offers limited but significant assistance in clarifying things for us. We can also put rhetoric to work to protect the relationships that make communication possible from the power of things or facts to subvert them.

Two rhetorical concepts I am not going to discuss thematically are argument (enthymeme) and the appeal to the emotions. From Aristotle to Chaïm Perelman and Jeffrey Walker, rhetorical theorists have written an enormous amount about enthymeme. Yet it is often forgotten that when you wish to move your audience to action, setting forth explicitly your premises, your inferences, and your conclusions often causes incredulity to creep back from your conclusions to your premises. Aristotle says that examples are no less persuasive than arguments, but here we will go along with Russell H. Conwell, the man who built Temple University from his proceeds on the lecture circuit: "People are more impressed by illustrations than by argument."[30]

---

30. Aristotle, *Rhetoric* 1.2.10, 1356b22–25 (all translations of extracts from the *Rhetoric* are mine); Robert Shackleton, "The Author's Life and Achievements," in Russell Herman Conwell, *Acres of Diamonds* (Joshua Tree, Calif.: Tree of Life Publications, 1993), 63–149, 138.

Arguments make the things argued for unclear or dubitable, where assertion or illustration makes things manifest or, even better, self-evident. Argument has acquired much of its luster illegitimately, because rhetorical theorists have failed to clarify the difference between argument and factual assertion, between the rational and the reasonable. It is far more important that our actions be justified in the light of the facts, that they be *reasonable,* than that they be justified in the light of our beliefs, that they be *rational.* Yet arguing is a substitute for providing facts—argument, as Jay Heinrich points out, "allows us to skip the facts when we have to."[31] Moreover, for arguments, changing beliefs is an end in itself, whereas for rhetoric, changing beliefs is only a means to the end of making the audience more prone to do what the speaker desires.[32] On those occasions when inference is necessary, the speaker should to the extent possible make his or her audience do the inferring.

When do we resort to argument? Aristotle claims that arguments excite the audience more than do examples, but real speeches heavy on arguments seem to aim to present the speaker as calm, serious, and knowledgeable.[33] In public life, one argues typically not to prove the claim for which one is arguing but to show that one shares the common prejudices or values that appear in the presuppositions and conclusions of one's argument and to demonstrate mastery of the subject matter by displaying relevant knowledge in coherently organized detail. Lincoln, appearing before a sophisticated New York Republican audience in his February 1860 Cooper Union address, displays his conservative commitment to constitutional government and his radical commitment to slavery restriction with a view to slavery extinction. Lincoln displays these judgments he shares with his audience by giving a detailed argument purporting to show that a majority of the members of the Philadelphia convention believed that putting slavery in the course of eventual extinction by preventing its territorial expansion was both desirable and compatible with the constitutional limitations on federal power. Lincoln does not need to convince his audience of the merits or constitutionality of slavery restriction—he needs to convince them that he is solid on slavery restriction and at the same time concerned (and competent) to manage slavery with a view to its eventual extinction in a manner compatible

31. Jay Heinrichs, *Thank You for Arguing: What Aristotle, Lincoln, and Homer Simpson Can Teach Us About the Art of Persuasion* (New York: Three Rivers Press, 2007), 122.

32. John C. Maloney, "The First 90 Years of Advertising Research," in *Attention, Attitude, and Affect in Response to Advertising* (Hillsdale, N.J.: Lawrence Erlbaum, 1994), 40.

33. Aristotle, *Rhetoric* 1.2.10.

with the Constitution. The knowledge, commitments, and sobriety of Lincoln's speech revealed him to possess the traits of character Americans then and now describe as "presidential." To quote Michael Leff and Gerald Mohrmann, Lincoln "presents himself as the voice of Republicanism," that is to say, "the text constructs Lincoln as persona for his party."[34] Arguing is thus a way of presenting things to show one's character, and in that fashion I analyze arguments in public life in chapter 1 and in chapter 3.

I do not discuss the appeal to the emotions because there is nothing distinctive and positive that passions as varied as lust, sorrow, and anger share, though these are all passions we speakers of contemporary English would call "emotions." Since emotion is a junk category, the rhetorical concept of an appeal to the emotions lumps together unrelated rhetorical devices.

The notion that there is a fundamental distinction between techniques of persuading with argument and techniques of moving the emotions was apparently introduced into rhetorical theory by Cicero.[35] Contemporary historians of the rhetorical tradition and its influence, such as Brian Vickers and Quentin Skinner, have by and large not recognized that the concept of emotional appeal with which they are working is distinctively Ciceronian.[36] Aristotle's original category of *pathos* in rhetoric at least defines emotion more narrowly, describing the passions for rhetorical purposes as "those, which changing, alter us in respect of our judgments (*kriseis*), that is, those judgments upon which pleasure and pain attend, such as anger, pity, fear, and however many others are of this sort, and the ones opposed to these."[37]

But whatever may have been Aristotle's concept of pathos, the received concept of emotional appeal (dominant from Descartes and Locke through the beginning phases of academic psychology, and strongly present in the rhetorical theorist most heavily influenced by academic psychology, Kenneth

---

34. This account of Lincoln's purposes is taken from Michael Leff and Gerald Mohrmann, "Lincoln at Cooper Union: A Rhetorical Analysis of the Text," *Quarterly Journal of Speech* 60, no. 3 (1974): 346–58 (I have quoted 352); Leff, "Lincoln at Cooper Union: Neoclassical Criticism Revisited," *Western Journal of Communication* 65, no. 3 (2001): 232–48; and Harold Holzer, *Lincoln at Cooper Union: The Speech That Made Abraham Lincoln President* (New York: Simon and Schuster, 2004).

35. See Cicero, *De partione oratoria* 1.4–5, 1.8, 8.27, 13.46, 15, 19.67, 21.71, 36.128.

36. On the reduction of rhetoric in the early modern period to an art of manipulating emotions through style and delivery, see Thomas Conley, *Rhetoric in the European Tradition* (Chicago: University of Chicago Press, 1994), 128–33, 152, 158–79. Even Brian Vickers, who contends that the rhetorical tradition emphasizes "persuasion by moving the feelings," admits that the appeal to the emotions acquired centrality in early modern rhetorical teaching, noting that "Renaissance rhetoric laid increasing stress on its power to move the reader's or listener's feelings" (*In Defence of Rhetoric* [Oxford: Oxford University Press, 1989], x, 53; cf. 75).

37. Aristotle, *Rhetoric* 1378a20ff.

Burke) presumes that there is a world of emotionally insignificant bodies in motion onto which we willfully impose emotional loadings or perspectives. This presumption, I contend, falsifies the rhetorical phenomena: things are presented to us, at least originally, as raising or subduing our feelings; Cicero himself, though he thinks that there are distinctive verbal tools for raising emotions, admits in addition that things themselves (*res*) work on the passions. We can see things as devoid of impact on our feelings only by bracketing the impact we immediately feel.[38]

William Grimaldi, commenting on Aristotle's *Rhetoric*, writes "in men the presence of ideas carries with it the presence of emotions."[39] That means that belief and the usual modern concept of "emotion," or even the narrower Aristotelian concept of passion, are abstracted from some more basic unity—it is that unity, which we might call a judgment (Aristotle's *krisis*), that is of principal concern in thinking about rhetoric. Accordingly, as I contend in chapter 3, a speaker stirs up anger, by pointing to or depicting the things that stir up anger; fear, by presenting fearful things; or avarice, by presenting opportunities for gain.[40]

This inquiry, in sum, illuminates the human path to things through our judgments of character and action. It shows how speech and writing are used to defend the fabric of social life from things or facts. It explores the fundamental practices of public life, what Susan Wells has called "the conditions under which, in contemporary societies, things manage to get said at all."[41] Once we see what these conditions are, we can think about them and consider whether they need to be shored up against the other areas of our lives together or whether they need to be altered to suit changes in other areas of our lives together. Finally, I show how conscious reflection on the

38. Cicero, *De partione oratoria* 15.53.

39. William M. A. Grimaldi, *Aristotle, Rhetoric 2: A Commentary* (New York: Fordham University Press, 1988), 13.

40. More generally, I would subscribe to Robert Solomon's and Martha Nussbaum's (and the Stoic Chrysippus's) claim that emotions are judgments. See Solomon, *The Passions* (Garden City, N.Y.: Doubleday, 1976); Nussbaum, *Love's Knowledge: Essays on Philosophy and Literature* (Oxford: Oxford University Press, 1990), 292; Nussbaum, *The Therapy of Desire: Theory and Practice in Hellenistic Ethics* (Princeton: Princeton University Press, 1994), 366–86; Nussbaum, *Upheavals of Thought: The Intelligence of Emotions* (Cambridge: Cambridge University Press, 2001), chaps. 1–2. On emotions as judgments in Aristotle, see W. W. Fortenbagh, *Aristotle on Emotion* (New York: Barnes and Noble, 1975), 12, 87. On the disutility of the category of emotions for experimental research on persuasion, see Gerald R. Miller, "On Being Persuaded," in *The Persuasion Handbook: Developments in Theory and Practice*, ed. James Price Dillard and Michael Pfau (Thousand Oaks, Calif.: Sage, 2002), 6.

41. Susan Wells, *Sweet Reason: Rhetoric and the Discourses of Modernity* (Chicago: University of Chicago Press, 1996), 140.

means of persuasion, or the art of rhetoric, aids us in not only in clarifying things but also in protecting our relations from the vicissitudes of things. The two kinds of rhetoric are two modes for dealing with the future. Communicating things is an attempt to present and thus anticipate the unseeable possibilities of the future, while saying nothing is an attempt to guard existing human relations and institutions against the uncertain possibilities of the future.[42]

Some of the rhetorical moments we will explore are well known, while others were famous in their time and place but have since been obscured. To remember and rethink these lost words, and these lost deeds, is to renew our understanding of the elements from which we weave our life together.

42. In historical terms (though the purposes of this book are conceptual rather than historical), I first explore rhetoric by reviving Aristotle's and Quintilian's understanding of character. In chapter 2, I take up the way action appears in speech, using an approach that resembles the Hellenistic theory of issues (*staseis*). The third chapter expounds vividness (*enargeia*), for which Quintilian's discussion is the primary classical guide, and the fourth chapter builds on contemporary social scientific understandings of speech as not just a medium for offering persuasive reasons or illustrations but also a medium for reaffirming social bonds. Finally, the fifth chapter returns to the old question of the utility of the effort to think systematically about persuasion; I attempt to show how stripping away the emotional and ornamental, thereby letting facts themselves appear to the audience, makes speech more effective.

1

CHARACTER

Do not cite an author except in a matter of doubtful credit.

—FRANCIS BACON

"Life is with people"—what the inhabitants of the Jewish shtetls in Eastern Europe said about themselves is true of every form of human existence.[1] And yet, as Gilbert Ryle has noted, "Philosophers have spent too much time asking what and how do I know, when they should have been asking what and how do we know."[2]

Ryle's observation is seen for its true importance when we recognize that facts are collectively produced: facts "are made, as their name [factum] implies," writes Richard McKeon, "and their making depends on structures of knowledge, action, and art from which they derive their being and interpretation."[3] Facts are made or fabricated; they are made within a structure, a network of persons and things: "An isolated person builds only dreams, claims, and feelings, not facts."[4] Here is the Afrikaner dissident poet Breyten Breytenbach, attempting to speak freedom on his return to South Africa from exile: "Nothing I say here this evening will sound new or strange to you. We all know it. What I discover myself means nothing. What we realize

Chapter 1's epigraph comes from aphorism 3 of Bacon's "Outline for a Natural and Experimental History" (*The New Organon*, ed. Lisa Jardine, trans. Michael Silverthorne [Cambridge: Cambridge University Press, 2000], 225).

1. Mark Zborowski and Elizabeth Herzog, *Life Is with People: The Culture of the Shtetl* (1952; repr., New York: Schocken, 1962).

2. C. A. J. Coady, *Testimony: A Philosophical Study* (Oxford: Clarendon Press, 1992), ix.

3. Richard P. McKeon, "Character and the Arts and Disciplines," *Ethics* 78, no. 2 (1968): 109–23, 120; Yaron Ezrahi, *The Descent of Icarus* (Cambridge, Mass.: Harvard University Press, 1990), 62.

4. Bruno Latour, *Science in Action: How to Follow Scientists and Engineers Through Society* (Cambridge, Mass.: Harvard University Press, 1987), 41.

as a group, as a society—that is important, for that is a shared possession. It has true value because it is on the way to truth."[5]

In being collectively produced, I should note, facts are no different from other things, such as transcontinental railroads or cellular telephone networks. As Jürgen Habermas writes, "Rationality has less to do with the possession of knowledge than with how speaking and acting subjects acquire and use knowledge." This acquiring and using is something that we do, in the plural. The acquisition and use of knowledge is a matter of collective or coordinated action rather than shared belief.[6]

Thus almost all the knowledge that we act on we learn from others. Hugh Blair began his celebrated *Lectures on Rhetoric and Belles Lettres* by depicting for his students what we might call the role of persuasive speech in the mobilization of knowledge:

> One of the most distinguished privileges which Providence has conferred upon mankind, is the power of communicating their thoughts to one another. Destitute of this power reason would be a solitary, and, in some measure, an unavailing principle. Speech is the great instrument by which man becomes beneficial to man: and it is to the intercourse and transmission of thought, by means of speech, that we are chiefly indebted for the improvement of thought itself. Small are the advances which a single unassisted individual can make towards perfecting any of his powers. What we call human reason, is not the effort

5. Breyten Breytenbach, *A Season in Paradise,* trans. Rike Vaughan (London: Faber and Faber, 1976), 156–57.

6. Jürgen Habermas, *Theory of Communicative Action,* trans. Thomas McCarthy, 2 vols. (Boston: Beacon Press, 1984–89), 1:8; Steve Fuller, *Philosophy, Rhetoric, and the End of Knowledge: The Coming of Science and Technology Studies* (Madison: University of Wisconsin Press, 1993), xvii. The collective nature of fact production was first emphasized by Ludwik Fleck in 1935 in *Entstehung und Entwicklung einer wissenschaftlichen Tatsache* (published in English as *Genesis and Development of a Scientific Fact,* ed. Thaddeus J. Trenn and Robert K. Merton, trans. Fred Bradley and Thaddeus J. Trenn [Chicago: University of Chicago Press, 1979]). Fleck wished to answer the sort of epistemological questions that subsequent work in the sociology of science has taught us to disparage. He understood the fact to be an achievement of cognition, the residue of collective thought style (*Denkstil*), rather than the result of communication. It is one of the advantages of Latour's focus on the production of scientific facts as the production of material inscriptions in scientific papers that it enables us to dispense with Fleck's collective mind as an actor in our stories of fact making. Peter Galison gives a compelling account of how certain highly valued facts were socially produced in the community of particle physics; he also describes how shared experimental techniques and devices bind scientists together even when language and beliefs divide rather than unite (*Image and Logic: A Material History of Microphysics* [Chicago: University of Chicago Press, 1997], esp. 498–500, 629, 829).

or ability of one, so much as it is the reason of many, arising from lights mutually communicated, in consequence of discourse and writing.[7]

Yet we must not only clarify the facts but even our own interests for ourselves through the processes of public discussion and decision—"nothing is more certain than that all classes of men are in constant perplexity as to what their interests are."[8] We need to understand the political process as the process by which facts are produced and common interests are formed. Steve Fuller has explained the distinction between this notion of the public as productive of facts and shared interests and the Habermasian conception of the idealized public sphere: "The Athenians took pride in their ability to change course quickly. . . . Today's democratic theorists often suppress this embarrassing legacy, as it suggests that democracies can work only if people are sufficiently impressionable to be swayed by public debate. Had the Athenians followed Habermas, who recommends that people determine their real interests before entering the forum, they would probably have been so preoccupied with defining and protecting those interests that they would have never been receptive to negotiating their differences in the name of collective action."[9] Even in learning those few things we do find out for ourselves, we rely on an enormous amount of information about things that we have learned from others. We accept a lot on trust, and we have to, because we simply cannot afford the time and the money it would take to question everything others tell us. In our struggle to learn from others we cannot become experts on everything, and we cannot become experts on anything without putting a great deal of trust in other experts.

More than four decades of work on the role of authority in science have demonstrated the centrality of trust in the mobilization of knowledge. The structure of science, as the sociologists of science have elucidated it, is a network of variably credible scientists and variably credible facts, experiments, effects, and observations. "For a working scientist, the most vital question is . . . 'Is he reliable enough to be believed? Can I trust him/his claim? Is he going to provide me with hard facts?' Each scientist needs the other in order to increase his production of credible achievements."[10] This

7. Hugh Blair, *Lectures on Rhetoric and Belles Lettres,* 13th ed., 2 vols. (London: Cadell and Davies, 1819), 1:1.

8. Walter Lippmann, *Public Opinion* (1922; repr., New York: The Free Press, 1965), 119.

9. Steve Fuller, *Thomas Kuhn: A Philosophical History for Our Times* (Chicago: University of Chicago Press, 2000), 48–49.

10. Bruno Latour and Steve Woolgar, *Laboratory Life: The Construction of Scientific Facts* (1979; repr., Princeton: Princeton University Press, 1986), 202, 203.

analysis was already sketched out by Friedrich Nietzsche: "Morality of the learned—Regular and rapid progress in the sciences is possible only when the individual is not obliged to be too mistrustful in the testing of every account and assertion made by others in domains where he is a relative stranger: the condition for this, however, is that in his own field everyone must have rivals who are extremely mistrustful and are accustomed to observe him very closely. It is out of the juxtaposition of 'not too mistrustful' and 'extremely mistrustful' that the integrity of the republic of the learned originates."[11]

In exploring the web of trust that is science, sociologists have followed up on Thomas Kuhn's insight that scientific education is more dogmatic, that is, puts more trust in the authority of others, than any other mode of education ever devised in the West, including that of Catholic dogmatic theology. As Fuller writes, "Faith in science marks a degree of deference to authority that is unparalleled in human history."[12] Sharon Traweek thus describes the paradigmatic scientists of the second half of the twentieth century, the elementary particle physicists: "One [particle-physics] experimentalist has told me that he believed that a successful postdoc had to be rather immature: a mature person would have too much difficulty accepting the training without question and limiting doubts to a prescribed sphere. He felt that this precondition kept most women and minorities from doing well: their social experience had taught them to doubt authority only too thoroughly."[13]

Traweek's high-energy physicists form a community that is, of course, meritocratic and hierarchical, not democratic. Particle physics, like the Catholic Church, is hierarchical because it must instill faith in numerous dogmas about "things not seen," faith in what Arabella Lyons and Susan Wells call "ghost stories."[14] In the case of physics, these dogmas or ghost stories are accounts of objects and properties too numerous and too difficult to observe for each physicist-in-training to acquire the necessary knowledge of through hands-on-experience. It is precisely the number of things on whose existence they jointly and dogmatically rely that links the physicists into a powerful community. Particle physicists learn to be dogmatic about

11. Friedrich Nietzsche, "Assorted Opinions and Maxims," no. 215, in *Human, All Too Human*, trans. R. J. Hollingdale (Cambridge: Cambridge University Press, 1996), 264.

12. Steve Fuller, *Science* (Buckingham, U.K.: Open University Press, 1997), 43.

13. Sharon Traweek, *Beamtimes and Lifetimes: The World of High Energy Physicists* (Cambridge, Mass.: Harvard University Press, 1988), 91–92.

14. Susan Wells, *Sweet Reason: Rhetoric and the Discourses of Modernity* (Chicago: University of Chicago Press, 1996), 64.

many things so as to be able to leverage skepticism about a few things: the most difficult lesson for budding experimentalists is learning when to challenge the authority of their seniors, and the very length of their training owes precisely to the enormous amount of very difficult material that they have to learn to be dogmatic about. Physicists' power is the quantity of people and things they can move with the levers of their skepticism.[15]

To change our beliefs is to change who and what we trust: it is "to discredit the old authorities or create new authorities."[16] Steve Fuller writes of "two interpretations of what 'trust in action' amounts to": first, "I have a live option to check up on someone, but don't do so in deference to the presumed character and ability of the person," and, second, "I have no such option because I lack the time and the skill to do so, and so I am forced to rely on that person's judgment."[17] Fuller goes on to note that the second option is more commensurate with our real epistemic situation than the first. The trick here is in Fuller's use of the definite article in "that person": Fuller assumes that someone is picked out for me as an expert, either because of reputation, credentials, or position in an institutionalized network. When no one is picked out for me out of the crowd of ordinary persons as an expert, when I run into a case where none of these markers are present, I do not trust. If the car mechanic's vacationing neurosurgeon brother-in-law is minding the store while the car mechanic makes a sandwich run, the customer who knows the family is not going to defer to the surgeon's judgment about her car.

The "impersonal" force of arguments must always be weighed in the same pan as the speaker's reputation for prudence, honesty, and public feeling. We usually think of appeals to feeling or character as deviations from or perversions of impersonal, rational argumentation. The privative etymology of "impersonal," however, implies that something—the person—has been removed from the argument. It would be more accurate to say that impersonal reason is a derivative or reduced form of ethical argumentation. It is hard to see this point in the glare of the reputation that impersonal reason has acquired from its supposed use in modern natural science and

15. The point here is not the *reductio ad physicam* that has perverted social inquiry since Edgeworth and Herbert Spencer. Nor, to repeat, do I wish to debunk science. The particle physics community makes a good case study because of that community's former social prestige and the enormous resources it commanded; from the accounts of this community we can most easily gain insight into the ways that human beings mobilize themselves and their material resources.

16. Edward L. Bernays, *Crystallizing Public Opinion* (New York: Boni and Liveright, 1923), 68.

17. Fuller, *Philosophy, Rhetoric, and the End of Knowledge*, 293.

mathematics. Yet the organization of science as a social enterprise requires scientists on whom we can rely to report their observations accurately and mathematicians on whom we can rely to write papers that correctly sketch the fully formalized proofs that we do not read, much less produce.[18] Such reliability is a trait of character. Even in science, impersonal reason is derived from ethical argumentation, in that we accept the impersonal argument only because we have come to trust its author as a reliable reporter of facts and minor details of arguments.

The man of good character, as Wayne Booth puts it, "somehow manages to build for himself sufficient respect concerning his past behavior to earn the right to influence any present or future crisis. He must do so, because he is not going to have time to give all the arguments."[19] For the rhetorician, the practitioner of the conscious art of persuasion, the question is, how does one person build for himself or herself the necessary respect and thereby present himself or herself as a trustworthy source of counsel? One part of this self-presentation, generally necessary for anyone who makes a claim to our faith, is constancy.[20] We need to be sure that someone has enough integrity that we can be sure what sort of person he or she will be in changing circumstances, that he or she is reliable.

But apart from the generic concern with reliability there are more specific qualities that might make a person trustworthy, depending on what sort of advice he or she aims to dispense. Plato's Socrates talks about how we recognize the craftsman or the technical expert. Peter Miller has written about the character of the early modern antiquarian, as exemplified by the Provençal scholar Nicolas-Claude Fabri de Peiresc.[21] Steven Shapin has famously described how in the seventeenth-century Royal Society the character

18. Steven Shapin and Simon Schaffer, *Leviathan and the Air-Pump: Hobbes, Boyle, and the Experimental Life* (Princeton: Princeton University Press, 1985); Steven Shapin, *A Social History of Truth: Science and Civility in Seventeenth-Century England* (Chicago: University of Chicago Press, 1994); Philip J. Davis and Reuben Hersh, *Descartes' Dream: The World According to Mathematics* (Boston: Houghton Mifflin, 1987). Aristotle abstracts from this choice of which steps in a proof to make explicit when he asserts that "mathematical discourses do not have ethos, because they do not show deliberate choice [*proairesis*]" (*Rhetoric* 3.16.8, 1417a19–20); for an exposition of Aristotle's claim, see Eugene Garver, *For the Sake of Argument: Practical Reason, Character, and the Ethics of Belief* (Chicago: University of Chicago Press, 2004), 81.

19. Wayne Booth, "The Power to Be a University," in *Now Don't Try to Reason with Me: Essays and Ironies for a Credulous Age* (Chicago: University of Chicago Press, 1970), 247–48.

20. Andrew Sabl, *Ruling Passions: Political Offices and Democratic Ethics* (Princeton: Princeton University Press, 2002), 43–49.

21. Peter N. Miller, *Peiresc's Europe: Learning and Virtue in the Seventeenth Century* (New Haven: Yale University Press, 2000).

of the scientist was formed on the model of the gentleman.[22] Our principal concern will be what makes someone trustworthy as a source of political advice in a democracy.

From Trust to Integrity

Trust in a speaker or writer is something that has to be earned and retained, and therefore it is always up for grabs. We trust people when we judge that they possess characters that make them reliable sources in their particular area of knowledge. Emerson pronounces in "Over-soul" that "the intercourse of society . . . is one wide, judicial investigation of character."[23] To move beyond the platitude of the worthy Emerson in attempting to understand how character is formed and assessed we need at least two more platitudes, which we can find in the maxims of La Rochefoucauld. First, a cynical maxim about the giving and seeking of advice: "Nothing is less sincere than the manner of seeking and giving advice. He who seeks advice seems to have a respectful deference for the sentiments of his friend, whereas he only thinks of making him approve his own, and to make his friend answer for his conduct. And he who advises repays the confidence he is shown with an ardent and disinterested zeal, even though most often he seeks in the advice he gives his own self-interest or glory."[24] We need to think about how we get by despite the apparent good sense of this maxim. Perhaps what we need is the equal and opposing maxim 231: "it is a great folly to want to be wise all alone." La Rochefoucauld means, of course, that it is a great folly to prefer to be alone in one's wisdom rather than be foolish with the many. But we will misread maxim 231 by taking it in a sense inspired by the work of the contemporary sociologist of science Bruno Latour: knowledge, to be power, must generally be shared. And what can be shared is, generally, what one really knows.

Consider the process by which expertise is validated: we are all called on to be sufficient judges of character in the sense that we can't take any advice from someone unless we trust our own competence in judging the

22. See Shapin, *A Social History of Truth*, and Shapin and Schaffer, *Leviathan and the Air-Pump*.

23. Ralph Emerson, "Over-soul" (1841), quoted in Kenneth Burke, *A Grammar of Motives* (1945; repr., Berkeley and Los Angeles: University of California Press, 1969), 277.

24. François duc de La Rochefoucauld, maxim 116, in *Maxims*, trans. Stuart D. Warner and Stéphane Douard (South Bend, Ind.: St. Augustine's Press, 2001).

trustworthiness of the advisor. This implies that there is no expertise in judging character: judging others is something that each of us must do for ourselves—which is not to say that it is something that we all succeed in doing well. In judging character, we rely on experience and good sense, what the Greeks called *phronēsis,* and it is to those who are more experienced than we are, to our elders, say, rather than to our experts, that we turn for advice in judging character.

One might think that this judgment of character was a kind of corruption of moral judgment. Habermas writes of the eighteenth-century English public sphere that experts "were permitted and supposed to educate the public, but only inasmuch as they convinced through arguments and could themselves be corrected by better arguments." Habermas is only speaking the conventional wisdom of the intellectuals when he valorizes the preference for "measures over men."[25]

Let us think through the asymmetry of expertise: there is expertise in judging measures but no expertise in judging men. Edmund Burke uses this necessary self-sufficiency in judging character as the basis for his argument for party government:

> When people desert their connexions, the desertion is a manifest fact, upon which a direct simple issue lies, triable by plain men. Whether a measure of government be right or wrong, is no matter of fact, but a mere affair of opinion, on which men may, as they do, dispute and wrangle without end. But whether the individual thinks the measure right or wrong is a point at still a greater distance from the reach of all human decision. It is therefore very convenient to politicians not to put the judgment of their conduct on overt acts, cognisable in any ordinary court, but upon such a matter as can be triable only in that secret tribunal, where they are sure of being heard with favour, or where at worst the sentence will be only private whipping. I believe the reader would wish to find no substance in a doctrine which has a tendency to destroy all test of character as deduced from conduct.[26]

25. Jürgen Habermas, *The Structural Transformation of the Public Sphere: An Inquiry into a Category of Bourgeois Society,* trans. Thomas Burger and Frederick Lawrence (Cambridge, Mass.: MIT Press, 1989), 259 n. 32.

26. Edmund Burke, *Thoughts on the Present Discontents,* in *Select Works of Edmund Burke,* 4 vols. (Indianapolis, Ind.: Liberty Fund, 1999), 1:151–52.

Michael McGee, in unearthing this passage, glosses it for us: "When potential [leaders] are pushed by journalists, academic, and opponents to 'stick to the issues,' to be specific 'on the issues,' to 'refrain from mudslinging,' the admonition is to avoid the only 'issue' which a voter is competent to judge, the general character and trustworthiness displayed by candidates for office."[27] As Christopher Hitchens put it, discussing the 2004 American presidential race, "The character of the candidate is itself the only 'issue,' and it is furthermore the only 'issue' about which a thinking voter can be expected to make up his or her mind."[28]

So our phenomenological question has become, what sort of traits make someone reliable as a source of information or counsel? Emerson's "judicial investigation of character" is the study of what is or can be made apparent or manifest. These are actions or motives that are immediately public or that are capable of being *discovered*. But consider this metaphor of discovery: whatever is concealing the actions or motives that are going to be discovered must be lifted—there is something public and removable, blocking us from the sight of something else that is capable of being made public. This "judicial investigation of character" is quite different from the search into the soul for unconscious motives. Bernard Asbell shows us the late Senator Edmund Muskie engaged in the judgment of character through action: "[Muskie] rarely describes anyone in terms of motivation, rarely judges or even characterizes anyone. He describes an action, or something said, or a vote cast, or a political person's general position—something observable and factual. As far as I can see, Muskie sees a person not as a bundle of passions but as a performer of external actions."[29] Asbell cannot see that Muskie is engaged in the judgment of the character of others because he thinks that judgment of others involves loose talk about motives or emotions rather than precise talk about what someone has said or done.[30]

27. Michael McGee, "'Not Men, but Measures': The Origins and Import of an Ideological Principle," *Quarterly Journal of Speech* 64, no. 2 (1978): 141–54; see also Harvey C. Mansfield Jr., *Statesmanship and Party Politics: A Study of Burke and Bolingbroke* (Chicago: University of Chicago Press, 1965), 179. On the more general issue of arguments about fitness for office, see John F. Cragan and Craig W. Cutbirth, "A Revisionist Perspective on Political ad hominem Argument: A Case Study," *Central States Speech Journal* 35, no. 4 (1984): 228–37. On the intentionally antidemocratic consequences of the emphasis on measures rather than men, see Michael E. McGerr, *The Decline of Popular Politics: The American North, 1865–1928* (Oxford: Oxford University Press, 1986), esp. 54–57, 65.

28. Christopher Hitchens, "All Against Bush: Whom Should the Democrats Nominate?" *Slate*, 9 February 2004, http://slate.msn.com//?id=2095158&.

29. Bernard Asbell, *The Senate Nobody Knows* (New York: Doubleday, 1978), 79.

30. See Roderick P. Hart, *Modern Rhetorical Criticism*, 2nd ed. (Boston: Pearson/Allyn and Bacon, 1997), 212.

The One Before the Many

To understand the production of character or ethos through speech we must first consider the fundamental paradox inherent in the rhetorical situation—what Harvey Yunis has described as the "inherent, unresolved discrepancy between the democratic insistence on amateurism in politics and the [people's] need for competent leadership."[31] In rising to speak, speakers single themselves out from their many listeners by speaking, but at the same time they must show themselves to be similar to the many in their interests and affections. This is what the communications scholars Karen Johnson-Cartee and Gary Copeland call "the Everyman/Heroic conflict": "Americans like for their candidates to be similar to themselves; yet they also want their candidates to excel in some particular area of character that they do not."[32] In getting the audience's attention, getting a hearing, it is just as important for the speaker to show himself or herself to have something special to contribute as to show that he or she is part of the community that he or she would address.[33] Here we are going to try and figure out what the relevant areas of excellence might be in the political-rhetorical situation most broadly defined.

Let us begin with those areas in which the political advisor must claim some excellence or understanding his or her audience lacks, since "the common man does, in the end, want uncommon leaders."[34] The notion that the orator is indeed special in virtue of his knowledge can be seen in the most striking passage in Demosthenes' *On the Crown:*

> It was evening, and a messenger came to the presidents announcing that Elatea had been captured. . . . The city was in an uproar. At dawn, the presidents called the Council into the Council chamber, and you made your way to the Assembly, and before the Council could get down to business and form the agenda, all you people were seated up on the Pnyx. Next the Council entered, the presidents reported the message that had come in to them, they introduced the messenger, and

31. Harvey Yunis, *Taming Democracy: Models of Political Rhetoric in Classical Athens* (Ithaca, N.Y.: Cornell University Press, 1996), 11.

32. Karen S. Johnson-Cartee and Gary A. Copeland, *Manipulation of the American Voter: Political Campaign Commercials* (Westport, Conn.: Praeger, 1997), 7.

33. See Quentin Skinner, *Reason and Rhetoric in the Philosophy of Hobbes* (Cambridge: Cambridge University Press, 1996), 129.

34. Garry Wills, *Nixon Agonistes: The Crisis of the Self-Made Man* (1970; repr., New York: New American Library, 1979), 144.

he spoke. Then the herald asked, "Who wishes to address the Assembly?" No one approached. The herald asked repeatedly, but still no one stood up, though the generals were there, and all the orators, and though your fatherland called with her common cry to the one who would speak for her salvation—for it is right to believe that the legally appointed cry that the herald hurled forth is the common cry of your fatherland. Well, had your city needed those who wished her to be saved, all of you and the rest of the Athenians would have stood up and made your way to the platform. For all of you, I think, wished that she be saved. If the wealthy had been needed, the Three Hundred would have stood up. If those who are both wealthy and benevolent toward the city had been needed, those who later laid out those great expenses would have stood up, since they did later lay out those expenses using their wealth and out of benevolence. But, it seemed, that moment and that day did not call for the man who was merely wealthy and benevolent but rather for he who had followed these matters from their beginning and deduced why Philip had done these things and what he wanted. For the one who did not know these things, nor had foreseen them when they were still distant, even if he were he benevolent or wealthy, would not know what was to be done, nor would it be possible for him to advise you. I then appeared, I approached, and I addressed you.[35]

It is not enough for a speaker to know the traditions of Athens, Demosthenes asserts. We evaluate the political speaker the same way Steve Fuller says we evaluate scientists: "Competence is judged in terms of an appropriate alteration of the tradition rather than a simple reenactment of it."[36] Demosthenes claims to have been exceptional at the moment of decision because he alone saw what action present circumstances required: Demosthenes alone saw how Athenian traditions and procedures could be put to work so that the city as a whole could form and execute a policy of opposition to Philip.

Now, to know what many do not know separates one from the many and puts a special burden on the speaker to prove that he or she shares in their concerns. As Josiah Ober writes: "He who thrusts himself forward to the [speakers' platform], abandoning his place in the mass, had by that act

35. Demosthenes, *On the Crown* §§169–73 (all translations of extracts from *On the Crown* are mine).

36. Fuller, *Philosophy, Rhetoric, and the End of Knowledge*, 30.

declared an individuality that was potentially suspect. His motive in choosing to address the people might be self-interest, rather than a desire to further the interests of the state as a whole."[37] Insofar as the speaker claims to know what others do not, the speaker draws attention to himself or herself, takes responsibility for his or her advice, and thereby puts himself or herself at risk. The speaker is risking that he or she will be treated according to the consequences of those collective actions that are attributed to his or her advice. Without the claim to uniqueness the speaker is just saying what anyone else could say and so we would find listening to him or her pointless and dull. Politics is risky, and political careers are frequently short, because politicians are often torn apart by this tension between having something special to say and sharing the general concerns of the audience to whom one says it.

At the same time, however, that the orator shows himself or herself to have special knowledge, he or she must also remain one of the people. As a t-shirt distributed by Ross Perot's admirers read "He's like us, only richer."[38] This does not necessarily mean that the speaker should patronize his or her audience by adopting the style or manners of it. It may be true that members of the U.S. House of Representatives "act differently around labor groups than around business groups. Their dress, comportment, demeanor, humor, diction, dietary preferences, small talk, and tastes are all likely to change in ways that are sometimes subtle and other times painfully obvious."[39] But these adjustments in style, even if they are easy for some speakers to pull off, are not essential for persuasive success. For every professional country boy, one can find a eccentric aristocrat such as Claiborne Pell, whose style (or persona) were utterly alien to his constituents, as well as, for that matter, such patrician populists as Franklin Delano Roosevelt, Winston Churchill, and Edward Kennedy. A famous anecdote from Teddy Kennedy's first run for the Senate makes the point: "Ted and his aides were at a factory gate to shake the hands of workers going in on the day shift. . . . 'Hey Kennedy,' yelled a worker. 'I hear you never worked a day in your life.'

37. Josiah Ober, *Mass and Elite in Democratic Athens: Rhetoric, Ideology, and the Power of the People* (Princeton: Princeton University Press, 1989), 296–97; see also 155. Sian Lewis, *News and Society in the Greek Polis* (Chapel Hill: University of North Carolina Press, 1996), 105.

38. Roderick P. Hart, *Seducing America: How Television Charms the Modern Voter*, rev. ed. (Thousand Oaks, Calif.: Sage, 1999), 52.

39. John R. Hibbing, foreword, in Richard F. Fenno Jr., *Home Style: House Members in Their Districts* (1978; repr., New York: Longman, 2003), vii–viii, and Fenno, *The Emergence of a Senate Leader: Pete Domenici and the Reagan Budget* (Washington, D.C.: Congressional Quarterly Press, 1991), 184.

Kennedy tightened. 'Well,' said the worker, 'I want to tell you something. You haven't missed a fucking thing.'"[40] Insofar as privilege is something we wish for ourselves and our children, we are not alienated from but identify with the privileged. Moreover, insofar as a privileged upbringing is a marker of a privileged education and privileged contacts, we esteem privilege as a sign of the special knowledge and capacities we require in our leaders. It is presumably true, as Yves Simon claims, that few among the privileged sympathize with the less privileged of the community. Yet it will nonetheless be the case that the unprivileged themselves will frequently elect privileged sympathizers over more "authentic representatives" of the unprivileged, since any sensible person prefers, other things being equal, to have his or her interests represented by the educated and suave rather than the uneducated and inarticulate.[41]

Still, in having something uncommon to say the speaker must combat the assumption that he or she has uncommon interests in the affairs at hand. In a democracy, to know what is to be done makes one automatically one of the few, the elite, who have prepared themselves through the study of politics in general and recent events in particular. Even (or especially) in a democracy the people know that the special knowledge and preparation required to have something to say are elite competencies. Yet even though the people would prefer to be represented by elite speakers, they can't help but be suspicious of them, since the elite are presumed to have very different interests from the people at large.[42] Those who know are always presumed by the many to have some class interest, as one can see in popular

40. The Kennedy anecdote is quoted from Sidney Blumenthal, *The Permanent Campaign*, rev. ed (New York: Simon and Schuster, 1982), 278. On Pell, see Richard F. Fenno Jr., *Senators on the Campaign Trail: The Politics of Representation* (Norman: University of Oklahoma Press, 1996), 262–63. One should also keep in mind the observation of Stuart Stevens that "not very likeable people with odd personalities get elected all the time—New York mayor Rudy Giuliani is a perfect example" (*The Big Enchilada: Campaign Adventures with the Cockeyed Optimists from Texas Who Won the Biggest Prize in Politics* [New York: The Free Press, 2001], 148). Although personality is (as Aristotle notes [*Nicomachean Ethics* 4.6.1126b12–1127a12]) a virtue, it is not a very important virtue.

41. Cf. Yves Simon, *Philosophy of Democratic Government* (Chicago: University of Chicago Press, 1951), 222. Simon refuses the implications of his own insight into the power of what he calls "intentional communion," in this case the capacity of the privileged to think themselves into sympathy with the unprivileged, in consequence of his habitual inability to grasp the effects of competition.

42. On the many and the few in Athenian political rhetoric, see Ober, *Mass and Elite*; Ober, *The Athenian Revolution: Essays on Ancient Greek Democracy and Political Theory* (Princeton: Princeton University Press, 1996); Yunis, *Taming Democracy*. Sian Lewis notes that if an Athenian orator gives a source for a fact about another city, the source is almost always a man of standing (*News and Society*, 86).

political culture from Aristophanes' *Clouds* down to latter-day conspiracy theories about the Council on Foreign Relations, the Trilateral Commission, and the neoconservative Straussian cabal.[43] To combat these presumptions speakers must show that, although they are members of the elite in their qualifications, they are men or women of the people in their sentiments and values.[44] "The advantage of a superior education," Richard Nixon once said, "should result in a deep respect for—and never contempt for—the value judgments of the average person."[45] The speaker must show that he or she identifies with the people's sentiments and values in his or her speeches: we have therefore arrived at the rhetorical problem of character or ethos.

The speaker in a democracy must show that he or she is "one of the boys," in the sense of being comfortable with others, and that he or she is concerned with the going on of the ways that they are together, of the continued existence of the community that they together constitute. This is what Churchill meant by "Tory democracy": the speaker grants his or her audience respect in order to show that their interests and concerns are worthy of being respected. You may not be like them in education, speaking style, or economic circumstances, you *must not* be like them in that you have some special knowledge relevant to the matter at hand, but you are like them in the sense that to you and to them can be ascribed an identity of moral values and political interests.

The Components of Ethos

Some speakers come to the rhetorical situation with a reputation earned not by previous advice but by previous deeds. The task of the speaker is to parlay that reputation in such a way as to serve his or her present ends. What the artful rhetorician must consider is the opportunity the rhetorical situation provides to show character in the speech. "Character," says Aristotle "provides just about the most powerful proof" of that for which the speaker contends, and the art of rhetoric shows how one can use speeches to show

43. It is not only the many who are suspicious of those who claim to know; here is an expression of populist suspicion from John Dewey, a member of the "few," usually identified as a "progressive": "A class of experts is inevitably so removed from common interests as to become a class with private interests and private knowledge, which in social matters is not knowledge at all" (*The Public and Its Problems* [1927; repr., Denver, Colo.: Alan Swallow, 1954], 207).

44. Cf. Aristotle, *Rhetoric* 1377b25–29 with Thucydides, *History of the Peloponnesian War* 6.12.

45. William Safire, *Before the Fall: An Inside View of the Pre-Watergate White House* (New York: Belmont Tower Books, 1975), 647. I do not want push for any measure of Nixon revisionism, but readers who cannot live by this Nixonian sentiment are hereby advised against a career in electoral politics.

forth the character of their speaker.[46] The principal purpose of expressing character in one's speeches "lies in making it seem that all that we say derives directly from the nature of the facts and persons concerned and in the revelation of the character of the orator in such a way that all may recognize it."[47] This is what Neil Postman refers to demeaningly as "the impression of sincerity, authenticity, vulnerability, or attractiveness (choose one or more) conveyed by the actor/reporter."[48] Or as in the old Woody Allen quip, if you can fake sincerity, you've got it made.

Postman and Allen run together two issues that have to be separated. While there are no generally reliable ways of faking honesty or sincerity, there are generally reliable ways of communicating honesty. There are indeed traits that make someone appear dishonest or insincere, and to the extent that one can avoid exhibiting them one is a better liar—but by the same token, avoiding exhibiting them makes one better at communicating the truth. To some extent this avoidance can be learned, and in that way one's character as honest and knowledgeable can be made apparent. That task is the rhetorical problem of character, that is to say, it is the problem of character for a conscious art of persuasion.

For a single speaker to persuade a mass audience, Aristotle says, he must show his audience that he possesses three traits of character. These three traits are practical knowledge (*phronēsis*), virtue (*aretē*), and benevolence toward his audience (*eunoia*). The orator needs to manifest his virtue in order to show that he grasps what is really good for his audience, that he does not have a perverted view of their good. He needs to show himself to be benevolent toward his audience, so that his listeners are confident that he advises them for their own good. Finally, the orator needs to manifest practical knowledge in order to show that he knows what is to be done, both in the specific case at hand and in the more general situation.[49]

46. Aristotle, *Rhetoric* 1356a13; for an example of such a showing forth, see *Rhetoric* 1395b12–17. Aristotle states famously that the political community ought not to be so large that the characters of those who address the public are unknown to most of their audience (see *Politics* 7.4.7, 1326b14–20). The Athenians, however, did not have newspapers, which philosophers at least since Hegel have seen as a pillar of the modern state.

47. Quintilian, *Institutio oratoria* 6.2.13.

48. Neil Postman, *Amusing Ourselves to Death* (New York: Viking, 1985), 102.

49. See Aristotle, *Rhetoric* 1359b16–1360b1, 1378a. Modern communications studies have confirmed that audiences can distinguish between the question as to whether a communicator is competent and the question as to whether that communicator shares group affiliation with them. These studies have, however, left open the question as to whether we do in fact distinguish between those who share our values and those who share our interests; see Sik Hung Ng and James J. Bradac, *Power in Language: Verbal Communication and Social Influence* (Newbury Park, Calif.: Sage, 1993), 14–15.

These three traits named by Aristotle—knowledge, benevolence, and virtue—are the traits that Richard Fenno, the leading student of how American politicians build and keep the trust of their constituents, calls competence, identification, and empathy.[50] Competence includes knowledge of what is at issue: in the 2000 presidential election campaign, Gore's partisans objected to Bush on the grounds that he lacked competence.[51] To show that one is competent one must endeavor to display one's qualifications. As I suggest in chapter 3, this may require that one present evidence—not to prove the truth of one's assertions but rather to establish that one possesses expertise.

The speaker cannot afford to give the audience the impression that his or her superior knowledge is being concealed behind condescendingly simplified expressions. On this point one can learn much from former Carter speechwriter James Fallows's critique of his old boss:

> Carter's problems as an explainer were compounded by his tendency to talk down to his audience. . . . While working on the first fireside chat, I received a lecture from the President. I should not use words such as "cynical," because average people wouldn't understand them. Carter said that whenever he worked on a speech he thought of a man at a certain gas station in central Georgia (not his brother). If that man couldn't understand it, it should be changed. . . .
>
> The sentiment was admirable but too broad. When simplifying words, Carter too often simplified ideas as well. I always thought the public could tell the difference between a clear, simple image—such as Franklin Roosevelt's garden hose to symbolize Lend-Lease—and a deceptively simple thought. When they heard Carter's constant talk of harmony, respect among nations, happy times at home, the men at the gas stations knew they were hearing less than the full truth.[52]

Carter "talked down" because he wished to benefit from being seen as "a populist president, one whom the people should respect because he was fundamentally like themselves."[53] In the aftermath of Nixon's scandals, Carter

50. Fenno, *Home Style*, 57–60.

51. James W. Ceaser and Andrew E. Busch, *The Perfect Tie: The True Story of the 2000 Presidential Election* (Lanham, Md.: Rowman and Littlefield, 2001), 33, 117–18.

52. James Fallows, "The Passionless Presidency," *Atlantic Monthly*, May 1979, 43.

53. Colin Seymour-Ure, *The American President: Power and Communication* (London: Macmillan, 1982), 96.

wished to show himself a president "as good as the American people" so that he would be able to use the presidential authority that made him unlike those he governed. In "talking down" the speaker assumes a superiority that he or she makes no effort to demonstrate. The speaker may thereby leave the audience with the impression that he or she cannot demonstrate his or her superior knowledge or judgment in the matter at hand. The speaker cannot demonstrate his or her superior knowledge, the audience is liable to infer, because he or she possesses no genuine superiority. Alternatively, as Fallows hints, the audience may infer that the speaker is concealing something—either his or her peculiar interest or his or her peculiar standards for judging interests—because he or she is endeavoring to deceive the audience.

Identification or *eunoia* means that the speaker shares the interests of the audience or cares about their interests. If the audience thinks that the speaker, while knowledgeable, is speaking in pursuit of interests other than or even hostile to their own, they will be unreceptive to the speaker's message. In England, regional accents mark group identification, while regionally unmarked pronunciation has greater prestige. Yet in an experimental study, audiences of a message arguing against capital punishment were more likely to be swayed when they perceived the speaker to be one of their own because he or she spoke with a regional accent than when they perceived the speaker to be knowledgeable and authoritative because he or she spoke with the regionally unmarked standard pronunciation.[54] That the speaker cannot show an identity of interests with the audience does not necessarily make him or her blameworthy, and he or she may not be condemned by them: a foreign ambassador is merely doing her job when she presents her own country's interests as identical with ours, but to the extent that we are aware of who sent her and of what interests she is striving to realize, we will find her presentation less persuasive.[55]

Finally, empathy is the correct judgment of right and wrong, or what we would call shared values.[56] "If given the choice, politicians would rather

54. See Howard Giles, "Communicative Effectiveness as a Function of Accented Speech," *Speech Monographs* 40, no. 4 (1973): 330–31; see also Howard Giles and Peter F. Powesland, *Speech Style and Social Evaluation* (London: Academic Press, 1970), 89–100.

55. See John C. Turner et al., *Rediscovering the Social Group: A Self Categorization Theory* (Oxford: Basil Blackwell, 1987), chaps. 3–4. For a helpful summary of current social science research on identification, see Cass Sunstein, *Republic.com* (Princeton: Princeton University Press, 2001), 69–71.

56. Fenno himself considers personal honesty and competence together to be "qualifications" and separates other "values issues" such as "empathy" from them (*Home Style*, 57–60). In the tripartite division I take over from Aristotle all values issues are considered together as empathy.

discuss national values than anything else," as Roderick Hart has noted.[57] The standard way of praising the Americans to the Americans is praise them for their commitment to "American values," just as the standard way of praising the Athenians to the Athenians was to praise them for their commitment to Athenian values such as freedom, equality, and zest for competition in excellence. Judging by the reactionary advice to women in Pericles' funeral oration, we can even speak of "Athenian family values."[58]

Often we judge public figures positively not because they are successful in preserving what we cherish but because they make it clear they believe it deserves to be cherished. Garry Wills explains the popularity of the Reagans' defense of traditional values thus: "[Ronald Reagan] did not really take people back to the past, but he made a dizzy rush toward the future less disorienting. He did so by clinging uncritically to notions that reassured people, despite their lack of practical impact. Neither the sexual nor the drug revolution was reversed, or even held static, by the Reagans' exhortation to 'say "no,"' but these developments were made somehow endurable by being treated as anomalous. Reagan made it possible to live with change while not accepting it."[59] The appeal to "law and order" in the late 1960s similarly allowed a politician to display his or her sympathy with the values of his or her audience. To quote former Lyndon Johnson speechwriter Harry McPherson:

> The voters were becoming quietly enraged by crime and disorder and by what they regarded as permissiveness on the part of institutional authority. Politicians who wanted to escape that rage should identify themselves with the forces of law and order. It was not necessary that they countenance ruthless acts of suppression, or even that they defend the police against the charges that had been made against them. Just that they show whose side they were on: the mugger, the looter, the sniper, the violent protester, or the law enforcer. If there was any doubt in the voters' minds about that, all the magnanimity and progressivism in the world would not suffice to save the candidate. If the doubt was removed, the candidate was free to promote whatever liberal schemes he wished.[60]

57. Roderick P. Hart, *Campaign Talk: Why Elections Are Good for Us* (Princeton: Princeton University Press, 2000), 142; see also Aristotle, *Rhetoric* 2.21, 1394a19–1395b19.

58. Thucydides, *History of the Peloponnesian War* 2.45.2.

59. Garry Wills, *Under God: Religion and American Politics* (New York: Simon and Schuster, 1990), 35–36.

60. Harry McPherson, *A Political Education* (Boston: Little, Brown, 1972), 77–78.

To show one's commitment to the commonly valued the speaker will frequently trespass beyond the realm of practical possibilities and invoke shared wishes or prayers. Consider this Reagan voice-over from "Roosevelt Room," a 1984 reelection campaign advertisement: "Just across the hall here in the White House is the Roosevelt Room; draped from each flag are battle streamers signifying every battle campaign fought since the revolutionary war. My fondest hope is that the people of America give us the continued opportunity to preserve a peace so strong and so lasting, never again will we have to add another streamer to those flags."[61] Although Reagan's second term was indeed pacific by comparison with other modern presidents, comparable sentiments expressing a preference for peace over war could probably be extracted from the speeches of any president since Theodore Roosevelt.[62]

The most familiar way to show that one shares the values of the audience is to display the integrity or strength of character that every audience values. It was the perceived lack of such integrity that the Bush partisans objected to in Al Gore. Bush himself described his opponent at a March 2000 press conference as "a man who will say anything to get elected"— that is to say, Gore, according to Bush and Bush's supporters, valued nothing more than getting elected.[63] Gore certainly fed this image himself: "I'm not like George Bush. If he wins or loses, life goes on. I'll do anything to win." Indeed, the turning point of the campaign came when the public made a judgment about Gore's character. Ceaser and Busch argue that the single greatest setback for Gore's campaign (prior to the vote!) was the public perception that Gore took advantage of the Elian Gonzales situation. Gore objected publicly to the Clinton administration forcing the Cuban orphan, who was brought to the United States after his mother drowned in the passage to Florida, to be returned to his father. Though Gore seems to have been sincere in his objections, Americans were so unused to a sincere Gore

61. Quoted in Hart, *Campaign Talk*, 129; the same sentiments can be found in another 1984 Reagan campaign ad, "Peace," available at http://www.youtube.com/watch?v=PyzrMigqslc (accessed 14 October 2007).

62. Shared values are not necessarily healthy or correct values. Aristotle asserted that the Spartans believed that virtue is desirable not because it leads to noble actions but because it helps its possessors to attain what is naturally good. This Spartan view is a perversion possessed by the audience as a whole, which would tend to make them find unpersuasive a speaker who was truly virtuous and thus endorsed an action on the grounds that it was virtuous (and it would be all the more virtuous for bringing no profit but merely reputation to the doer or his regime). See Aristotle, *Eudemian Ethics* 7.15, 1248b37ff., and Aristotle, *Politics* 2.9, 1271b6–10, 7.14, 1333b5–1334a10, and 7.15, 1334a40–b5.

63. Daniel M. Shea and Michael John Burton, *Campaign Craft: The Strategies, Tactics, and Art of Political Campaign Management*, rev. ed. (Westport, Conn.: Praeger, 2001), 99; Ceaser and Busch, *The Perfect Tie*, 33, 118–19.

that they couldn't believe in him, and so his advocating that Elian be allowed to stay was seen as further proof of his insincerity.[64]

Integrity is so central a value in politics that it can bridge the widest gaps between divergent interests and values. When Hitler invaded the Soviet Union in June 1941, Churchill offered all possible help to Stalin while affirming his own opposition to Communism: "The Nazi regime is indistinguishable from the worst features of Communism. It is devoid of all theme and principle except appetite and racial domination. It excels in all forms of human wickedness, in the efficiency of its cruelty and ferocious aggression. Noone has been a more consistent opponent of Communism than I have for the last twenty-five years. I will unsay no words that I've spoken about it. But all this fades away before the spectacle which is now unfolding."[65] This is a strange note to strike, one might think, in proffering an alliance. Yet as George Orwell noted at the time, "[Churchill's] hostile references to Communism were entirely right, and simply emphasized the fact that this offer of help was sincere. One can imagine the squeal that will be raised over these by correspondents in the *New Statesman* etc. What sort of impression do they think it would make if Stalin stood up and announced 'I have always been a convinced supporter of capitalism'?"[66] Since loyalty to one's own side is a value audiences share with speakers, speakers at least show that both they and their audience esteem it by making clear the difference in interests between themselves and the audience. Such a sharing of values can help make more plausible a speaker's claims of a temporary common interest with an audience whose interests are fundamentally opposed to those of him or her.

The Art of Appearing as You Are

In the matter of Elian Gonzales, Gore failed to persuade because he failed to show his sincerity. The public was not able to appreciate Gore's sincerity owing to his peculiar reputation for insincerity; it was distracted by his reputation from hearing his message: that he supported the Cuban exile

64. Ceaser and Busch, *The Perfect Tie*, 174 (quoting *Newsweek*, 11 November 2000), 34, 119.

65. Winston Churchill, "Minister Winston Churchill's Broadcast on the Soviet-German War," 22 June 1942, available at http://www.ibiblio.org/pha/policy/1941/410622d.html (accessed 26 October 2007).

66. George Orwell, "War-time Diary," 23 June 1941, in *My Country Right or Left, 1940–1943*, vol. 2 of *Collected Essays, Journalism, and Letters of George Orwell*, ed. Sonia Orwell and Ian Angus (New York: Harcourt, Brace, Jovanovich, 1970), 404–5.

community against the Clinton Administration. In order to keep one's audience focused on one's message, one ought to present oneself in such a way that one's peculiarities go unremarked.

This does not mean concealing one's bias or special interest, but it does mean helping people to see through one's bias or interest to the things that one is talking about. Because negative facts about one have greater salience than positive facts, one wants to be as unmarked by facts as possible, while presenting oneself as possessing those traits of character that mark one as a trustworthy voice in public debate.[67]

The man or woman of good character is in a sense empty—like the guardians of Plato's *Republic,* he or she is ideally as far as possible free of private or, rather, hidden interests. Richard Posner writes, "charismatic political leadership—the most dangerous kind—depends on the leader's ability to control information about himself."[68] The most straightforward way of controlling public information about oneself is to control one's conduct so that there is nothing discreditable to be reported. Cicero offers a striking example in the undelivered second speech *Against Verres,* when he depicts the Roman official Lucius Piso setting the goldsmith "to reforge [Piso's] ring in the middle of the marketplace, having first weighed out the gold in the sight of all."[69]

The best person of this sort is hollow; there is no whole to grasp or study, no treasures of a rich inner life hidden and thus available to be revealed by "the picklocks of biographers."[70] "Reagan forcefully conveyed the message that he was neither more nor less than he appeared to be," writes the rhetorical critic Edwin Black, but Black does not seem to mean this as praise.[71] Nietzsche writes thus of the hollowness or transparency for which public speakers strive: "Becoming Empty.—Of him who surrenders himself to events there remains less and less. Great politicians can thus become complete empty men and yet have once been rich and full."[72] The politician must minimize his personal style. As Roderick Hart has shown, successful

67. Johnson-Cartee and Copeland, *Manipulation of the American Voter,* 21–22.

68. Richard A. Posner, *Public Intellectuals: A Study of Decline* (Cambridge, Mass.: Harvard University Press, 2001), 254.

69. Cicero, *Against Verres* 2.4.25.56–57 (my translation). See Daniel Patrick Moynihan, *Secrecy: The American Experience* (New Haven: Yale University Press, 1998), 82, for a similar anecdote about Andrew Jackson.

70. Steven Vincent Benét, "Army of Northern Virginia," from *John Brown's Body* (New York: Doubleday, Doran, 1928).

71. Edwin Black, *Rhetorical Questions: Studies of Public Discourse* (Chicago: University of Chicago Press, 1992), 91.

72. Nietzsche, "Assorted Opinions and Maxims," no. 315, in *Human, All Too Human,* 284.

politicians speak in less distinctive, more average ways than their unsuccessful rivals. The "more unique a politician's language, the more likely he is to lose." Hart finds that "most of the winning candidates—people like Dwight Eisenhower and George Bush, for example—were average in every measurable way" in their speaking style.[73] "To listen to a political speech," Hart writes elsewhere, "is to listen to a group discussion"; the political speaker tries to minimize his or her peculiarities and to talk in a way acceptable to the group who listens.[74] "Public people," writes Meg Greenfield, "almost eagerly dehumanize themselves. They allow the markings of region, family, class, individual character, and, generally, personhood that they once possessed to be leached away. At the same time they construct a new public self that often does terrible damage to what remains of the genuine person."[75] For Greenfield the genuine person is his or her past, his or her origins. She recognizes that political actors can literally remake themselves but asserts, without argument, that the remade self is counterfeit rather than genuine. But if character is a stamp that people through a long labor of self-fashioning have stamped on themselves, then people are really as they appear, genuinely possessing the qualities they have cultivated.

Greenfield is correct that part of the public person's self-fashioning involves eliminating his or her "natural" idiosyncrasies—peculiarities of speech, dress, or mannerism: "In public life it is sometimes necessary in order to appear really natural to be actually artificial." That is to say, don't do things that seem affected. Coolidge, for example, realized that as president, a perpetual subject of newsworthy photographs, he could no longer wear his father's work apron since it appeared when publicized to be a falsely rustic affectation.[76] To use a theater anecdote retold by David Mamet, "Stanislavski was once doing a play about a terrorist at Yalta. He imported to Moscow, at a terrible expense, real palm trees, but when he put them on stage they looked phony. So he had to make artificial ones that would look real."[77] If you are the dovish candidate Michael Dukakis—who had served in the United States Army at the bleak post of 1950s Korea—don't be televised driving a tank. If you are Nixon in 1968, the clever and sophisticated political operator,

73. Hart, *Campaign Talk*, 20, 96–101.

74. Roderick P. Hart, "A Commentary on Popular Assumptions About Political Communication," *Human Communication Research* 8, no. 4 (1982): 366–79, esp. 369–70.

75. Meg Greenfield, *Washington* (New York: PublicAffairs, 2001), 7.

76. Calvin Coolidge, *The Autobiography of Calvin Coolidge* (New York: Cosmopolitan Book Corporation, 1929), 20.

77. David Mamet, *David Mamet in Conversation*, ed. Leslie Kane (Ann Arbor: University of Michigan Press, 2001), 43.

don't be filmed walking on the beach, gathering shells.[78] If you are John Kerry, preppie child of former diplomats, don't show yourself off going duck hunting in the Ohio swamps. Even if you know that what you are doing is actually unaffected, you will likely never convince other people that you aren't faking sincerity. In the conscious avoidance of what seems affected or artificial, we have the first glimmer that there may be an art of appearing natural. The gap between the truly and the apparently natural opens up because the public has little information about the speaker but must judge based on that little.[79]

The successful political speaker is remarkable for his or her good qualities rather than for the peculiar details of his individual life story, and his good qualities are those that are present in numerous others, though these others possess fewer of these qualities and possess them to lesser degrees. One can tell a story about how such a man grew from a child into a man of good character, but each such story is more or less the same as all the others of its kind. A collection of such stories would be monotonous, repetitive, and hagiographical rather than biographical—not because such a collection would conceal what was interesting about its subjects but because apart from their deeds and speeches, all similar in kind, there would be nothing interesting about them to reveal.

For all their virtues, political leaders, insofar as they have successfully eliminated everything that interferes with their presentation of their public self, are dull, both intellectually and, one might say, aesthetically. Their characters are distinctive only in those qualities that make those characters admirable. In particular, an estimable public character cannot comprehend certain features of a human life that we moderns regard as desirable and worthy—religious sentiments that go beyond the conventional pieties, refined aesthetic sensibilities, romantic passions.[80]

78. Joe McGinniss, *The Selling of the President, 1968* (1969; repr., New York: Penguin, 1988), 161.

79. The upside, in some rare cases, is that a true accusation may be too terrible to be believed. Reviewing the 1992 U.S. presidential race, Dennis W. Johnson writes: "Voters simply didn't believe that the worst charges could be true. Both Bush and Clinton campaigns believed that one of the most damaging indictments against Clinton was a successful lawsuit charging that the state of Arkansas was criminally negligent in treating poor and abused children under its care. Years had elapsed before Governor Clinton did anything to clean up this problem, and it would have been easy to charge him with inept leadership. But when the issue was tested before focus groups, participants essentially dismissed the charge as 'as a fairy tale; it sounded too horrible to be true'" (*No Place for Amateurs* [London: Routledge, 2001], 80).

80. See Cicero's disavowal of knowledge of Greek sculpture in the *Verrine Orations,* ed. and trans. L. H. G. Greenwood (London: Heinemann, 1928–35), 2.4.2§3–2.4.3§5, 2.4.6§12, 2.4.7§13, 2.4.14–15§33 (vol. 2, 319), 2.4.43§94; see also Greenwood's comments at 2:284 n. a. For more

"There is only one man better and more uncommon than the patrician, and that is the individual," says T. S. Eliot.[81] Few today would argue with Eliot, but whatever the man of good character may be, whether patrician or plebian, aristocrat or man of the people, he is not an individual. He may even be lacking in personality, for, as John M. Barry writes of members of Congress, "there are personal things more important than personality. Most important: is that member reliable? Reliability offers the only security in politics. Members want it from all their colleagues; they demand it from their leaders."[82]

No one, of course, is born hollow, with virtues instead of personality. Rather one makes oneself hollow. The paradigmatic example of someone who hollowed himself out is George Washington, both the clearest and the most successful example of the self-invention of a political man in America. Washington "was acutely aware of his public persona, and he took care to write and speak so as to create a favorable view of his motives, character, and achievements."[83] One could say that Washington, like Homer's Achilles, wanted to be a fictional character, taking as his own exemplar Addison's Cato; George Washington, writes Forrest McDonald, "was self-consciously both more than a mere man and less than a man: his people craved a myth and a symbol, and he devoted his life to fulfilling that need."[84] Washington succeeded in assimilating himself to one of Plutarch's heroes, whom, according to Gertrude Stein, Plutarch did not really feel "had any life except the life they . . . [were] given by their telling."[85] Washington succeeded in becoming a myth and a symbol, someone whose *whole* life could be captured in a Plutarchan "Life of Washington"—and without significantly distorting the genuine facts of Washington's life, the facts as he had fabricated them.

Washington gradually hollowed himself out particularly in his public presentation of his own private life, his performance of the role of Washington,

---

on the norm of hiding one's Greek learning more generally, see *De oratore* 2.1.4, and Bryan Garsten's discussion in "Saving Persuasion: Rhetoric and Judgment in Political Thought" (Ph.D. diss., Harvard University, 2003), 214–18. Contempt for Greek things continued to be a standard for old Roman virtue long after Cicero; see Juvenal (fl. c. 120 C.E.), *Satire* 6.184–99.

81. T. S. Eliot, "Imperfect Critics," in *The Sacred Wood*, 6th ed. (London: Methuen, 1948), 32.

82. John M. Barry, *The Ambition and the Power* (New York: Penguin, 1989), 17.

83. Stephen E. Lucas, "George Washington and the Rhetoric of Presidential Leadership," in *The Presidency and Rhetorical Leadership,* ed. Leroy G. Dorsey (College Station: Texas A&M University Press, 2002), 44.

84. Forrest McDonald, *The Presidency of George Washington* (Lawrence: University Press of Kansas, 1974), xi.

85. Gertrude Stein, *Narration* (Chicago: University of Chicago Press, 1935), 60–61. Stein, of course, contends that there must be something more to a life than is captured by Plutarch, something more than can be captured by "the historian who really knows everything and an historian really does he really does."

which was supposed to be all there was to the man Washington. In the last age the West has seen of ostentatious dress by the male members of the ruling classes, Washington as chief magistrate wore a plain brown suit of Connecticut cloth as his uniform and carried an unornamented sword.[86] Washington was ostentatious only in his publicly and repeatedly professed preference for private life over public life.

Unlike Washington, who won global and lasting fame by his successful self-fashioning, Nixon was accused of being a "self-made man." According to Edwin Black, "Nixon's preoccupation with self-creation made him impatient with modesty. It brought him to talk of himself too much, to solicit attention to his struggles, to his defeats and triumphs. . . . His public image became one to which his sense of himself had to adapt instead of, as in most of us, the reverse."[87] Black's criticism seems a bit odd, since most of "us" are not public persons and therefore have no public image: it would seem that Black is blaming Nixon for self-fashioning in public.[88]

After quoting a critique of Nixon's speaking style that he wrote for Nixon, William Safire remarks that "if I had to write that critique again, I would certainly add, 'Too much self-pity.' He found too much pleasure in recounting how the fashionable people would never appreciate what he did, a part of the 'us v. them' syndrome, and would lay too much stress on the courage it took to pursue the unpopular course."[89] Safire's observation is amply borne out by Nixon's broadcast speech on "The War in Vietnam" of 14 May 1969: "I know that some believe that I should have ended the war immediately after the Inauguration by simply ordering our forces home from Vietnam. This would have been an easy thing to do. It might have been a popular thing to do. But I would have betrayed my solemn responsibility as President of the United States if I had done so."[90] Washington hollowed himself out, leaving us with no subjective motives to distract us from his objective reasons for actions, so that his virtues became manifest in his public deeds and not in his claims about his own good intentions. Nixon put his whole self on display for his American viewers and audience, including his alleged inner motives.

---

86. On Washington's control of his own iconography, see Garry Wills, *Cincinnatus: George Washington and the Enlightenment* (Garden City, N.Y.: Doubleday, 1984).

87. Edwin Black, "The Invention of Nixon," in *Beyond the Rhetorical Presidency,* ed. Martin J. Medhurst (College Station: Texas A&M University Press, 1996), 121, 106.

88. See Wills, *Nixon Agonistes,* 155–61.

89. Safire, *Before the Fall,* 533.

90. Richard M. Nixon, "The War in Vietnam," in *American Rhetoric from Roosevelt to Reagan: A Collection of Speeches and Critical Essays,* 2nd ed., ed. Halford Ross Ryan (Prospect Heights, Ill.: Waveland Press, 1987), 134.

Nixon was successful for a time, but his success was one that we would not choose for ourselves—and not only because his success culminated in the disaster of Watergate, which Safire argues was the logical outcome of Nixon's understanding of politics as divided between policy making and image making. Two decades before Watergate there was Nixon's 1952 Checkers speech, in which he had exonerated himself from charges of corruption by displaying for all to see the scantiness of his means and the simplicity of his private life. Washington had thinned out his private life to the point of transparency; Nixon, on the other hand, flaunted his: "It was as if somehow in saving himself Nixon had paid too high a price. He had made himself even more the issue—not just his politics but himself. There was a growing feeling among the political and journalistic taste makers of the country that Nixon was not quite acceptable for very high office."[91] To be "suitable for very high office," to be "presidential," it is not enough to put on a convincing mask, a persona: Nixon's Checkers speech indeed succeeded in convincing listeners that he had not enriched himself out of his public activities. To be "presidential" is to persuade others that there is nothing about one's character to be revealed behind one's public performances.

Character and Advocacy

For Aristotle, men only have characters in what they say or in what they do, provided that what they say or do can itself be made to appear in public speech.[92] Eugene Garver claims "the character of the speaker is what is revealed in the speech."[93] This is true, but in a much stronger sense than Garver means. There is nothing else to character—whatever else there might be in the life of the one whose character it is—except what can be revealed in the speech.

In stating the point thus, we depart from the usual view: it is almost a commonplace of the literature on Aristotle's *Rhetoric* to make a distinction

91. David Halberstam, *The Powers That Be* (New York: Knopf, 1979), 330, quoted in Kathleen Hall Jamieson, *Packaging the Presidency,* 3rd ed. (New York: Oxford University Press, 1996), 79.

92. One can therefore radicalize Humphrey House's statement that in Aristotle's *Poetics,* the characters in a drama "only exist as characters in what they say and do" (*Aristotle's* Poetics [London: Rupert Hart-Davis, 1956], 72). What House notes as the Aristotelian view of drama is true of actual public life, not merely its theatrical re-creation.

93. Eugene Garver, *Aristotle's* Rhetoric: An Art of Character (Chicago: University of Chicago Press, 1994), 51.

between the real character of the speaker and the speaker's artful character, and it is frequently claimed that for Aristotle a speaker uses the rhetorical art to put on a mask of good character in order to persuade.[94] In making a distinction between the orator's real character and the character that he or she should craft into his or her speeches, Garver invokes an alleged feature of forensic rhetoric: namely, that, although the advocate in a trial must win our trust, we do not expect him or her to mean what he or she says.[95]

Garver brings forward no textual evidence from Aristotle to ground his appeal to forensic rhetoric but instead relies on features of modern advocacy that did not obtain in fourth-century Athens or even, to a certain extent, in Rome. The Athenians did not generally permit citizens to be represented in court—a forensic speaker generally spoke either as a personal prosecutor, whether on behalf of his own cause or the cause of the city, as a defendant pro se, or as a friend of the defendant.[96] They had no notion that a suspect was entitled to the best possible defense from the best possible advocate— indeed, they frequently punished those who in court assisted scoundrels.[97] The Athenians also felt little need to require proof of guilt "beyond a reasonable doubt" because they judged every case as a matter not only of justice but also of the public interest. In Athens speakers spoke in a fundamental sense only on their own behalf, for they only spoke for the sake of their private interest, for the sake of a friend or relative, or for the sake of their supposed personal interest as citizens in the welfare of the city.[98] The Athenian jury judged the merits of the speech, and thus the case, in the light of the apparent merits of the speaker. As an interpretation of Aristotle, Garver's appeal is thus anachronistic and must therefore be rejected.

94. See, for example, George E. Yoos, "A Revision of the Concept of Ethical Appeal," *Philosophy and Rhetoric* 12, no. 1 (1979): 41–58, who speaks of Aristotle's "emphasis on feigned *ethos*." See also James L. Kinneavy and Susan C. Warshauer, "From Aristotle to Madison Avenue: *Ethos* and the Ethics of Argument," in *Ethos: New Essays in Critical and Rhetorical Theory*, ed. James S. Baumlin and Tita French Baumlin (Dallas, Tex.: Southern Methodist University Press, 1994), 171–90.

95. Garver, *Aristotle's Rhetoric*, 195–96.

96. See George Kennedy, "The Rhetoric of Advocacy in Greece and Rome," *American Journal of Philology* 89, no. 4 (1968): 419–36.

97. See, for example, Lycurgus, *Against Leocrates* §§138–40; interestingly, at §6, Lycurgus justifies his prosecution of Leocrates for abandoning Athens in the crisis after Chaironeia not by invoking his own public spirit but by claiming that "the just citizen . . . will consider those who commit crimes against the fatherland to be private enemies" (my translation). Mere public spirit was apparently, for the Athenians, neither a credible nor a creditable motive for prosecuting one's fellow citizen.

98. On the need to justify advocating another's case in terms of one's own personal stake in the outcome, see, for example, Isocrates, *Against Euthynus* 1, and Demosthenes, *On the Crown* §5.

Part of the problem is that Garver has gotten the Greek word "ēthos" confused with the Latin "persona"; the Roman rhetorician Quintilian, by contrast, tells us that "ēthos" is "a word for which in my opinion Latin has no equivalent."[99] Indeed, Aristotle's notion of ethical proof as central to the art of rhetoric plays little or no role in Cicero's treatises on rhetoric.[100] For example in *De oratore*, the Academic Charmadas is said to have claimed that the knowledge of how the orator can *be* such a man as he desires to seem to be "lay thrust away and buried deep in the very heart of philosophy, and these rhetoricians had not so much as tasted it with the tip of the tongue."[101]

If we turn, however, from Cicero's teachings to his practice, the ethos or character of the Roman advocate, as distinct from the ethos of his client, appears in pleadings where representation is permitted. Consider this passage from the defense of Milo:

> You never, O judges, will inflict such grief upon me, (although, what grief can be so great as this?) but you will never inflict this particular grief upon me, of forcing me to forget how greatly you have always regarded me. And if you, yourselves, have forgotten it, or if any part of my conduct has offended you, why do you not make me atone for that offense rather than Milo? For I shall have lived gloriously enough if I die before seeing any such great misfortune happen to him.
>
> At present one consolation supports me, that no exertion that affection, or that zeal, or that gratitude could possibly make, has been wanting on my part to promote your interest, O Titus Annius. For your sake I have courted the enmity of powerful citizens; I have repeatedly exposed my person and my life to the weapons of your enemies; I have thrown myself as a suppliant at the feet of many for your sake; I have considered my fortunes and those of my children as united with yours in the time of your necessities. Lastly, on this very day, if any violence is prepared against you, or any struggle, or any danger of death, I claim my share in that. What remains now? What is there that I can say, or that I can do in return for your services to me, except considering whatever fortune is yours mine also? I do not object, I do

---

99. Quintilian, *Institutio oratoria* 6.2.8, trans. H. E. Butler (Cambridge, Mass.: Harvard University Press, 1920–22), cited in Richard Leo Enos and Karen Rossi Schnakenberg, "Cicero Latinizes Hellenic *Ēthos*," in *Ethos*, ed. Baumlin and Baumlin, 192.

100. See William M. Sattler, "Conceptions of *Ethos* in Ancient Rhetoric," *Speech Monographs* 14, no. 1 (1947): 55–65, 61, 64–65.

101. Cicero, *De oratore*, trans. E. W. Sutton and H. Rackham (1948; repr., Cambridge: Harvard University Press, 2001), 1.87.

not refuse so to consider it. And I entreat you, O judges, either to add to the kindnesses which you have already conferred on me by granting me this man's safety, or else to take notice that they will all perish in his fall.[102]

As Berry comments: "If an advocate is speaking on behalf of someone else, his speech will naturally seek to make capital out of his own character as well as that of the defendant and his opponent. Sometimes the advocate's character and standing might compensate for his client's character failings: if the jury like the speaker and approve of him, they may perhaps give his client the benefit of the doubt. In the speeches of his consulship and afterwards, Cicero makes much of his own authority (*auctoritas*): this is something he could deploy against an opponent, particularly a young one, with devastating results."[103] Cicero acknowledges in his speech in defense of the son of the dictator Sulla that judgment of his client depends in part on judgment of Cicero's own activity in appearing on his behalf: "If I am inconsistent and unstable, no . . . authority [*auctoritas*] should be given to my defense." Cicero even appeals from the judges' opinion of his own character to their opinion of the characters of his fellow advocates: "What do you think of these leading figures and distinguished citizens, men of drive and distinction, whom you can see thronging this court, making this case famous and proclaiming my client's innocence?"[104]

Despite their practice of advocacy, then, even among the Romans the advocate had to show himself to be a man of good character if he was to succeed in persuading the court on behalf of his client. Not least the advocate had show himself to be possessed of a good reason for defending the accused. Cicero himself ticks off the possible excuses one might use in appearing for a guilty man in the second Verrine oration: "Quintus, this man is not your kinsman, he is not your personal friend; of the pleas by which you have often in the past excused your lack of impartiality, none are at your disposal in your defence of Verres. When he was governing his province he used to say, openly and frequently, that he was doing what he was doing because he had confidence in you; and unless you are very careful, it will be

---

102. Cicero, *Pro Milone* 100, in *The Orations of Marcus Tullius Cicero*, trans. C. D. Yonge (London: George Bell, 1891).

103. D. H. Berry, introduction, in *Cicero: Defence Speeches*, trans. D. H. Berry (Oxford: Oxford University Press, 2000), xxviii.

104. Cicero, *Pro Sulla* §§10, 4, in *Pro Murena, Pro Sulla, Pro Flacco, Bks. 1–4*, trans. Coll Macdonald, new ed. (Cambridge, Mass.: Harvard University Press, 1977) (translation of 10 modified).

thought that he had good reason for saying so."[105] The English barrister, or at least the English barrister as described in the English court procedure novel, is obliged to accept any brief if his or her fee is paid. The Roman advocate, by contrast, stood for his client as a man who believed in his client's cause and endorsed his client with the full weight of his name and reputation.

In the knowledge mobilization model, the character of the knower is obviously crucial, since in that model knowledge is put to use by altering the position of the knower in the network of people and things.[106] But even in the knowledge diffusion model championed by Bernays, character reappears in the professional ethos of the "public relations counsel." The public relations counsel's crucial asset is good will, for which truthfulness is indispensable.[107] The public relations counsel "won't deal in spurious goods. They know that one such error would be fatal. The public may forget, but the editor never." "The standards of the public relations counsel are his own standards and he will not accept a client whose standards do not come up to them." The public relations counsel will shun "those whose cases in a law court would be valid, but whose cases in the higher court of public opinion are questionable." To sum up, the public relations counsel "should be candid in his dealings": "It must be repeated that his business is not to fool or to hoodwink the public. If he were to get such a reputation, his usefulness in his profession would be at an end. When he is sending out propaganda material, it is clearly labeled as to source. The editor knows from whom it comes and what its purpose is, and accepts or rejects it on its merits as news."[108] There is, it turns out, a network of ethical knowledge, knowledge of character, within which the propagandist or public relations specialist must act, a network that encompasses the editors and journalists whom the public relations specialist needs to get his message out to the public. If by "ethical" we mean not adhering to some code of ethics but manifesting ethos, then the public relations person is ethical toward the client and toward the journalist but not toward the public. This is not because it is the duty of the public relations person to cheat the public by seducing the journalist on behalf of the client but because the public relations

105. Cicero, *Verrine Orations* 5.176, trans. Greenwood, cited in Matthias Gelzer, *The Roman Nobility*, trans. Robin Seager (Oxford: Basil Blackwell, 1969), 118; see also *Pro Sulla* 6.

106. On the knowledge mobilization model and the knowledge diffusion model, see the introduction, 7–12.

107. Edward L. Bernays, *Public Relations* (Norman: University of Oklahoma Press, 1952), 5, 128.

108. Bernays, *Crystallizing Public Opinion*, 198, 215, 216; Edward L. Bernays, *Propaganda* (New York: Liveright, 1928), 45–46.

counselor does not appear before the public. The public relations specialist is what fourth-century B.C.E. Greeks called a logographer, one who writes speeches for a plaintiff or defendant to speak in his own name: it is the public relations specialist's job to present the client's ethos, not his or her own ethos, to the public. It is no accident that advertisements are issued in the name of the advertiser and not the copywriter.[109]

Such a distributed, interconnected knowledge system, in which the public relations specialist must win the trust of media personnel, is quite different from the centralized knowledge bureau that Bernays is thinking of in describing the then new field of public relations. Bernays's knowledge diffusion model turns out to be unable to account for his own success in public relations.

The public relations counsel "does not accept a client whose case he believes to be hopeless or whose product he believes to be unmarketable." Or as a more recent practitioner, George W. Bush campaign aide Stuart Stevens, puts the point, "The secret to success in political consulting is to work for candidates who were going to win anyway."[110] To avoid a reputation with media personnel as untrustworthy, the public relations counsel must refrain from trying to sell a view that the media will be see as implausible.

Character and the Art of Publicity

Aristotle never makes a distinction between artful—or apparent—and real character.[111] The closest he comes is when he acknowledges that "since all accept speeches that are spoken in their own character or similar to it, it is not unclear how we employ our speeches so that we and our speeches will appear their sort."[112] We can certainly shade our speeches somewhat to

---

109. Leon H. Mayhew contrasts public relations work as advocacy (and therefore as lacking a publicly visible professional ethos), as opposed to auditing professions like accounting, where the information is supposed to be presented to the public according to generally known and accepted standards (*The New Public: Professional Communication and the Means of Social Influence* [Cambridge: Cambridge University Press, 1997], 204). Accountants, of course, present their reports in their own name even though they are paid by the organizations they are auditing. Mayhew fails to recognize that public relations people, too, present their ethos, but to media personnel, not to the public.

110. Bernays, *Propaganda*, 45; Stuart Stevens, *Big Enchilada*, 97; see also John Joseph Brady, *Bad Boy: The Life and Politics of Lee Atwater* (Reading, Mass.: Addison-Wesley, 1997), 135.

111. As Jan Swearingen writes, "Aristotle neither defines nor implies the notion of a selfhood, authenticity, or essential identity for a speaker or actor, a univocal 'true' self that contrasts with the voice and character taken on for rhetorical speech or acting" (*"Ethos:* Imitation, Impersonation, and Voice," in *Ethos*, ed. Baumlin and Baumlin, 121).

112. Aristotle, *Rhetoric* 2.13.16, 1390a25–28.

correspond to the characteristics of the audience. Yet since knowing what virtue looks like is part of actually being virtuous, our ability to appear trustworthy is dependent, if only partially, on actually possessing the qualities of people who are likely to be trusted by a certain audience. Just as the typical way to appear knowledgeable is to possess the relevant knowledge together with the rhetorical skill to make one's knowledge manifest, so too the typical way to appear of good character is to possess the proper qualities and the skill to ensure that those qualities are revealed in what one says.[113]

The virtues, says Quintilian, are matter for the rhetorician as much as for the philosopher.[114] Rhetoric, public relations, and campaign management are matters of the representation of ethos, not of the creation of a persona. In this respect nothing vital has changed since the age of private streetcar lines: "The public relations man who tries to camouflage a reactionary chief executive may as well try to get blood out of a turnip, get up heat without steam, lift himself by his bootstraps or attempt any other impossible stunt. . . . When I was asked in New York, a few months ago, what a director of public relations for a street railway should do first of all, I answered without hesitation: 'He must choose the right kind of president.'"[115] Despite the claim of Joe McGinniss in *The Selling of the President* that Nixon's advertising and media men invented "the New Nixon," Richard Nixon's aides generally felt "their job was to let the public see Nixon as he is."[116] It would, in any case, be impossible for a U.S. presidential candidate to perform a persona over the length of time a campaign takes. For a public figure like Nixon, the task of the artful persuader is not to contradict the impressions people already have of him but to supplement these impressions with other, favorable ones. As a former Edward Kennedy aide commented on Kennedy's 1980 presidential campaign: "They tried to make out that [he] was a happily married man. I call that image re-touching. You can't tell people something when they know the opposite."[117]

It is true that the speaker must attempt to assimilate his or her character to the character of his or her audience, but this too is a form of ethical proof. Take as an illustration Aristotle's discussion of the speaker who seeks

113. Cf. E. M. Cope, *An Introduction to Aristotle's* Rhetoric (London: Macmillan, 1867), 248–49 n. 1.

114. See the preface in Quintilian, *Institutio oratoria* 1.9–12.

115. Thomas Dreier quoted in Eric F. Goldman, *The Two-Way Street: The Emergence of the Public Relations Counsel* (Boston: Bellman, 1948), iv n. 39.

116. Jamieson, *Packaging the Presidency*, 265 (quoting Price memo).

117. Jamieson, *Packaging the Presidency*, 263–69, 382 (Kennedy aide quote); see also Garry Wills, *Reagan's America: Innocents at Home* (Garden City, N.Y.: Doubleday, 1987), 381.

to persuade an aged audience. Now, according to Aristotle, the old do not merely love advantage more than honor; the old believe that to love advantage more than honor is an aspect of the character of virtuous men.[118] They thus fear lest even the speaker who speaks only in terms of advantage and disadvantage harbors a secret love of honor. The man most successful at showing himself to prefer advantage to honor will, other things being equal, be the most successful at persuading an audience of the aged. The speaker will be most naturally persuasive if he truly loves advantage more than honor. Deception can and certainly does occur, but rhetoric is not the skill of deceiving; it is the skill of communicating or making manifest.

Such a skill should not be exercised too openly, however. As Aristotle advises, "Introduce yourself right away as being of a certain sort, so that they will look on you as this sort, and your opponent [as being of a certain sort]—but do this invisibly."[119] What is to be concealed here is not one's true character but one's art in making one's own character and that of one's opponent appear to the audience.

Character in the context of the true art of rhetoric is the same ethos that is the subject of Aristotle's ethical philosophy. Instead of contrasting real with merely artfully apparent character, we are more faithful to the phenomena of political life Aristotle sought to explain if we understand character in both ethics and rhetoric as essentially that which generally ought to appear in artful speeches, if the speeches are correctly written and if the audience is not corrupted in its judgments of character by its own vices.[120] We, under the influence of Cartesian dualism, assume that to articulate character in one's speeches is to present something that is external and other to one's inner, real self.[121] We readily combine this post-Cartesian disdain for the world of appearances with our conception of the narrative self. Thus we come to believe that the speaker uses rhetoric in general and the argument from character in particular to hide rather than to reveal his story.[122] This

---

118. Aristotle, *Rhetoric* 2.13.9, 1389b36–1390a2.

119. Aristotle, *Rhetoric* 3.16.10, 1417b7–8.

120. See Aristotle, *Rhetoric* 1.1.12, 1355a22ff., and Larry Arnhart, *Aristotle on Political Reasoning: A Commentary on the* Rhetoric (DeKalb: Northern Illinois University Press, 1981), 11, 27–28. Garver himself comes close to recognizing this when he says that "in a flourishing polis, and in artful rhetoric at its best, *logos* and *ethos* are aligned" and "the moral virtues in Aristotle's hands look more like rhetorical and strategic skills than a modern reader might expect" (*Aristotle's* Rhetoric, 171, 214).

121. Swearingen, "*Ethos:* Imitation, Impersonation, and Voice," 129.

122. The central difficulty for us in assessing Aristotle's understanding of rhetoric is that Aristotle always connects the normative with the typical, generic, or normal, while we tend to see the normative as superordinate or extraordinary; see, for example, Jürgen Sprute, "Aristotle

peculiarly modern cynicism ignores the fact that pretense could only be effective if it were rare—lying, or pretending to virtues or knowledge that one lacks, can only help a speaker if nearly all speakers nearly all of the time are speaking in order to reveal the truth about themselves and the matter under discussion.[123]

Yet surely there are limits to what even an ethically virtuous speaker can hope to convey in his speeches to an ethically uncorrupted audience. Indeed, it is a crucial aspect of the rhetorical situation that the members of the audience always fear something is being hidden from them: opposing speakers frequently endeavor to persuade them that the speech they just heard arose from the speaker's private, hidden interests or was corrupted by the speaker's private, hidden vices. It should come as no surprise that for Aristotle drawing out the contradiction between a politician's public praise of the noble and the just and his private wish for the advantageous is the most powerful "commonplace" of political rhetoric.[124] That is to say, one can make other speakers' claims unpersuasive by making an inference from their open to their secret professions or vice versa.[125] Private conduct, not only private opinions, affects public judgment: there is every evidence that the Athenians were as fascinated with the sexual misbehavior of political figures as are present-day Americans, though the transgressions that brought obloquy were not the same then as now.[126] As soon as the speaker's private character is questioned, the speaker is in trouble, trouble from which it is very

and the Legitimacy of Rhetoric," in *Aristotle's* Rhetoric: *Philosophical Essays,* ed. David J. Furley and Alexander Nehemas (Princeton: Princeton University Press, 1994), 121, and C. D. C. Reeve, "Philosophy, Politics, and Rhetoric in Aristotle," in *Essays on Aristotle's* Rhetoric, ed. Amélie Oksenberg Rorty (Berkeley and Los Angeles: University of California Press, 1996). In consequence, Aristotle's claim that the true and ethically worthy speech is typically more persuasive than the false but artfully expressed one (*Rhetoric* 1.1.12, 1355a22ff., 1355a37–38) is often misunderstood as "idealistic" and therefore dismissed as naive.

123. See Ruth W. Grant, *Hypocrisy and Integrity: Machiavelli, Rousseau, and the Ethics of Politics* (Chicago: University of Chicago Press, 1997), 13–14; Richard A. Posner, *An Affair of State: The Investigation, Impeachment, and Trial of President Clinton* (Cambridge, Mass.: Harvard University Press, 1999), 142, 187.

124. Aristotle, *Rhetoric* 2.23.16, 1399a28–32.

125. See Aristotle, *Sophistical Refutations* 12, 172b35–172a30, and Edward Meredith Cope, *The* Rhetoric *of Aristotle with a Commentary,* ed. John Edwin Sandys, 3 vols. (Cambridge: Cambridge University Press, 1877), commentary to *Rhetoric* 2.23.16 on 274–75.

126. See Aeschines' *Against Timarchus* and the literature that has grown up around it following K. J. Dover, *Greek Homosexuality* (Cambridge, Mass.: Harvard University Press, 1978), especially Michel Foucault, *The Uses of Pleasure,* vol. 2 of *The History of Sexuality,* trans. Robert Hurley (New York: Vintage Books, 1985), David M. Halperin, "The Democratic Body: Prostitution and Citizenship in Classical Athens," in *One Hundred Years of Homosexuality and Other Essays on Greek Love* (New York: Routledge, 1989), 88–112, and David Cohen, *Law, Violence, and Community in Classical Athens* (Cambridge: Cambridge University Press, 1995).

unlikely that he or she will ever fully extricate himself or herself. If one charge is successfully refuted, people will simply suspect that he or she is hiding something else.

In elections, we choose the man (and now the woman) not the measure. But we can choose the man or woman on the basis of the measures he or she proposes or on our assessment of his or her ability to carry them out, including his or her ability to manage affairs in the face of unanticipated difficulties.[127] The very concept of rhetoric is threatened by the assignment of all things to one or another substantive area of expertise: what, we may wonder with Socrates, can the rhetorician add to a deliberation about war that the general is not better equipped to supply?[128] The need to influence and clarify judgments of character provides a minimum content for rhetoric. Judgment of character provides a minimum role for rhetoric in that there is no peculiar area of expertise to which it can be assigned. In that sense rhetoric has no subject matter. Rhetoric is not about things or about human beings understood as things: rhetoric is reflective manipulation of the distinction between our relations to each other and our relations to things.

Character is in between the individual and the impersonal. Character is central in understanding politics because it is as characters, as bearers of qualities of character such as honesty, integrity, intelligence, opportunism, or greed, that human beings appear to each other when they come together to discuss and decide. But character manifests itself only in action: to understand what, say, Edmund Muskie was doing in judging others by judging their actions, we will next explore the political activity of giving advice.

127. See Samuel Popkin, *The Reasoning Voter: Communication and Persuasion in Presidential Campaigns* (Chicago: University of Chicago Press, 1994), 61–62.

128. On the problem of the content of rhetoric vis-à-vis substantive expertise, see Plato, *Gorgias* 449a–456a; Karl R. Wallace, "The Substance of Rhetoric: Good Reasons," *Quarterly Journal of Speech* 49, no. 3 (1963): 240–49.

2

ACTION

It's a wonder how much will get done when people are concerned with who gets the credit.

—DICK ARMEY

We judge someone, that is to say, we judge someone's character, by his or her actions. Actions provide the opportunity for judging character, Aristotle demonstrates, because character, which is potential, becomes visible in action: "We praise and blame all looking toward their deliberate preference [*proairesis*] rather than their actions, although the activity [of a virtue] is preferable to the virtue [if it is not active], because under compulsion anybody may do worthless acts, though no one deliberately prefers to do them. Still, because it is not easy to see the deliberate preference, what sort it is, on account of this we are compelled to judge from his acts what sort someone is."[1] It is through action one shows oneself as one is. The greater one's opportunities for action, the more we can see of one's possibilities and limitations. The wider the scope for action, the more definitive the grounds of judgment. The nineteenth-century historian Lord Acton claimed famously that "absolute power corrupts absolutely," that one's character will be corrupted if one has an unhindered scope for action. Aristotle, by contrast, quotes with approval the proverb that ruling will show what a man is worth and will show it more clearly insofar as his scope for action is broader.[2]

Chapter 2's epigraph comes from *Armey's Axioms* (Hoboken, N.J.: John Wiley, 2003), axiom 19.

1. Aristotle, *Eudemian Ethics* 2.11.12, 1228a15–16 (my translation); cf. Thomas B. Silver, *Coolidge and the Historians* (Durham, N.C.: Carolina Academic Press, 1982), 63, and Charles Taylor, "Action as Expression," in *Intention and Intentionality: Essays in Honor of G. E. M. Anscombe* (London: Harvester Press, 1979), 87.

2. Aristotle, *Nicomachean Ethics* 5.1.16, 1130a1–2; on the distance between Acton's claim and Aristotle's contention that power exposes rather than corrupts, see Tom Shippey, *The Road*

To show character, whether in describing another or in presenting ourselves, we must show that character in action. David Mamet's advice to the
playwright has general application: "Characterization is taken care of by
the author, and if the author knows what he is about, he also will avoid it
like the plague, and show us what the character does rather than having the
character's entrance greeted with 'Well, well, if it isn't my ne'er-do-well
half brother, just returned from New Zealand.'"[3] To show character, show
an action; to show an action, tell a story. "Examinations of character often
rely on the 'telling anecdote'—the vignette or story that illuminates a larger
point and, in a vivid shorthand, explains more than the vignette itself."[4] The
story is an account of an action that reveals the actor. Only in that way can
the writer show character as alive, as possessing the potential for action.

The record of actions of a politician's life is his or her career, and as Joseph
Bessette says of his former employer Richard M. Daley, "The most effective
way to convince the citizenry . . . that he was doing a good job was, most
simply, by doing a good job."[5] A public figure without a record has a problem, as Richard Fenno records of Senator Pete Domenici: "In those early
months of 1979, Domenici expressed some sense that he was still thrash-
ing about, that he had not settled into any recognizable pattern of congressional activity."[6] Note well the mention of what is "recognizable"—a senator
ought to have a communicable record of legislation to be reelected, and a
record is successfully communicated only to the extent that voters understand the incumbent's actions and their purposes.[7] A first-time candidate's
prior career likewise ought to be capable of being understood by voters as
constituting a record of political actions. For example, American voters might

---

to *Middle-Earth: How J .R. R. Tolkien Created a New Mythology*, rev. and exp. ed. (Boston: Houghton Mifflin, 2003), 137.

3. David Mamet, *Some Freaks* (New York: Viking, 1989), 61–62. As Anna Kochin pointed
out to me, this greeting reveals a great deal about the greeter's character, if not that of the Kiwi
brother. Wayne Booth famously emphasized the role of telling rather than showing in *The Rhetoric of Fiction* (Chicago: University of Chicago Press, 1961). Yet as Booth demonstrates at length,
what an author shows through telling is the character of the implied author or the narrator.

4. Dayton Duncan, "The Miscovered Campaign," *Boston Globe Magazine*, 11 June 1989,
quoted in John Joseph Brady, *Bad Boy: The Life and Politics of Lee Atwater* (Reading, Mass.:
Addison-Wesley, 1997), 173.

5. Joseph Bessette, *The Mild Voice of Reason: Deliberative Democracy and American National
Government* (Chicago: University of Chicago Press, 1994), xiv; cf. Richard F. Fenno Jr., *Senators
on the Campaign Trail: The Politics of Representation* (Norman: University of Oklahoma Press,
1996), 19.

6. Richard F. Fenno Jr., *The Emergence of a Senate Leader: Pete Domenici and the Reagan
Budget* (Washington, D.C.: Congressional Quarterly Press, 1991), 31.

7. Dennis W. Johnson, *No Place for Amateurs* (London: Routledge, 2001), 66.

have seen Eisenhower prior to his run for the presidency in 1952 as "apolitical" just because he was a figure whose popularity transcended partisan politics. But voters also understood that politics embraces actions that are not simply partisan and therefore that Eisenhower—who was not only hailed throughout the West as the architect of Allied victory in Europe but had also subsequently shouldered a musket in Truman's Cold War as commander of NATO—did have a relevant record of political actions.

Dan Quayle, by contrast, became a byword for political immaturity not only because of his boyish good looks but because—despite eight years in the Senate—he did not succeed in presenting a record that seemed relevant to executive office.[8] Another example that shows a failure to reflect on how to present one's record emerges in Richard Fenno's analysis of the political career of John Glenn. When running for president in 1984, Glenn could not explain why his astronaut past was relevant and failed to integrate it with his subsequent experience and achievements in public life. For this reason, the Glenn campaign discovered that, although "all their polling told them that Democrats preferred a candidate like John Glenn," the Democrats "did not yet prefer John Glenn." "We found that the opinions of an overwhelming number of Democrats match what John Glenn stands for," said one aide. But, he added, "what was startling was that most people were not connecting Glenn to the view that they had on the issues." The voters could not connect Glenn to their views on the issues because Glenn had done nothing readily comprehensible by the public that would enable it to connect his own record as, in Fenno's words, "America's greatest peacetime hero" to his own views on the issues or to his actions as senator.

Having discovered that he was politically vulnerable in his run for the presidency, Glenn rehabilitated himself in his 1986 Senate reelection campaign by linking himself with technological and military affairs: Glenn's principal television advertisement showed him talking about the Chernobyl nuclear accident in the Ukraine. Glenn left the Senate Foreign Relations Committee for the Armed Services Committee, and his prominence as an astronaut suddenly become directly relevant—for the first time in his political career—after the space shuttle *Challenger* disaster.[9]

8. On looks, see James W. Ceaser and Andrew E. Busch, *Red over Blue: The 2004 Elections and American Politics* (Lanham, Md.: Rowman and Littlefield, 2005), 95; on Quayle's lack of a record, see Richard F. Fenno Jr., *The Making of a Senator: Dan Quayle* (Washington, D.C.: Congressional Quarterly Press, 1989).

9. Richard F. Fenno Jr., *The Presidential Odyssey of John Glenn* (Washington, D.C.: Congressional Quarterly Press, 1990), 10, 158–60, 262–63, 267, 275.

Men, Not Measures

To judge persons or parties solely by their policy views assumes that these policies can be implemented without regard for circumstances and events. We should look at enacted policy to see how these men and women responded to past contingencies, which should tell us something about how they will respond to future contingencies. The record is important, not because of what it says about the speaker's past achievements but as a means of judging his or her future prospects. A publicly visible record, to use Alexander Hamilton's words, "enable[s] the people, when they see reason to approve of [a politician's] conduct, to continue him in the station, in order to prolong the utility of his talents and virtues."[10] To understand how character is judged, then, we need to understand how records are judged. A record is a record of actions; thus to judge character is to judge action.

Policy is past accomplishments or present efforts, but character, as we infer it from past actions and present aspirations, is our predictor of future actions. When voters judge candidates by considering how they would invent and implement policies for unanticipated circumstances, they are making the case for choosing the best man or woman over the most suitable party platform.[11] Indeed, as James Ceaser has shown, American political parties originally constituted themselves not as conglomerates of interests but as institutions for choosing suitable characters to fill the presidential chair.[12]

Why, then, do politicians "take stands on the issues" when they "run" for office? We do get help in judging public figures when they put forward policy views, though not so much because we expect them to put these views straight into action but because these views indicate what that person is capable of. As a student of political advertising has put it, "The best way to make a positive image impression on the voter is to use issues."[13] Fenno writes that, on the campaign trail, "policies count, but mostly as vehicles

---

10. *Federalist Papers*, no. 72, cited in Ceaser and Busch, *Red over Blue*, 3.

11. Pace Neil Postman, *Amusing Ourselves to Death* (New York: Viking, 1985), 133. See also Michael McGee, "'Not Men, but Measures': The Origins and Import of an Ideological Principle," *Quarterly Journal of Speech* 64, no. 2 (1978): 141–54, and Tony Schwartz, *The Responsive Chord* (New York: Doubleday, 1973), 102–3.

12. James W. Ceaser, *Presidential Selection: Theory and Development* (Princeton: Princeton University Press, 1979).

13. L. Patrick Devlin, "An Analysis of Presidential Television Commercials, 1952–1984," in *New Perspectives on Political Advertising*, ed. Lynda Lee Kaid, Dan Nimmo, and Keith R. Sanders (Carbondale: Southern Illinois University Press, 1986), 26; Karen S. Johnson-Cartee and Gary A. Copeland, *Inside Political Campaigns: Theory and Practice* (Westport, Conn.: Praeger, 1997), 86–87.

through which each candidate displays and communicates a political persona. It matters that Senator Pell opposes the Vietnam War, but it matters more that he uses it to display his political independence. It matters that [Senator] Pryor investigates government consultants, but it matters more that he uses it to portray himself as a watchdog against bureaucratic waste."[14] Pell and Pryor, in these examples, are displaying their character by the action of taking stands. Issues matter, but character matters more.

Fenno's clearest case of the relevance of policy views for the judgment of character is the liberal Republican senator from Pennsylvania, Arlen Specter: "In a strategic sense, [Specter used issue papers] to help make the essential contrast with his opponent, who had none." Specter thus demonstrated his ability to act in a manner that helps voters bridge the gap between comparisons of policy views, which they make with relative ease but that are of limited use to them in deciding whom to support, and evaluations of character, which they make with relative difficulty. Most important, by articulating policy views Specter showed himself competent and concerned to master the details of policy. Second, since these views put him at odds with both the Republican and the Democratic party lines, Specter asked to be judged as a maverick. He "set the individualistic standards by which he would be judged[15]

To appear sufficiently presidential to be nominated, much less elected, George W. Bush, explains Jeff Greenfield, "had to demonstrate enough grasp of substance to erase the sense that he was nothing more than a fortunate son, gliding to the presidency on a path that had been greased by good connections and good fortune." To defeat Al Gore, who was, like Michael Dukakis and "wonder-boy" Herbert Hoover, perceived to be a "policy wonk," the campaign decided Bush would have to "spend four months talking about policy proposals."[16] As Bush campaign aide Stuart Stevens puts it, "No Republican primary candidate had ever gone as far as Bush had in laying out a governing framework of serious proposals involving the work of some of the leading talent in their fields. But it may also be true that no candidate had ever *needed* to go through this process as much as George Bush."[17]

14. Fenno, *Senators on the Campaign Trail,* 324.

15. Richard F. Fenno, *Learning to Legislate: The Senate Education of Arlen Specter* (Washington, D.C.: Congressional Quarterly Press, 1991), 6–7, 9–10.

16. Jeff Greenfield, *"Oh, Waiter! One Order of Crow": Inside the Strangest Presidential Election Finish in American History* (New York: G. P. Putnam's Sons, 2001), 37, 175.

17. Stuart Stevens, *The Big Enchilada: Campaign Adventures with the Cockeyed Optimists from Texas Who Won the Biggest Prize in Politics* (New York: The Free Press, 2001), 96.

Political candidates are certainly advertised, and even marketed, just as products are frequently and—perhaps a greater surprise—effectively endorsed by their company's CEOs.[18] Nonetheless there remains a distinction between a political platform and a product. Consider the following passage from Edward Bernays:

> An entire party, a platform, an international policy is sold to the public, or is not sold, on the basis of the intangible element of personality. A [c]harming candidate is the alchemist's secret that can transmute a prosaic platform into the gold of votes. Helpful as is a candidate who for some reason has caught the imagination of the country, the party and its aims are certainly more important than the personality of the candidate. Not personality, but the ability of the candidate to carry out the party's program adequately, and the program itself should be emphasized in a sound campaign plan. Even Henry Ford, the most picturesque personality in business in America to-day, has become known through his product, and not his product through him.[19]

A product is an achievement in the present: at the time Bernays was writing, the late 1920s, Henry Ford was rapidly losing market share to General Motors through his failure to innovate his product, his failure to deal with the possibility of change in the future by offering new model cars in place of the Model T. A platform is a set of promises about the future: the platform wins support by what it promises to do. It also provides a standard by which performance can be judged retrospectively.

The mere fact that the candidate puts forth a standard can be more important than the content of the standard: just ask George H. W. "Read my lips, no new taxes" Bush. This was a promise that most Americans would probably have preferred that Bush had never made, but the very act of taking a stand helped get him elected (and he ultimately failed to get reelected in part because he did not keep this campaign promise).[20] In American presidential campaigns, the platform matters primarily because putting it together

18. Dulcie Straughan, Glen L. Bleske, and Xinshu Zhao, "Modeling Format and Source Effects of an Advertising Message," *Journalism and Mass Communication Quarterly* 73, no. 1 (1996): 135–46, cited in Xinshu Zhao, "A Variable-Based Typology and a Review of Advertising-Related Persuasion Research During the 1990s," in *The Persuasion Handbook: Developments in Theory and Practice,* ed. James Price Dillard and Michael Pfau (Thousand Oaks, Calif.: Sage, 2002), 499–500.

19. Edward L. Bernays, *Propaganda* (New York: Liveright, 1928), 101.

20. See Johnson, *No Place for Amateurs,* 64–65.

creates a scope for action, not because of its content. The platform, like other elements of the campaign and convention, provides an example of political action from which we judge a candidate's competence in managing.[21]

Since judgment of character is judgment of action, our next step must be to clarify the canons for the judgment of political action in order to show how these canons are put to work in speeches. Fortunately, there is a speech from Greek antiquity, *On the Crown* by Demosthenes, who, after Pericles, was the greatest orator of democratic Athens, that is not only classical in its provenance but also in the sense that it sets out some of the most central canons for the judgment of action.[22] Both Demosthenes and his modern interpreters put the question of judgment of action by its consequences at the center of their arguments. In order to understand what is at stake in the confrontation between Demosthenes and his rival Aeschines, some preliminary remarks are required about the different ways actions appear to actors and historians.

Political Time and Consequentialist Judgment: The Apology of Demosthenes

Although we generally act out of concern for the future, in our best moments we bracket anxieties about "what may happen" that do not relate to matters under our current control. David Mamet instructs us in this wisdom through the apology of Roma, his exemplary boiler-room real estate salesman, in *Glengarry Glen Ross:*

ROMA: If it happens, AS IT MAY for that is not within our powers, I will deal with it, just as I do today with what draws my concern today. I say, this is how we must act. I do those things which seem to me correct

---

21. Samuel Popkin, *The Reasoning Voter: Communication and Persuasion in Presidential Campaigns* (Chicago: University of Chicago Press, 1994), 62.

22. Here I will explore a single speech, Demosthenes' *On the Crown*, and a single aspect of judgment, the relation between judgment of an action and judgment of its consequences. Readers whose appetite is whetted for the rhetorical phenomenology of the judgment of action can explore the Hellenistic theory of issues (*staseis*), which is best understood as an attempt to set out all possible categories under which an action can be judged; making himself conscious of the categories helps the orator ensure that he addresses each category in making his case. See Hermogenes, *On Issues,* trans. Malcolm Heath (Oxford: Oxford University Press, 1995); George Kennedy, *Greek Rhetoric Under Christian Emperors* (Princeton: Princeton University Press, 1983), 80–86; D. A. Russell, *Greek Declamation* (Cambridge: Cambridge University Press, 1983), chap. 3, "Teachers and Theories."

today. I trust myself. And if security concerns me, I do that which today I think will make me secure. And every day I do that, when that day arrives that I need a reserve, (a) odds are that I have it, and (b) the true reserve that I have is the strength that I have of acting each day without fear.[23]

The category of action that concerns us here is the giving of political advice. To give political advice is not to raise hopes or make promises, not least because those on the receiving end of the advice listen in order to find out what they themselves are to do. As Calvin Coolidge said: "The country cannot be run on the promise of what it will do for the people. The only motive to which they will continue ready to respond is the opportunity to do something for themselves, to achieve their own greatness, to work out their destiny."[24] To give political advice is to speak about present things, about what opportunities or advantages or dangers are now present, so as to show what can be shown about the future. That is, the best political speakers avoid attempting to state what *will* happen, emphasizing instead what we aspire to make happen: "The progress of our arms, upon which all else chiefly depends, is as well known to the public as to myself; and it is, I trust, reasonably satisfactory and encouraging to all. With high hope for the future, no prediction in regard to it is ventured," to quote Lincoln's second inaugural.

To offer political advice is to see things beginning, to see where they are going, and to tell others about them before they happen.[25] But how do we judge political advice? We cannot judge it simply by judging the motives of the speaker, since if the advice is novel because the speaker's motives are novel, the speaker probably differs from us in either interests or values and so is unlikely to persuade.[26]

Nor can we judge advice by the actual consequences of our having accepted it. Our judgment of actions ex post facto is a judgment of the judgment on which these actions relied. Consequentialism, the belief that actions ought to be judged strictly by the state of affairs that result from them, is a vice of the historian. As the Lincoln scholar Don Fehrenbacher

---

23. David Mamet, *Glengarry Glen Ross* (New York: Grove, 1984), 1.3.

24. Calvin Coolidge, "The Foundation of Our Institutions," in *The Price of Freedom: Speeches and Addresses* (New York: Charles Scribner's Sons, 1924), 293; cf. 281.

25. Demosthenes, *On the Crown* §§191, 26, and Demosthenes, *Preambles* 21.4, 28.1.

26. As a rhetorical critic I can only say that I subscribe to Elizabeth Anscombe's disclaimer: "As for the importance of considering the motives of an action . . . I am very glad not be writing either ethics or literary criticism, to which this question belongs" (*Intention* [1957; repr., Cambridge, Mass.: Harvard University Press, 2000], 19).

puts it, "The historian, knowing what happens next, is excluded by the very certainty of his knowledge from the contingent world of those who make history."[27] The historian, echoes H. Stuart Hughes, "cannot give the full sense of events as reality in the process of becoming—*because he knows the outcome.* By no literary device or trick of false innocence can he recapture his historical virginity; it is idle for him to pretend to an unsophistication of judgment which fools nobody."[28]

The contrast between the canons of political judgment and the historians' canons of consequentialist judgment can be seen through an examination of Demosthenes' speech *On the Crown.* Demosthenes' speech is not only the greatest speech that remains to us from the Greek experience of politics; the speech has at its central theme the relation between the judgment of political actions and the judgment of their consequences.

Ever since 346 B.C.E., Demosthenes had striven to form an alliance of Greek cities capable of defying Philip of Macedon. In 339 Thebes and Athens at last came together as the pillars of such an alliance, but their confrontation with Philip ended in defeat at Chaeronea in 338. Demosthenes was not, however, disgraced politically by the defeat of his policy. He was given charge of the defenses of the city, and he oversaw the repair of the city wall and the reorganization of the city's finances so as to meet the emergency. Although Demosthenes was ultimately unsuccessful in his attempts to stop Philip and, later, to stop Philip's heir Alexander, Demosthenes' political friend Ctesiphon nonetheless proposed in 336 that he be recognized for his service to Athens by being presented with a golden crown in the theater of Dionysus, where the herald would "proclaim . . . before the Greeks that the Athenian People crown [Demosthenes] for his virtue and manly worth, because he continues saying and doing the best things for the People."[29] The proposal was passed by the Council (the *Boulē,* which set the legislative agenda for the Assembly), but Aeschines, Demosthenes' principal rival, immediately charged Ctesiphon with having proposed an illegal decree. Aeschines thereby blocked the decree from being considered by the Athenian People in their assembly.

When Aeschines finally brought Ctesiphon to trial in 330, he alleged three

27. Don Edward Fehrenbacher, *Prelude to Greatness: Lincoln in the 1850's* (Stanford, Calif.: Stanford University Press, 1962), 26–27.

28. H. Stuart Hughes, quoted in Robert Sobel, *Coolidge: An American Enigma* (Washington, D.C.: Regnery, 1998), 393–94. On consequentialism as the vice of the historians, see Michael S. Kochin, "Time and Judgment in Demosthenes, *De Corona,*" *Philosophy and Rhetoric* 35, no. 1 (2002): 77–89.

29. Aeschines, *Against Ctesiphon* §49 (all translations of extracts from *Against Ctesiphon* are mine).

violations of the law in Ctesiphon's decree: first, it illegally proposed award-
ing Demosthenes his crown in the theater before a mixed audience of Athenians and foreign Greeks, even though the law demanded that all crowns
awarded by the People could be proclaimed only in the Assembly, from which
foreigners were excluded. Second, Ctesiphon had proposed crowning Demosthenes even though Demosthenes was ineligible to receive honors at the
time, since Demosthenes had not yet made an accounting to the People of
the offices he held. Third and most important, Ctesiphon had proposed to
engrave false claims among the decrees passed by the People, since, as the
defeat at Chaeronea and the failure of Demosthenes' whole policy had shown,
to use Aeschines' own words, that Demosthenes "has not even begun to
speak the best things, nor does he now continue to do what has the most
advantageous consequences for the People."[30]

In *On the Crown* Demosthenes advocates acquitting the defendant, Ctesiphon, for proposing an illegal decree. As Stephen Usher has observed,
the speech does not easily fit into any one of Aristotle's three rhetorical
genres, the forensic, deliberative, and epideictic. *On the Crown* is forensic
in that it is a speech advocating the case of the defendant, Ctesiphon, but
its concern is the deliberative prowess of the two real contestants, Demosthenes and Aeschines. The speech is evocative of epideictic in that Demosthenes argues that his actions and advice were the only possible ones worthy
of Athens.[31] To defend Ctesiphon for proposing to honor Demosthenes,
Demosthenes delivers a speech in defense of his whole career.

What time is it, when we sit down to read and imagine that we hear the
speech *On the Crown?* It is time for thinking about politics, a moment of
contemplation (*theoria*), one might say, of meditation on the spectacle of
the confrontation between Philip and Athens. We can only watch because,
as Demosthenes puts it, the time for action to save Athenian freedom has,
for the moment, passed. Yet "even if the opportunity [*kairos*] for action has
passed," he says, "the opportunity to know these sorts of things is always
present for those who are sensible."[32]

His whole life, Demosthenes says, including his private life and his political actions for the commonalty of Athens, is being judged in this trial.[33]

---

30. *Against Ctesiphon* §50.
31. Stephen Usher, *Greek Oratory: Tradition and Originality* (Oxford: Oxford University Press,
1999), 270 n. 91, 275; *Demosthenes*: On the Crown, ed. Harvey Yunis (Cambridge: Cambridge
University Press, 2001), 15–17.
32. Demosthenes, *On the Crown* §§ 46, 48.
33. Demosthenes, *On the Crown* §8.

That is to say that judgment of Demosthenes' public life disaggregates into judgment of his political acts. In contemporary moral philosophy we are used to a distinction between agent morality, or virtue ethics, and a morality of motives, or, to use the Kantian term, maxims. Political judgment, as Demosthenes invited his audience to exercise it, would be judgment of an agent through his acts, or judgment of an actor as he appears in his acts.

What the jury was asked to do was to judge whether Demosthenes' actions undertaken in defense of the freedom of the Athenians were worthy ones. Now there are two obvious ways time can feature in the assessment of actions. Actions can be assessed based on the motive with which they are undertaken: motives are prior to action in time. Actions can also assessed based on their consequences, and consequences are posterior to actions in time, of course.

Yet to acquit Ctesiphon and thus defend his own life and all his public actions, Demosthenes has to convince his listeners that neither the assessment of an action based on its motives nor an assessment based on its consequences is the fundamental form of the judgment of actions already completed. Demosthenes does not deserve to be crowned simply because of his motives at the decisive moment. The jury, and all patriotic Athenians, wished that Athens be saved, Demosthenes says, during his account of the crucial moment of his intervention in the Assembly, when Philip had captured Elatea: "Well, had your city needed those who wished her to be saved, all of you and the rest of the Athenians would have stood up and made your way to the platform. For all of you, I think, wished that she be saved."[34] Nor can Demosthenes contend that he deserves to be crowned because of the consequences of his actions. The final consequences, as Aeschines points out at length in the accusation of Ctesiphon, were apparently bad: Athens and her allies lost at Chaeronea.[35]

Demosthenes asks his audience to judge him as one deserving of honor despite the consequences of his policy and despite the fact that he could

---

34. Demosthenes, *On the Crown* §171. For other uses of the commonplace that "all Athenians have patriotic intentions," see Demosthenes, *Letter* 1.8, and Demosthenes, *Preamble* 41.1.

35. Aeschines, *Against Ctesiphon* §§154–58, 244–25. When Polybius, writing long after the events, reminds his readers of the disastrous consequences of Demosthenes' policy for Athens (*Histories* 18.14), he does not explicitly deprecate the policy on that score but rather points to these consequences to exculpate from the charge of treason those men in other Greek cities who persuaded their fellow citizens to join Philip. This is not the same thing, obviously, as saying that the policy pushed by Demosthenes was the wrong policy for Athens to adopt, and I am not sure that we should infer that Polybius thought that it was. On this point, see N. G. Hammond and G. T. Griffith, vol. 2 of *A History of Macedonia* (Oxford: Oxford University Press, 1979), 480.

hardly be due extraordinary honors for his motives, since by his own admission his wish to preserve the freedom and security of Athens was that of every decent citizen. Political judgment would then be distinct from what we think of as judgment of actions based on their motives, as well as from judgment of actions based on their consequences.

Political judgment in the sense in which Demosthenes invites of his fellow citizens is some third kind of way of assessing actions. It is judgment after the fact but not judgment in the light of the consequences only. Consequences are part of the evidence to which judgment is applied: Demosthenes claims that Aeschines is unworthy in part because he has never successfully proposed any decree that has had good consequences for the city.[36] As regards Demosthenes' own policy, he argues that Athens, for all her ills, has fared better than those cities that gave her over for alliance with Philip.[37] Certainly an actor must take account of the foreseeable consequences, if his or her action is to be deemed worthy: Demosthenes condemns Aeschines because his single most notable action, his intervention in the Amphictyonic Council, brought, as was foreseen by Demosthenes, the bad consequence of an Amphictyonic war down on Athens.[38] Yet consequences are not the whole of the matter for judgment. Manly virtue can be recognized and esteemed even in failure, Demosthenes tells the jury, since "You justly honor alike those who fell in victory and those who fell in defeat." That is to say, it may be justifiable in rendering judgment to conclude that an action was worthy of praise and honor even though its consequences were bad.[39]

What, then, are the temporal criteria of a worthy act? A worthy act must in the first place be properly oriented in the present toward the future. "What are these things" for which an orator is responsible, Demosthenes asks. His answer is that the orator must "see affairs in their beginnings, . . . foresee [their consequences], and . . . foretell them to others."[40] My proposals

---

36. Demosthenes, *On the Crown* §139.

37. Demosthenes, *On the Crown* §254. In the funeral oration ascribed to Demosthenes, the speaker claims that Philip decided not to press his attack on Athens lest he have to face more men as brave as those who fought and fell and Chaeronea (20).

38. Demosthenes, *On the Crown* §143; cf. Demosthenes, *Preambles* 9, 33.3.

39. Demosthenes, *On the Crown* §208. In the speech *Against Androtion*, Demosthenes says, "I wonder at this, that he considered it worthy to crown the Council for the things that had gone wrong. For I, for my part, believed that these sorts of honors were restricted to deeds done correctly" (§17 [my translation]). Yet in that speech the failure of the Council is to make adequate provision for the navy: it is a failure to bring an act to completion, to do it right, not a failure to achieve the intended consequences.

40. Demosthenes, *On the Crown* §192. Cf. *On the Crown* §246 and Demosthenes, *Preamble* 14.3.

have always been forward looking, Demosthenes claims; by reorganizing the finances of the fleet I enabled these important provisions to be made at the right time (*en kairōi*).[41] Ask, Demosthenes invites the jury, what I added to our means and resources to face what was then the future, and contrast me with Aeschines, who never added anything.[42]

In particular, a worthy political act should be oriented toward future benefits and harms rather than past grievances. In my previous speeches, I always advised the city to look to the future, not the past, claims Demosthenes. Your support of the Spartans, after their defeat at Leuktra, against the Thebans who had defeated them, served as the precedent for the alliance I proposed with Thebes against Philip. We will drive the Thebans into the arms of Philip, Demosthenes claims he said at the time, "if we will prefer at the present, if the Thebans have done something disagreeable to us, to recall this and to mistrust them as though they were in the ranks of our enemies."[43]

Nor are worthy actions oriented toward the recollection of past benefits.[44] In politics it is unworthy to remind others of what they have done to you or of what you have done for them.[45] Finally, one should not look for small gains in the face of great dangers. In the wake of the taking of Elatea, it is an *aischros kairos*, an "ugly moment," to be asking things of the Thebans.[46]

Given that "that which is to come is unclear to all human beings, since insignificant happenings [*mikroi kairoi*] are the causes of the greatest things" as Demosthenes says in the speech *Against Leptines,* how then, are we to descry the future toward which our actions ought to be oriented?[47] The possibilities of the future become visible to us from the study of the past actions of present men. Demosthenes offers an answer at the high point of the speech, when he shows Philip, having captured Elatea, menacing Thebes and Athens: "That moment and that day did not call for the man who was merely wealthy and benevolent, but for he who had followed these matters from their beginning and deduced why Philip had done these things and what he wanted. For the one who did not know these things, nor had foreseen them when they were still distant, whether he were benevolent or wealthy, would not know what was to be done, nor would it be possible for

---

41. Demosthenes, *On the Crown* §102. Cf. Demosthenes, *On the Symmories* §2 = *Preamble* 7.2 and *Preamble* 30.1.

42. Demosthenes, *On the Crown* §§233, 309–11.

43. Demosthenes, *On the Crown* §§96–101, 176.

44. Demosthenes, *On the Crown* §§268–69.

45. On the latter point cf. Aristotle, *Nicomachean Ethics* 4.3.24–25, 1124b10–17.

46. Demosthenes, *On the Crown* §178.

47. Demosthenes, *Against Leptines* §162.

him to advise you."[48] One might compare this description of the man for whom the moment called with what was said of a twentieth-century American leader: "The universal testimony of those who know him is that he is always thinking. Not mind-wandering, casual consciousness, but hard, disciplined, purposeful thinking upon his problems. He is, they say, forever thinking ahead. That is why he is never caught off his guard, never excited when the moment for decision and action comes."[49] This purposeful thinking is not so much historical thinking, in the sense practiced by historians, as intelligence, in the sense of political or military intelligence.

We are invited by Demosthenes to judge after the fact that an action had been oriented (pluperfect) toward the future. We must consider the future as its possibilities were humanly foreseeable then, at the moment of action. "The future as it was" is something that becomes cloudier for us as the moment of decision recedes into the past, Demosthenes reminds us. We must always keep in mind that to miss what cannot be seen is neither to do wrong nor to make a mistake but merely to be unfortunate. Having defined his ground Demosthenes can take his stand: "That I did not choose all the things that were present to the extent available to human reckoning and did not carry them through honestly and diligently and with energy beyond my strength or that I instituted acts ignoble and unworthy of the city and unnecessary: show these things, and then it will be time to accuse me." The statesman must rely on others to make use of what he provides: his task is to encourage them and hasten them on to what must be done. If the ship is adequately provisioned, the owner has done his part and cannot be blamed if it goes down, for neither the shipowner nor the statesman reigns over fortune.[50] Demosthenes teaches the Athenians that the right decision is no less right just because it did not save them. To have deliberated well, then, is to have judged well in the past what present facts indicated as the possibilities of the future. Demosthenes thus both praises himself and condemns Aeschines:

> It belonged to the just citizen to show to all then, if he had something better than the things [that I proposed], not now to chastise. For the

48. Demosthenes, *On the Crown* §172.

49. French Strother on Calvin Coolidge, quoted in Sobel, *Coolidge*, 138. Compare Edmund S. Muskie, *Journeys* (Garden City, N.Y.: Doubleday, 1972), 48: "The most effective spontaneity often has a basis in preparation. If you don't anticipate and prepare, the chances you will react intelligently are lessened. I had not specifically planned what happened, but I had been thinking about what might happen. I was flexible, and when the cue came I took it."

50. Demosthenes, *On the Crown* §§226, 275, 193, 246, 194.

counselor who deliberates and the malicious accusing sycophant—not that they are alike in any other respect—in the following respect differ most. The one reveals his judgment before the actions, and makes himself responsible to those who were persuaded by him, to fortune, to the moment, to any who would call him to account. But the malicious accusing sycophant, who shut his mouth when it was necessary to speak, if something disagreeable consequences, this that sycophant reproaches.[51]

Demosthenes, both in *On the Crown* and throughout his career, repudiates "the cheap glory of denouncing" the mistakes of others after the fact.[52] I will go so far to admit, he says at the moment of trial in 330 B.C.E.,

> that if someone now has something better to show, or, altogether, if there was then [in 339/8 B.C.E.] present any alternative apart from the things I then preferred, I agree that I did unjustifiable things. For if there is anything that someone sees now, which would have had beneficial consequences had it been done then, I say, it should not have eluded me then. But if there isn't anything nor wasn't anything nor would be anything for anyone to say at any time and even today, what was it necessary for the counselor to do? Was it not to choose the best of the things that were presently manifest? This is what I did then, for the herald was asking, Aeschines, "Who wishes to address the Assembly?" not "Who wishes to make accusations concerning the things that have gone?" nor "Who wishes to make promises about the future?"[53]

Like the doctor who advises only when the patient is dead, Aeschines seizes the opportunity to advise at the moment most unfortunate for the city, Demosthenes says.[54] It is a kind of perverted form of advice, advice offered after the opportunity for action has come and gone.

The last Demosthenic criterion for judging political action is that the action must befit Athens as a city that through all time seeks to achieve the first place in honor and glory.[55] It was therefore more fitting for the Athenians

---

51. Demosthenes, *On the Crown* §189.

52. Werner Jaeger, *Demosthenes: The Origin and Growth of His Policy* (Berkeley and Los Angeles: University of California Press, 1938), 159, discussing *On the Peace* (*Demosthenes* 5.2). For other versions of the commonplace that accusations about the past have no place in deliberations about the future, see Demosthenes, *Preambles* 11, 20, 30.2, 35.1–2, 40.3, 41.1.

53. Demosthenes, *On the Crown* §§190–91.

54. Demosthenes, *On the Crown* §308; cf. §§323, 233.

55. Demosthenes, *On the Crown* §§66, 99–101, 193, 203.

than for the people of any other Greek city to resist Philip, Demosthenes claims.[56] Demosthenes shows that he shares the highest values of the Athenians when he argues that present actions must be worthy of the city's past. In the affairs of private life we must act according to the ordinary laws and precedents, but in political life we must look toward what is worthy of our ancestors.[57] Harvey Yunis claims that Demosthenes contends for the rightness of his policy by arguing that "questions of self-interest are still subordinated to questions of honor, as they always have been in the Athenian tradition."[58] Yet even when Demosthenes invites his listeners to judge his counsels before Chaeronea as if "the things that were to be were clear beforehand to everyone," as if everyone had known in advance that Philip would triumph, he says, "Not even then ought the city to have distanced herself from this [the policy of resisting Philip], if she had been taking account of fame, ancestors, or the ages that will be."[59] Resistance to Philip served not just Athenian honor but the future of Athenian freedom. We read *On the Crown* with the foreknowledge that the future of Athenian freedom after 330 was to be short and dim, but here too our historical knowledge is but an anachronistic bar to rhetorical and political comprehension.

More important for our purposes, Demosthenes explicitly denies that he could be worthy of honor merely because his policies expressed the sentiments and traditions that are common to all patriotic Athenians. Demosthenes' actions fit the city so well that it would be unbecoming of him, he states, "to claim to have brought you to think things worthy of your forefathers."[60] Far be it from Demosthenes to remind Athenians how to be Athenians, nor is it for this that he deserves to be honored. In order to defend the exceptional honor that Ctesiphon proposed he receive, Demosthenes must show himself to be exceptional, and at the same time, in order to avoid alienating his audience, the jury, he must grant that they are as noble and just as he. For this reason, too, it is impossible to agree with Harvey Yunis that Demosthenes makes his case by appealing to the nobility of his actions, since the Athenian orator is rhetorically constrained to grant noble sentiments to all worthy Athenians.[61] Where Demosthenes can and must claim

56. Demosthenes, *On the Crown* §§66–72.
57. Demosthenes, *On the Crown* §210.
58. Demosthenes, *On the Crown* §15.
59. Demosthenes, *On the Crown* §199.
60. Demosthenes, *On the Crown* §206; cf. §293.
61. See Harvey Yunis, "Politics as Literature: Demosthenes and the Burden of the Athenian Past," *Arion*, 3rd ser., 8, no. 1 (2000): 97–118, and *Demosthenes: On the Crown*, 15–17, 219–20. Cf. Mr. Dooley: "Ivry man ought to be honest to start with, but to give a man an office just because he's honest is like ilictin' him to Congress because he's a pathrite, because he don't

to stand out from the crowd, as we have seen, is in his special knowledge of what was to be done at the time of the crisis in 339/8 B.C.E.

Do not, however, compare me with our ancestors, Demosthenes warns, with Themistocles, Pericles, or Cimon; rather, ask only whether I intended the same things as them. Here too, Demosthenes contrasts himself with the prosecutor Aeschines. I act, says Demosthenes, in anticipation, while you, Aeschines, anticipate misfortune and delight in it when it comes. You shine on the stage only when it is time to accuse others unjustly. Then you invoke our past glories—to calumniate our present citizens. I use the past to encourage us to emulate it, while you use the past to encourage us to be jealous of those who at present strive to emulate it. I resemble the heroes of the past, and you resemble the villains.[62]

Nonetheless, Demosthenes entreats the jury, compare me not to the men of the past but to those of the present, for it is in comparison to present men that I deserve all the crowns that I have received.[63] Demosthenes, of course, invites the very comparison that he modestly refuses. Yet by invoking the comparison while (by paraleipsis) denying its application to himself, Demosthenes benefits from the comparison and simultaneously diminishes the envy of his audience that he supposes the comparison to provoke.

The past should be a spur to emulation, not a just source of invidious comparisons, as in Lloyd Bentsen's devastating attack on Dan Quayle in the 1988 vice-presidential debate: "I knew Jack Kennedy, and you are no Jack Kennedy." Too often, as Socrates points out to Callicles in the *Gorgias*, the men of the present are found wanting compared to the men of the past because present men are mistakenly held responsible for the mistakes of those long-gone and so-admired leaders.[64] One could say, then, that there is a Socratic impulse at work in the writing of history, since it acts to purge us of our anger at our present leaders by showing that our past leaders are truly to blame for our present ills.

Splitting up the World into Actions

An action is the basic unit for judgment: it is the smallest unit in a story with a beginning, a middle, and an end. This is Aristotle's celebrated canon

---

bate his wife or because he always wears a right boot on th' right foot" (Finley Peter Dunne, *Observations* [New York: R. H. Russell, 1902], 165–73, quoted in Charles R. Schutz, *Political Humor: From Aristophanes to Sam Ervin* [Rutherford, N.J.: Fairleigh Dickinson University Press, 1977], 219).

62. Demosthenes, *On the Crown* §§315ff., 308, 313, 317.
63. Demosthenes, *On the Crown* §§319–20.
64. Plato, *Gorgias* 518e–519a.

of the unity of action in the *Poetics*. The contemporary playwright David Mamet never tires of professing his adherence to the Aristotelian canon of unity:

> I'm sure *trying* to do the well-made play. It is the hardest thing to do. I like this form because it's the structure imitating human perception. It is not just something made up out of whole cloth. This is the way we perceive a play: with a clear beginning, middle, and an end. So when one wants to best utilize the theater, one would try to structure a play in a way that is congruent with the way the mind perceives it. Everybody wants to hear a story with a beginning, a middle, and an end. . . . That's all theater is: storytelling. . . . To me recognizing the storytelling dimension of playwriting is a beginning of a mark of maturity. That's why I embrace it. Nobody in the audience wants to hear a joke without the punch line. Nobody wants to tell how feelingly a guy can tell a joke. But we would like to find out what happened to the farmer's daughter.[65]

Judgment of character is the integration of judgments of action to form a picture of the actor's future potentialities. And yet the world is not given to us neatly bounded off in indisputably atomic "least units of action." The world itself is not divided; rather we divide it. The world can be divided in various ways, but the way we divide it must be a way that we are capable of living with sensibly. By defining an action in one way rather than another, we are making a judgment on that action.

Judgment is the process by which we break life up into events and happenings. The way that an action is picked out and defined is the way that our judgment of it is determined. Our evaluation of an action is equivalent to a determination of what we will count as its consequences, as opposed to what we will count as the circumstances that are external to it. Controversies about the merits of an action already performed are generally controversies about what counts as part of it or how the various parts of it are to be described.

Consider the murder rate in New York City. In his book *Leadership*, former mayor Rudolph Giuliani invites us to judge his record by his success at reducing it. Giuliani writes that there were 642 "murders" in 2001, his last

---

65. David Mamet, *David Mamet in Conversation*, ed. Leslie Kane (Ann Arbor: University of Michigan Press, 2001), 49–50.

year in office, as against 1,946 "homicides" in 1993, the year before Giuliani took office.[66] Giuliani's figure of 642 for 2001 excludes, of course, the World Trade Center victims, by which standard Giuliani presided over one of the most murderous years in the history of the city.

Of course, we know that the September 11 attacks were beyond Giuliani's ability to prevent: as mayor of New York he had no air force or foreign intelligence operatives. In judging Giuliani, that is to say, in judging Giuliani's actions, we set aside the dictionary definition of the word "murder" and unconsciously redefine it in a way that makes it consonant with Giuliani's capacity for crime-fighting actions. We do not judge Giuliani's mayoral administration by reference to the event of September 11: we judge Giuliani's actions only on the basis of the consequences that we assign to his possibilities for action as mayor. We do judge Giuliani by the way he dealt with the municipal consequences of the World Trade Center attacks using the tools of his office as mayor.

We know how to act when we see how the continuum of existence is to be divided: in acting we define what is to count as a cause, as an agent, as a consequence, and so on. But the defining is not separate from the acting: we do not decide how to define and then act; rather, we act when we see how the world is or can be defined. To act in the world is to respond to its chunked-up or defined appearances.

Action in Theory

The way actors break up actions is very different from the way academic observers break them up. Richard Fenno summarizes his analysis of Dan Quayle's principal accomplishment as senator, the Job Training Partnership Act of 1982, thus: "[Quayle's] governing accomplishment with JTPA was indispensable and essential and necessary to his success at home. That cannot be proven. But in support of that judgment we have provided copious evidence of the clear intentions to use JTPA, of the widespread usage of it, and of the multiple positive effects flowing from that usage."[67] The reader is left with two questions. First, what would we need to *prove* that the JTPA was vital to Dan Quayle's political future, over and above the grounds Fenno himself has offered for *judging* that that the JTPA was vital to Dan Quayle's

66. Rudolph W. Giuliani with Ken Kurson, *Leadership* (New York: Hyperion, 2002), 117.
67. Fenno, *The Making of a Senator*, 165.

political future? And, second, what is the place in our form of life of this standard of proof? Fenno here is contrasting his own and Dan Quayle's actual mode of arguing with some way of proving that something happened in the past separate from the ways that political actors use the past to guide the present toward the future, that is, he is contrasting the practical engagement with the past with a theoretically informed history or social science.[68]

For the actor, on the hand, the past is available only to the extent that it is useful or usable. Calvin Coolidge, a Republican and racial liberal, said at an occasion that would seem to be weighted to the point of despair with the burdens of the past—for he was speaking on Memorial Day in 1924 at the Confederate Memorial in Richmond—that "it is not for us to forget the past but to remember it, that we may profit by it. But it is gone; we cannot change it. We must put our emphasis on the present and put into effect the lessons the past has taught us." Within the life of political activity, as Kenneth Burke tells us, "a history of the past is worthless except as a documented way of talking about the future."[69]

We are oriented *toward* the future *by* the past. To quote Coolidge again, this time eulogizing Ethan Allen and his Vermont Revolutionary followers, the Green Mountain Boys, in "The Green Mountains": "We review the past not in order that we may return to it but that we may find in what direction, straight and clear, it points into the future."[70] Coolidge shows us how to put the past to work in the peroration of that speech. Coolidge takes Ethan Allen's demand that the British fortress of Ticonderoga surrender "in the name of the Great Jehovah and the Continental Congress" to mean "For God and Country," whereas Allen, who in old age wrote anti-Bible screeds, probably just meant to blaspheme.[71]

Coolidge's appropriation of the past is uncontaminated by academic history. Moreover, his appropriation of the past is not constrained by either of the two most common ways our thinking about political actions is beclouded: on the one hand, by consequentialism, and on the other hand by moralism, the belief that actions ought strictly to be judged by their motives.

---

68. Compare the argument between George C. Edwards III and Martin Medhurst in *Beyond the Rhetorical Presidency*, ed. Martin J. Medhurst (College Station: Texas A&M University Press, 1996).

69. Calvin Coolidge, "The United Nation," in *Foundations of the Republic* (1926; repr., Freeport, N.Y.: Books for Libraries Press, 1968), 16; Kenneth Burke, *Attitudes Toward History*, 3rd ed. (Berkeley and Los Angeles: University of California Press, 1984), 159.

70. Calvin Coolidge, "The Green Mountains," in *The Price of Freedom*, 357; cf. 355.

71. Coolidge, "The Green Mountains," in *The Price of Freedom*, 374–75.

Moralism reflects a kind of broad application of the juridical notion of personal responsibility. Such a basic juridical distinction as that between murder and manslaughter obviously rests on the judgment of motive. Motive has a role in law, especially in criminal law, that it does not have in other areas of our life together. Even in law we judge motives by inference from our judgments of actions. That is what evidence of motive is: evidence of ancillary or instrumental actions that indicates the motive of the primary action.[72]

Juridical actions of punishment and exoneration are oriented toward the past, to what happened; political actions, on the other hand, are oriented toward the future, toward what may happen. As we learned from Demosthenes, political actions are to be judged by their orientation toward the future as it could have been perceived at the moment of decision. To have deliberated well is to have judged well in the past what then-present facts indicated as the possibilities of the unseeable future.[73] Montaigne sets out the canons of good judgment appropriately:

> In my business dealings several good opportunities have escaped me for want of the happy knack of conducting them: yet my decisions were well chosen *secundum quid* [that is, according to the events which they ran up against]; my decisions are so fashioned as always to take the easiest and the surest side. I find that I proceeded wisely, according to my rule, in my previous deliberations given the state of the subject

72. See Cicero, *De partione oratoria* 32–33.114; cf. Mark Alexander Pollock, "A Reconsideration of the Prospects for Rhetoric in Hannah Arendt's Political Philosophy" (Ph.D. diss., Northwestern University, 1989), 205: "In his discussion of character (*ethos*) in the *Rhetoric*, [Aristotle] made it clear that it is from a person's actions that we judge their character. This tradition might have offered Arendt better resources for grappling with the problem posed by Eichmann for legal theories grounding judgments of guilt or innocence largely on the basis of intent."

73. See Thomas Aquinas, *Summa Theologica* I[a] II[ae] Q20 art. 5, trans. the Fathers of the English Dominican Province (New York: Benziger Brothers, 1947–48), cited in Leo Strauss, *Natural Right and History* (Chicago: University of Chicago Press, 1953), 70 n. 29:

> The consequences of an action are either foreseen or not. If they are foreseen, it is evident that they increase the goodness or malice. For when a man foresees that many evils may follow from his action, and yet does not therefore desist therefrom, this shows his will to be all the more inordinate.

> But if the consequences are not foreseen, we must make a distinction. Because if they follow from the nature of the action and in the majority of cases, in this respect, the consequences increase the goodness or malice of that action: for it is evident that an action is specifically better, if better results can follow from it; and specifically worse, if it is of a nature to produce worse results. On the other hand, if the consequences follow by accident and seldom, then they do not increase the goodness or malice of the action: because we do not judge of a thing according to that which belongs to it by accident, but only according to that which belongs to it of itself.

as set before me: and in the same circumstances I would do the same a thousand years from hence. I pay no regard to what it looks like now but to how it was when I was examining it. The force of any advice depends upon the time: circumstances endlessly alter and matters endlessly change. I have made some grievous mistakes in my life—important ones—for want of good luck not for want of good thought. In the subjects which we handle, and especially in the natures of men, there are hidden parts which cannot be divined, silent characteristics which are never revealed and which are sometimes unknown to the one who has them but which are awakened and brought out by subsequent events. If my wisdom was unable to penetrate through to them and foresee them I bear it no grudge: there are limits to its obligations. What defeats me is the outcome and if it favors the side I rejected, that cannot be helped. I do not find fault with myself: I blame not what I did but my fortune. And that is not to be called repenting.[74]

Eisenhower, exemplifying the wise man who finds nothing more useless than regrets, said, "I never worry about what I did the day before."[75] One does one's best to see what needs to be done, one does it, and then one moves on. One ought to learn from one's mistakes, but one also has to learn to recognize, as Montaigne advises, that some bad results cannot be explained by one's own errors—or the errors of others. To ascribe these bad results to bad luck is to assert that there is nothing one can learn from them about what one should have known or done.

It is not easy to face the world without a narrative interposed between it and us, to live without providential delusions about how things were meant to turn out. Our lives are a mixture of intended actions and their frequently accidental consequences. Stories are when practical thinking goes on holiday. In our human-all-too-human moments we all want to be comforted by stories, and so "television tells complete stories [while] politics is naggingly unfinished." Our love of plot," writes Norman Mailer, "comes out of our need to find the chain of cause and effect that so often is missing in our own existence."[76] To describe what has happened as "a tragedy" is to

74. Michel de Montaigne, "On Repenting," in *The Complete Essays*, trans. and ed. M. A. Screech (London: Penguin, 1991), 917.

75. Fred I. Greenstein, *The Hidden-Hand Presidency: Eisenhower as Leader* (New York: Basic Books, 1982), 42.

76. Roderick P. Hart, *Seducing America: How Television Charms the Modern Voter*, rev. ed. (Thousand Oaks, Calif.: Sage, 1999), 93; Norman Mailer, *The Spooky Art: Some Thoughts on Writing* (New York: Random House, 2003), 89.

imply that the tragic conclusion was somehow foreshadowed, that what happened ought to be understood as the reasonable—and not merely accidental—working out of prior events. Such a description in dramatic form, in this case the form of a tragedy, has, as Edward Black writes, "the epistemological function of fixing human events into a condition that enables us to comprehend them." Yet action in the realm of practice is a responding to things, not a comprehension of events. The comprehension that the historians wish to provide is an action in the realm of theory.[77]

77. Edwin Black, *Rhetorical Questions: Studies of Public Discourse* (Chicago: University of Chicago Press, 1992), 16. See also Michael Oakeshott, "On the Theoretical Understanding of Human Conduct," in *On Human Conduct* (Oxford: Oxford University Press, 1975), 1–107, who rejects the attempt to assimilate the historian's timeless reasoning to the timely deliberation and decision required of political actors. For an example of such an attempt, see Arlene W. Saxonhouse, "Democratic Deliberation and the Historian's Trade," in *Talking Democracy: Historical Perspectives on Rhetoric and Democracy*, ed. Benedetto Fontana, Cary J. Nederman, and Gary Remer [University Park: Pennsylvania State University Press, 2004], 57–86.).

3

THINGS

That notorious pair, speech and deed, constitute the two linked means of showing things to be the way you say they are and making things be the way you say they are. Toward the end of showing that things are as he says they are, a carpenter shows us sample works. In order to persuade us of the truth of her theorems a mathematician accumulates proofs, which are, practically speaking, never complete but nonetheless are sufficient to show that they could be completed by an expert. In place of proofs or sample appliance carts an experimental scientist accumulates experimental evidence.

A political actor, for his or her part, accumulates a record based on the advice he or she has offered in the past. Character, we have seen, is made visible in action: to show character, show the actions that express the potentials of the character. To show action, in turn, show the action's traces in the world in the alteration it effects in things. Actions appear in things that direct us toward them. Pericles in his funeral oration shows the greatness of Athenian military deeds by inviting his audience to see with the eyes of

Chapter 3's epigraphs come from Hugo von Hofmannsthal, *The Lord Chandos Letter*, ed. and trans. Russell Stockman (Marlboro, Vt.: Marlboro Press, 1986), 13 (translation modified), and from Richard P. McKeon, "Creativity and the Commonplace," in *Essays in Invention and Discovery*, ed. Mark Backman (Woodbridge, Conn.: Ox Bow Press, 1987), 33.

the mind the trophies the Athenians have erected throughout the Greek world, "since we have left everywhere memorials of the good things [we have done] and the bad things [we have inflicted]."[1]

Because we can only see action in its effects on things it is always tempting to judge actions simply by assessing their effects. The trouble is that such consequentialism is not a humanly available position because we are not capable of seeing all the effects of our actions.[2] To cultivate political judgment is to learn to look at things not in order to say what is actual but to try to see how what is actual reveals what could have been. Action occurs in the realm of what could be—as the cliché goes, politics is the art of the possible. To assess political action we need to know what is or was possible. To engage in retrospective judgment we must reconstruct the possibilities that existed in the past from the traces they leave in the things that are present. To engage in prospective judgment we must envision the possibilities of the future from the signs in the things that are present. To persuade to a course of action is to present things so as to elicit from the audience the judgment you desire concerning the possible. "The most persuasive of all rhetorical stances is to write as if one is not trying to persuade at all but simply presenting truth."[3]

To present truth, present things themselves rather than make demands or requests. When the premier public relations firm of Hill & Knowlton counseled the Kuwaiti government on its propaganda efforts after Saddam Hussein's 1990 invasion and occupation of Kuwait, the firm "advised the Kuwaitis to eschew talking in public about what the US government should do, and just talk about what the Iraqis are doing in Kuwait."[4] It is rhetorically more effective to leave one's demands or requests implied rather than stated, so as not to emphasize them unduly: demands or requests must always be *your* demands or requests, and so separate you from the audience you are trying to persuade.

The material of rhetoric is in things, as Quintilian teaches us, not in words. Not that Quintilian himself has this insight constantly in view: "A speech

1. Thucydides, *History of the Peloponnesian War* 2.41.4.

2. Cf. Francis Sparshott's exposition of Aristotle's critique of the idea of the good in the *Nicomachean Ethics* (*Taking Life Seriously: A Study of the Argument of the* Nicomachean Ethics [Toronto: University of Toronto Press, 1996], 31–32).

3. Francis-Noël Thomas and Mark Turner, *Clear and Simple as the Truth: Writing Classic Prose* (Princeton: Princeton University Press, 1994), 119.

4. Jarol B. Manheim, "Strategic Public Diplomacy: Managing Kuwait's Image During the Gulf Conflict," in *Taken by Storm: The Media, Public Opinion, and U.S. Foreign Policy in the Gulf War*, ed. W. Lance Bennett and David L. Paletz (Chicago: University of Chicago Press, 1994), 143.

consists of that which is signified and that which signifies, that is to say things and words [*rebus et verbis*]."[5] This is ontological confusion on a par with saying that a stop sign consists of two parts, the command to stop, which is signified, and the word "stop," which signifies the command.[6] Speeches are not made up of two elements, things and words: rather, speeches present things in words.[7] To sway the audience is to move them by presenting in words the things that move them, as Cicero says.[8]

Rhetoric and the Possibilities of Things

Crises (the Greek term is "kairoi") render action necessary. A crisis is phony or illusory if there is no real necessity for action. In a spurious crisis, a spurious necessity is imagined, due to a mistake in judgment, or, worse, manufactured in order to conceal idiosyncratic and therefore discreditable motivations. As Carole Blair and Davis Houck write, "To the extent that the context seems unreadable as a crisis, or that it seems readable as a crisis only to the interests of the speaker, the critic may rightfully be concerned about questions of perception or honesty."[9] To urge action is to present matters or things as in crisis; otherwise, the audience might conclude that action could be postponed. The crisis must be presented in terms of what caused it and what constitutes it. By presenting the things relevant to the crisis the speaker presents objective justifications for acting as he or she advises, so that his or her advice is more than a product of his or her personal, idiosyncratic motives.[10] In order to show the crisis, the opportunity for action, the speaker has to have some proposal as to what must be done.

The usual view of rhetoric, the one that dismisses rhetoric as "mere rhetoric," sees possibilities as given prior to speech. Rhetoric is thus maligned

5. Quintilian, *Institutio oratoria* 2.21.4, 3.5.1.

6. I would direct those who think that the ontological confusion I note in the example in the text of an imperative "STOP" is uncommon to the examples offered by J. L. Austin in lectures 9–12 of his *How to Do Things with Words*, 2nd ed., ed. J. O. Urmson and Marina Sabisà (Cambridge, Mass.: Harvard University Press, 1975); see also Wayne Booth, *A Rhetoric of Irony* (Chicago: University of Chicago Press, 1974), 15 n. 10.

7. See, for example, Robert Sokolowski, *Presence and Absence: A Philosophical Investigation of Language and Being* (Bloomington: Indiana University Press, 1978), 46.

8. *Quod unum est oratoris maxime proprium, quocumque res postularet, impellare* (Cicero, *Brutus,* 322).

9. Carole Blair and Davis W. Houck, "Richard Nixon and the Personalization of Crisis," in *The Modern Presidency and Crisis Rhetoric,* ed. Amos Kiewe (Westport, Conn.: Praeger, 1994), 99.

10. See pseudo-Aristotle, *Rhetoric to Alexander* §29, 1437b18–28; Henry Fairlie, *The Kennedy Promise* (New York: Dell, 1974), 292.

as the conscious effort to pervert deliberation about the already given options. Yet it is in speech that the options are collectively constituted, not just collectively known.[11] Rhetoric is not just about sharing ideas but about sharing things, and thereby sharing collective options or possibilities.[12] In that way rhetoric, as Steve Fuller notes, "enables large numbers of people to move in a common direction without having to reach explicit agreement on a label for that direction."[13] Rhetoric helps to present things (say, Philip of Macedon's army advancing on Thebes) and thus helps constitute the audience's relation to those things (inducing the Athenians to make an alliance with the Thebans and order their citizens out to fight Philip). Rhetoric helps the audience mobilize to produce other things (an allied Theban-Athenian army facing Philip's host on the field of Chaeronea).

Rhetoric is the effort to reflectively form and narrow options, to move the audience from seeing infinite and infinitely unimportant possibilities to seeing, and being mobilized to act out, only a few salient possibilities.[14] Typically, the speaker wishes to urge the audience to one particular action, and so only one of the presented options is presented as viable, that is to say, as possible in the fullest sense. All rhetoric thus aims at minimum to forestall, anticipate, and thus "foreclose dissent."[15]

Rhetoric is not about mere appearances, though even a rhetorician such as Roderick Hart is prone to move from the claim that "the people" are rhetorically constituted to the claim that the people's existence is "mythical."[16] It is things themselves that are constituted and then communicated, so that there is no irreducible distinction between facts and objects. What is said or stated is what is, what is in the world: being said is simply another

11. See Michael McGee, *Rhetoric in Postmodern America: Conversations with Michael Calvin McGee*, ed. Carol Corbin (New York: Guilford Press, 1998), 130–31.

12. Gerard Hauser, *Vernacular Voices: The Rhetoric of Publics and Public Spheres* (Columbia: University of South Carolina Press, 1999), 64, citing Robert Park, "News as a Form of Knowledge: A Chapter in the Sociology of Knowledge," *American Journal of Sociology* 45, no. 4 (1940): 669–86, 677. Subsequently Hauser writes that "importantly, common understanding reflects judgments about propositions of value or belief, such as the repugnance of Hitler's 'final solution,' rather than of truth or facts such as that six million Jews were exterminated by the Nazis" (100). But the intimate relation between contemporary anti-Semitism and Holocaust denial suggests, in keeping with Hauser's earlier statement, that common understanding is in the primary sense the shared understanding of facts, from which shared judgments generally arise.

13. Fuller, *Philosophy, Rhetoric, and the End of Knowledge: The Coming of Science and Technology Studies* (Madison: University of Wisconsin Press, 1993), 188.

14. See Roderick P. Hart, *Modern Rhetorical Criticism*, 2nd ed. (Boston: Pearson/Allyn and Bacon, 1997), 7.

15. See Blair and Houck, "Richard Nixon and the Personalization of Crisis," 106.

16. Hart, *Modern Rhetorical Criticism*, 243.

possibility of things. "I see that John is crossing the street." "I said that John is crossing the street."[17]

To say something is to present it, to point to it, to engage in what we ought to call pointing, indication, which is the etymological meaning of the Greek term *epideixis*.[18] To inspire feeling, show the things that will communicate feeling. Reagan's famous 1984 "Morning in America" arouses emotion by showing "a rolling montage of American symbols" from church weddings to the Capitol.[19] T. S. Eliot's once notorious term "objective correlative" instructed us that poets describe an emotion by describing the things as they are seen by someone undergoing that emotion. This is reversed by rhetoric, which instructs one who would inspire an emotion to present those things that ought to provoke that emotion. If you aspire to seduce, "the point is not to speak the desire but to speak that which is most likely to bring about the desire"—don't think "I want to sell this pinball game," but, as 1970s ace copywriter Joseph Sugarman put it, "I want to make this pinball game easy to buy and seem like fun."[20] One inspires anger by presenting the things that make us angry; one inspires pity by presenting the things that are pitiable. "Sympathy," summarizes Adam Smith, "does not arise so much from the view of the passion, as from that of the situation which excites it."[21]

17. John Searle, *Speech Acts: An Essay in the Philosophy of Language* (Cambridge: Cambridge University Press, 1969), 93–94. See also Martin Heidegger's statement that "man [is] a being which has its world in the mode of something addressed" (*Ontology: The Hermeneutics of Facticity*, trans. John van Buren [Bloomington: Indiana University Press, 1999], 17). See further John McDowell, *Mind and World* (Cambridge, Mass.: Harvard University Press, 1994), 23–29, and Ludwig Wittgenstein, *Philosophical Investigations*, trans. G. E. M. Anscombe (Oxford: Blackwell, 1953), §§95, 97. The very notion of a distinction between facts and objects is an artifact of Indo-European linguistic conventions: whereas Indo-European languages distinguish words and things, *verbum et res, logoi kai erga*, the Hebrew "davar" comprehends the semantic fields of thing, word, fact, and event (Walter J. Ong, *Orality and Literacy: The Technologizing of the Word* [London: Methuen, 1982], 32).

18. On presentation in general, see Chaïm Perelman and Lucie Olbrechts-Tyteca, *The New Rhetoric*, trans. John Wilkinson and Purcell Weaver (Notre Dame, Ind.: University of Notre Dame Press, 1969), §29.

19. John Boiney and David L. Paletz, "In Search of the Model Model: Political Science Versus Political Advertising Perspectives on Voter Decision Making," in *Psychological Processes*, vol. 1 of *Television and Political Advertising*, ed. by Frank Biocca (Hillsdale, N.J.: Lawrence Erlbaum, 1991), 22. The "Morning in America" ad is available at http://www.youtube.com/watch?v=EU-IBF8nwSY (accessed 27 October 2007).

20. David Mamet, *David Mamet in Conversation*, ed. Leslie Kane (Ann Arbor: University of Michigan Press, 2001), 75; Joseph Sugarman, *Advertising Secrets of the Written Word* (Las Vegas: DelStar, 1998), 97.

21. Adam Smith, *Theory of Moral Sentiments*, ed. D. D. Raphael and A. L. Mcfie (1976; repr., Indianapolis: Liberty Press, 1982), 1.1.1.10, cited in Daniel Gross, *The Secret History of Emotion: From Aristotle's* Rhetoric *to Modern Brain Science* (Chicago: University of Chicago Press, 2006), 173.

There is a moment of recognition, where we see that things as they are presented are pitiable and thus feel pity, and a second moment of judgment, which may or may not occur, when we judge that things are, in truth, as the speaker has presented them.[22]

"The emotions take place in the *audience*," not in the orator.[23] The way to get the audience to feel is to present the audience, as impassively as possible, with a detailed story or anecdote. Ronald Reagan, the "Great Communicator," was a master of the anecdotal style: "In Chicot County, Arkansas, James Wier over-planted his rice allotment. The government obtained a $17,000 judgment, and a U.S. marshal sold his 960 acre farm at auction. The government said it was necessary as a warning to others to make the system work."[24] One of Reagan's strengths as a speaker was that he was never averse to making up details in order to make a story even more moving, just as when, as a sportscaster in the 1930s practicing what used to be called "recreations" in the radio world—in which a sportscaster in a studio far from the game would recreate it for the radio audience from a stream of Western Union wires—he used to make up foul pitches and crowd news. The level of concreteness in the James Wier anecdote is striking, and, as Reagan always said, "An example is better than a sermon."[25] A sermon tempts us with disobedience, while an anecdote presents something to us with such vividness that we feel that there is no alternative but to respond in the manner in which the speaker has (perhaps invisibly) directed us.[26] To quote

22. Edwin Black's critique of the Aristotelian account of the relation between judgment and emotion seems to rest on a confusion of these two moments (*Rhetorical Criticism: A Study in Method* [New York: Macmillan, 1965], 116–17). I. A. Richards rightly points out that presenting things in speech or writing does not necessarily mean asking the audience to visualize an image in the eye of the mind (*The Philosophy of Rhetoric* [Oxford: Oxford University Press, 1965], 98, 130–31).

23. The quote is from David Mamet, *Conversations with David Mamet*, 51. The claim that the actor must out of dispassionate study perfect the movements and attitude that excite the audience is the famous "paradox of the actor" of Diderot ("The Paradox of the Actor," in *Selected Writings on Art and Literature*, trans. Geoffrey Bremmer [London Penguin, 1994], 98–158).

24. Ronald Reagan, "A Time for Choosing," 27 October, 1964, in Kurt Ritter and David Henry, *Ronald Reagan: The Great Communicator* (New York: Greenwood Press, 1992), 16, 141ff.; see also Rick Perlstein, *Before the Storm: Barry Goldwater and the Unmaking of the American Consensus* (New York: Hill and Wang, 2001), 501.

25. Ronald Reagan, *An American Life* (New York: Simon and Schuster, 1990), 246, cited in Ritter and Henry, *Ronald Reagan*, 121; cf. the account of Lincoln's use of humorous stories in Charles R. Schutz, *Political Humor: From Aristophanes to Sam Ervin* (Rutherford, N.J.: Fairleigh Dickinson University Press, 1977), chap. 5, "Lincoln, Satyr Statesman," esp. 151–52.

26. The anecdotal style thus exploits what Daniel Kahneman and Amos Tversky called the "availability heuristic": we tend to "answer a hard question about probability by asking whether examples come readily to mind" (cited in Cass R. Sunstein, *Why Societies Need Dissent* [Cambridge, Mass.: Harvard University Press, 2003], 91–93).

another great Californian, John Steinbeck, "It means very little to know that a million Chinese are starving unless you know one Chinese who is starving."[27] It is the anecdote, like the photograph of the eight-year-old girl with hollow brown eyes and a smudge on her cheek on the front of a brochure from Save the Children, that brings us face-to-face with a single victim and demands that we respond.[28]

Ronald Reagan and his speechwriters understood well how to use his ability to communicate things to help achieve their most important political goals, as one can see from Reagan's most important and—if George H. W. Bush is a competent judge—his most stirring speech as president, the speech given at Pointe du Hoc in Normandy at the commemoration of the fortieth anniversary of D-Day on 6 June 1984.[29] The speech moves us through two short sentences: "These are the boys of Pointe du Hoc, these are the men who climbed these cliffs." In these sentences the president points to the assembled Ranger veterans, seated in rows before him at the ceremony. These were the most moving lines in Reagan's entire public career; these lines move the reader of the speech more than two decades after it was given by pointing to the aged veterans to recall their heroism. We imagine ourselves seeing these men, and in seeing them we recall what they did, their actions, in the teeth of Hitler's army.

The speech at Pointe du Hoc is especially illustrative because its force was harnessed to prospective political action, though to recall that action requires delving back into the arcana of the Cold War.[30] The goal of the speech was to cement the Western allies behind Reagan's complex policy regarding "Euro-missiles," intermediate-range ballistic missiles based in West Germany as part of the deterrent to conventional or nuclear Soviet attack. The missiles themselves were intended primarily as bargaining chips.

27. Quoted in Michael Osborn, "Rhetorical Depiction," in *Form, Genre, and the Study of Political Discourse*, ed. Herbert W. Simons and Aram A. Aghazarian (Columbia: University of South Carolina Press, 1986), 87.

28. On the power of stories about real people, or rather, "about specific people whether they are real or not," see Michael J. Graetz and Ian Shapiro, *Death by a Thousand Cuts: The Fight over Taxing Inherited Wealth* (Princeton: Princeton University Press, 2005), 81, and Robert E. Goodin, *Reflective Democracy* (Oxford: Oxford University Press, 2003), 187.

29. See George H. W. Bush and Brent Scowcroft, *A World Transformed* (New York: Knopf, 1988), 16–17. Bush also relates that Reagan claimed that he could deliver stirring speeches calmly by rereading them until the emotional effect on him was dulled by repetition, precisely the method described by Diderot in "The Paradox of the Actor" (145).

30. On the policy behind the Pointe du Hoc speech, see Peggy Noonan, *On Speaking Well* (New York: HarperCollins, 1999), 71–75; and Douglas Brinkley, *The Boys of Pointe du Hoc: Ronald Reagan, D-Day, and the U.S. Army 2nd Ranger Battalion* (New York: William Morrow, 2005).

The ultimate American goal was the "Zero Option"; no short- or intermediate-range ballistic missiles in Europe on either side of the Iron Curtain. Deploying the missiles was in fact part of Reagan's grand vision of a world made safe through the elimination of nuclear weapons; since, as Paul Nitze once put it, the Soviet Union was a third-world country without its missiles, a world liberated from nuclear terror would be a world in which the Soviet empire in Europe would become untenable.[31] This would complete the liberation of Europe from tyranny, from the cliffs of Pointe du Hoc to the castles of Bohemia and the shipyards of the Baltic.

Bill Clinton, by pointing out Richard Dean sitting next to Hillary Rodham Clinton in the First Lady's box, gave similar force to his 1996 State of the Union address. Dean, a federal civil servant, was a hero of the Oklahoma City bombing, President Clinton asserted, but this did not keep him from becoming a victim of the 1995–96 government shutdown brought about by the Republicans. Clinton had lost the battle in 1994, which resulted in the Republicans assuming a majority in Congress, but by using this one concrete figure, Richard Dean, he was able to link the Republicans' partisan zeal with an antigovernment fanaticism that most Americans had rapidly learned to abhor.[32] It took September 11 for the Republican Party to recover from Richard Dean.

Nullius in verba

The method of anecdote is but a species within the more general class of the rhetoric of examples. To draw inferences in one's speech one must derive one's arguments from "the necessities of the things themselves" (*ipsa rerum necessitas*)—or at least present them as so derived.[33]

The rhetoric of modern scientific communication assumes that the way to communicate these necessities is through an appropriate selection of numeric facts. The early members of the Royal Society took as their motto "nothing in words" (*nullius in verba*), thereby instructing would-be "experimental philosophers" to inscribe figures, numbers, and illustrations into

---

31. See George P. Shultz, *Turmoil and Triumph: My Years as Secretary of State* (New York: Scribner's, 1993), and Peggy Noonan, *When Character Was King: A Story of Ronald Reagan* (New York: Viking, 2001), 285.

32. Michael Waldman, *POTUS Speaks: Finding the Words That Defined the Clinton Presidency* (New York: Simon and Schuster, 2000), 112–13.

33. Quintilian, *Institutio oratoria* 7.1.35.

their writing in order to persuade.[34] In the world those seventeenth-century men have made for us, their advice on how to persuade is now understood even by politicians, as Rudolph Giuliani's memoirs of his service as mayor of New York suggest: "Throughout the book, I seek to demonstrate the effectiveness of the lessons I have learned with hard evidence. I believe in proof more than theories, results more than rhetoric, so I have included a range of before and after examples."[35] Giuliani quotes crime statistics. Similarly, Calvin Coolidge, speaking as vice president to the American Legion in 1921, informs the legionnaires that:

> The Veterans' Bureau and the agencies now included in it, up to October 1 have paid $71,000,000 for medical and hospital services, $267,000,000 for compensation, $254,000,000 for insurance awards, $582,000,000 for allotments and allowances, $171,000,000 for vocational education. The amount disbursed by this Bureau in September was $34,237,000. This reaches a total of $1,345,000,000, about one-third of all pensions paid by the government from its beginning up to our entry into the World War. The yearly expenditures of the Veterans' Bureau are running at a rate of about $411,000,000, which is more than one-half the entire expense of the government before this war.[36]

34. On the rejection of words, see Thomas Sprat, *The History of the Royal Society for the Improving of Natural Knowledge* (1667; Chestnut Hill, Mass.: Elibron Classics, 2003), 105, 332, 422, 423–24, and Jackman I. Cope and Harold Whitmore Jones, introduction, in their edition of Sprat (St. Louis: Washington University Press, 1959), xxv–xxxii. On the rhetoric of figures, see the tables and illustrations reprinted from reports to the Royal Society in Sprat, *History of the Royal Society*, 228–39; see also Steven Shapin, *A Social History of Truth: Science and Civility in Seventeenth-Century England* (Chicago: University of Chicago Press, 1994), Mary Poovey, *A History of the Modern Fact: Problems of Knowledge in the Sciences of Wealth and Society* (Chicago: University of Chicago Press, 1998), and Theodore M. Porter, *Trust in Numbers: The Pursuit of Objectivity in Science and Public Life* (Princeton: Princeton University Press, 1995). Paradoxically, the turn in artful persuasion from words to things, that is, to figures, is connected to the Gutenberg revolution because before the invention of printing it had not been possible to accurately transmit numbers and illustrations (Elizabeth L. Eisenstein, *Printing Press as an Agent of Change* [Cambridge: Cambridge University Press, 1980], 69–70, 200–201, 262–67, 460–61, 467–70, 482–83, 485–87, 588–90, 596–97, 698). Numbers and illustrations are therefore distinctive not just of written as opposed to oral rhetoric but of printed as opposed to manuscript rhetoric.

35. Rudolph W. Giuliani with Ken Kurson, *Leadership* (New York: Hyperion, 2002), xi.

36. Calvin Coolidge, "The Title of American," in *The Price of Freedom: Speeches and Addresses* (New York: Charles Scribner's Sons, 1924), 89. Note that even when numbers appear in an orally delivered speech, the figures themselves are almost always present before the speaker in writing, and the speaker will frequently (as in Coolidge's case) disseminate the speech himself in printed form.

These numbers, in their place, are as eloquent in expressing *The Price of Free-dom*, the title Coolidge gave to this collection of his speeches, as the more high-falutin' language of patriotism that Coolidge always had ready for use.

When numbers are put through their paces in the proper bureaucratic form of cost-benefit analyses, mighty dams spring from the earth or vanish into might-have-beens, and the great persuaders of the American political class armed merely with words are stunned into speechlessness by those armed with figures as though they had attempted to trade repartee with Churchill or insults with Demosthenes. Pity poor George Norris, the giant of Nebraska Progressivism, pinned down by the thin but unbreakable cords of Army Corps of Engineers numbers: "It was explained to Senator Norris . . . that the cost of these reservoirs would be between 40 and 60 million dollars; and that the cost-benefit ratio will not be better than 2:1, and will probably be nearer to 3:1 even with very liberal assumptions as to benefits. He was told that we were making every effort to improve the showing of the project, that we have not yet found a justifiable project for him, have scant hope of doing so, but are exhausting our ingenuity to make the report convincing to all concerned."[37] The choice to speak or write numbers is a rhetorical choice, a choice among the available means of persuasion, even if those who appeal to numbers to persuade often belittle other ways of speaking as "mere rhetoric." Numbers like those thrust at Norris persuade not because the audience can assess their validity or their relevance but because they give the impression that the speaker or writer has mastered the field.

Real speech is much more factual, and even more numerate, than we usually imagine. Comparing George Patton's July 1944 address to his troops with its Hollywood re-creation by George C. Scott in the opening scene of the film *Patton*, Roderick Hart observes: "Students who compared the real Patton speech to the movie version found 50% fewer [f]actual [assertions] in the latter, indicating that real soldiers need hard data but the movie audiences were primarily interested in 'color.'"[38] By presenting hard data you purport to invite judgment of the facts (and Hart seems to have fallen under the spell of the real General Patton's apparent invitation), and, more important, you compel your audience to infer that you are master of the relevant facts, that you know what needs to be known about the matter at hand. As

---

37. Quoted in Porter, *Trust in Numbers*, 180, from whom the discussion of cost-benefit analysis as a mode of rhetoric is drawn.

38. Hart, *Modern Rhetorical Criticism*, 74.

Bob Woodward describes the thinking of Andrew Card, George W. Bush's chief of staff, at the beginning of the war in Afghanistan, "The president had to be familiar enough with the details, sufficiently immersed in the tactics, so that he never appeared ignorant in public. That would be a true disaster."[39] "Technical explanations can add a great deal of credibility," counsels advertising copywriter Joseph Sugarman, "but before you write them, make sure you indeed become an expert. If not, the customer will see right through this ploy."[40] Detailed factual presentation thus persuades not because audiences absorb the facts but because the facts give them impression that a speaker knows all relevant detail, even though audiences have neither the time nor the knowledge to assess the presentation: "The sheer copiousness of information . . . may suggest to a potential voter that there is substance in the candidate's position" and thus that there is substance in the candidate.[41] As Sugarman puts it, more pithily, "By being specific, you sound like you're an expert."[42]

A comparison of two numbers can make what you are saying evident to all.[43] A forest of numbers can persuade, however, not because they give the audience a sense of the things involved but because numbers persuade the audience that the speaker or writer has mastered the things involved. Detailed numerical data does not invite the audience to think about the things presented; on the contrary, it attempts to suppress thought about the subject by drawing the audience's attention to the speaker instead and eliciting the audience's approval of the speaker.[44] Numerical data presents reasons and

39. Bob Woodward, *Bush at War* (New York: Simon and Schuster, 2002), 176.

40. Sugarman, *Advertising Secrets,* 117; for a review of the experimental evidence showing that detailed and clear arguments make the speaker seem more credible and authoritative, see Mark A. Hamilton, "Message Variables That Mediate and Moderate the Effect of Equivocal Language on Source Credibility," *Journal of Language and Social Psychology* 17, no. 1 (1998): 109–43.

41. Thomas N. Edmonds, "Print Ads," in *The Manship School Guide to Political Communication,* ed. David Perlmutter (Baton Rouge: Louisiana State University Press, 1999), 159.

42. Sugarman, *Advertising Secrets,* 167; see also Daniel J. O'Keefe, "Justification Explicitness and Persuasive Effect: A Meta-Analytic Review of the Effects of Varying Support Articulation in Persuasive Messages," *Argumentation and Advocacy* 35, no. 2 (1998): 61–75.

43. John Kline, "Interaction of Evidence and Readers' Intelligence on the Effects of Short Messages," *Quarterly Journal of Speech* 55, no. 4 (1969): 407–13.

44. Rodney A. Reynolds and J. Lynn Reynolds, "Evidence," in *The Persuasion Handbook: Developments in Theory and Practice,* ed. James Price Dillard and Michael Pfau (Thousand Oaks, Calif.: Sage, 2002), 431; Charles R. Berger, "Processing Quantitative Data About Risk and Threat in News Reports," *Journal of Communication* 48, no. 3 (1998): 87–106, 87–88, and the studies cited there. In "Affective and Cognitive Reactions to Narrative Versus Statistical Evidence Organ Donation Messages" (*Journal of Applied Communication Research* 26, no. 3 [1998]: 279–300), Jenifer E. Kopfman, Sandi W. Smith, James K. Ah Yun, and Annemarie Hodges purport to examine which is more thought provoking, anecdote or statistics. Yet their "statistical message" has only two numbers in it, which is hardly a numerically rich enough message

therefore presents the speaker as reasonable but does not invite the audience to *reason with the speaker*. John F. Kennedy, recalls the reporter James Reston, "either overwhelmed you with decimal points or disarmed you with a smile and a wisecrack."[45] Speeches should therefore be less numerate if speakers aim to make the audience understand. But to present a plethora of numbers is often the right rhetorical choice when the speaker invites the audience to consent to actions he or she has already undertaken.

To reason with others is to offer them reasons that they can make their own. In scientific communications such an invitation is offered in principle, as when the author of a social science paper, in keeping with present norms, states that the numerical data on which his or her argument is based is available to readers through a data repository. Yet the author does not expect that he or she will persuade the readers if and only if that invitation is acted on. To move one's readers through sight of the things themselves, and not just through deference to one's knowledge and expertise, one must argue on the basis of things that one has made present for the readers and thus available to their contemplation. Not words, not numerical figures, but things made vivid in words though concrete depiction, through example, or through analogy.

Enargeia: The Power of Detail

The ancient rhetoricians knew the power of detailed circumstantial description as *enargeia*. Quintilian explains the matter pedantically: "I am complaining that a man has been murdered. Shall I not bring before my eyes all the circumstances it is reasonable to imagine must have occurred in such a connection? Shall I not see the assassin burst [forth] suddenly from his hiding place, the victim tremble, cry for help, beg for mercy, or turn to

---

to unlock the peculiar features of the processing of quantitative messages. Compare the eight numbers in the Coolidge paragraph quoted above or the four numbers in the memorandum of the briefing for George Norris. Kopfman and her collaborators appear merely to have replicated the demonstration of the effect of specific numerical evidence made in the 1960s by Kline. Likewise, the potentially valuable study of studies by Mike Allen and Raymond W. Preiss ("Comparing the Persuasiveness of Narrative and Statistical Evidence Using Meta-Analysis," *Communication Research Reports* 14, no. 2 [1997]: 125–31) uses experiments that presented subjects with only two or three numbers in order to demonstrate that "statistics" are slightly more persuasive than anecdotes; compare their study with such studies in their sample as Peter R. Dickson, "The Impact of Enriching Case and Statistical Information on Consumer Judgments," *Journal of Consumer Research* 8, no. 4 (1982): 398–406.

45. Henry Fairlie, *The Kennedy Promise* (New York: Dell, 1974), 174.

run? Shall I not see the fatal blow delivered and the stricken body fall? Will not the blood, the deathly pallor, the groan of agony, the death rattle, be indelibly impressed on my mind? From such impressions arise that *enargeia* Cicero calls illumination and actuality."[46] *Enargeia* is defined by Joseph Williams as "the extensive use of concrete description, instead of abstract nominalizations."[47] In the process of taking in the speaker's concrete description, the members of the audience create for themselves the images that the speaker describes. "A work of art," writes Sergei Eisenstein, in a statement that applies no less to speeches than to painting or film, "is the process of the birth of an image in the spectator's senses and mind."[48]

Now that we have grasped the ancient concept of *enargeia,* we can understand both the power and, in a way, the disingenuousness of some statements of the great Afrikaner poet, painter, and former political prisoner Breyten Breytenbach:

> I believe it is the primary function of the painter or poet to present an image. To present an opinion would be authoritarian. Similarly I believe the primary confrontation to be between the viewer or the reader and the image presented, face to face as it were, with neither intermediary nor a priori.
>
> The painting as anonymous or masked messenger, as a reflection of breathing, a continuous shaping of consciousness, can be a weapon also. Let me explain. If you can look without projecting a meaning you will be confronted head-on by an embodiment of being. "Meaning," "Understanding"—these neutralize the threat of the unknown or the unexpected. After all, you can control meaning, but you cannot regiment seeing. Thus the instant relationship between the viewer and the image (and the one is inexistent without the other) is an uncontrollable expression of freedom, ideally the establishment of a free zone not embattled by convention or by fashion, but also one of confrontation. To sum up: when the mind has no meaning, seeing becomes a weapon for liberation.[49]

46. Quintilian, *Institutio oratoria* 6.2.31–32, trans. H. E. Butler (Cambridge, Mass.: Harvard University Press, 1920–22) (translation slightly modified). For commentary on this passage, see Skinner, *Reason and Rhetoric,* 182–88.

47. Joseph M. Williams, *Style: Ten Lessons in Clarity and Grace,* 6th ed. (New York: Longman, 2000), 75–76.

48. Eisenstein, "Montage in 1938," in *Notes of a Film Director* (New York: Dover, 1970), 69.

49. Breyten Breytenbach, *The Memory of Birds in Times of Revolution* (New York: Harcourt Brace, 1996), 69–70.

Breytenbach claims that judgments can be authoritarian whereas pictures—whether word pictures or painted pictures—are liberating.[50] Breytenbach does not wish to present us with something we can dismiss as "Breytenbach's judgment" or "Breytenbach's view" but to show us things as they are.[51] Yet what Breytenbach obscures is that judgments can be ineffective because they invite a "judgmental" response to the speaker's own judgment, whereas images presented can move viewers to adopt as their own the perspective of the creator of the images. "The social content of a definite creed or an explicit message is consciously realized by the speaker and consciously accepted or rejected by the hearer," Arnold Hauser explains.[52]

What is wrong, or even self-deceiving, about Breytenbach's supposed self-denial becomes visible when Breytenbach's condemnation of "judgmental" art is laid beside André Bazin's critique of the technique of montage in movie editing. Breytenbach valorizes painting because it presents the viewer with the image to which the viewer freely responds; Bazin condemns montage because the film director chooses images to which the viewer, without any guidance external to the flow of images, will respond, compelling him or her to judge the action the images depict in the way that the director has foreseen and intended. Bazin excoriates the montagist precisely because he or she conceals his own judgment in his choice of images in imposing his own view of the actions depicted on the audience—as Sergei Eisenstein, the master of montage put it, "the spectator is compelled to proceed along that selfsame creative road that the author traveled in creating the image."[53]

50. Cf. Edwin Black's critique of sentimentalism, "The Sentimental Style as Escapism," in *Rhetorical Questions: Studies of Public Discourse* (Chicago: University of Chicago Press, 1992), 97–112.

51. As Daniel Markovits pointed out to me, Breytenbach appears to be echoing Keats's claim that a poet "has no Identity—he is continually in for—and filling some other body. . . . Not one word I ever utter can be taken for granted as an opinion growing out of my identical nature—how can it, when I have no nature" (letter to Richard Woodhouse, in *Letters of John Keats*, ed. Robert Gittings [Oxford: Oxford University Press, 1987], 157–58). See also Daniel Markovits, "Legal Ethics from the Lawyer's Point of View," *Yale Journal of Law and the Humanities* 15, no. 2 (2003): 273.

52. Arnold Hauser, *The Philosophy of Art History* (New York: Knopf, 1959), 29; and see Murray Edelman's discussion of Arnold Hauser in *From Art to Politics: How Artistic Creations Shape Political Conceptions* (Chicago: University of Chicago Press, 1995), 49–50, to which I owe this reference.

53. See André Bazin, "The Evolution of the Language of Cinema," in vol. 1 of *What Is Cinema?* ed. and trans. Hugh Gray (Berkeley and Los Angeles: University of California Press, 1967), 25–26; Sergei Eisenstein, *The Film Sense*, ed. and trans. Jay Leda (New York: Harcourt, 1975), 32, cited in V. F. Perkins, *Film as Film* (London: Penguin, 1972), 33; Noël Carroll, *Philosophical Problems of Classical Film Theory* (Princeton: Princeton University Press, 1988), 161–62. Bazin prefers the deep focus shot, where all elements in a complex scene are available to the viewer's visual attention, to the montage. For Bazin, the superiority of the deep focus shot to the montage

Breytenbach, like the montagist, is not disarming himself rhetorically so much as renouncing the ineffective, ornamented weapons, easily dismissed by the audience as mere rhetoric, in favor of the concrete, vivid, style of depiction that rarely fails of impact.[54] "What can rhetorical depiction [*rhetorikē phantasia*] do?" Longinus asks, and his answer is, "Much, but especially it adds persuasive pull and fellow feeling to your speeches, and mixed with the facts that are ready to hand it does not just persuade your listener but enslaves him."[55]

In the speech that won the 1981 election for Likud prime minister Menachem Begin, what every Israeli recalls is the inflammatory conclusion, comparing the disparagement of Moroccan immigrants by Israel's Labor elite with the acceptance, honor, and responsibility those immigrants were offered by Begin's movement. Begin devoted much of this speech to a highly purple account of the Iraqi nuclear threat that no one can remember. But every Israeli of even modest political awareness knows of the end of the speech, in which Begin describes how at the Labor party rally the previous night a celebrity entertainer used an ethnic slur to silence hecklers:

> Last night, in this square, a young actor got up, what was his name? Dudu? Dudu To . . . Paz, Dudu Topaz. Here he said the following words—silence, not even a fly should be heard, absolute silence. Listen:—Dudu Topaz, in the ears of 100,000 members of the [Labor] Alignment, he said these words: "Tzach-tzachim [dirty Moroccans],

---

is that the deep focus shot creates the impression that the things in the scene are revealed to us without interference from the director's intentions or persona. What is really at stake, of course, in this argument about film directing is a theological quarrel between humanism and Catholic theism over the problem of evil. For the humanist, evil is to be excluded by editing, and since God hasn't done the job it is up to us to recut the world. For the theist Bazin, evil is significant only as a part of a world the whole of which is offered by the Creator to our invariably selective attention.

54. Although vivid, concrete language is more likely to make an impression on the audience, there is surprisingly little experimental evidence that vivid language is more likely to *persuade* the audience to adopt the views of the speaker; see Shelley E. Taylor and Suzanne C. Thompson, "Stalking the Elusive Vividness Effect," *Psychological Review* 89, no. 2 (1982): 155–81; Rebecca L. Collins, Shelley E. Taylor, Joanne V. Wood, and Suzanne C. Thompson, "The Vividness Effect: Elusive or Illusory?" *Journal of Experimental Social Psychology* 24, no. 1 (1988): 1–18; Lawrence A. Hosman, "Language and Persuasion," in *The Persuasion Handbook*, ed. James Price Dillard and Michael Pfau (Thousand Oaks, Calif.: Sage, 2002), 375–78. As I note at the end of this chapter, speakers therefore avoid vivid speech when they have more to fear from creating a negative impression of themselves than from leaving no impression at all.

55. Longinus, *On the Sublime*, 15.9 (translation mine). Eisenstein himself discusses what he calls the use of montage in literature in "Word and Image" (in *The Film Sense* [New York: Harcourt Brace, 1942], 1–65).

those in Metzudat Ze'ev [Likud headquarters], those who with difficulty make it as battalion MPs, if they go to the army at all. Here are
the soldiers and the officers of the combat units."

I will admit and confess before you that until today I never heard
the word "tzach-tzachim," and I didn't know what it meant. In the
underground, in the days of the movements of the revolt [against the
British], Galili [of the Labor Zionist-dominated Haganah] asked me,
after taking counsel with Nathan Yellin-Mor, may his memory be for
a blessing, of the Lehi [a Zionist terrorist organization founded in
1940], when we planned an operation together against British rule,
and he said to me in these words exactly, Galili said to me: "How did
you solve the problem of the Oriental Jews in the Irgun?" And I look
at him in surprise and I say to him: "Israel, what are you asking?
What problem?" And he says: "Nu, you don't know, you haven't heard?
The problem of the Oriental Jews." So I say to him: "What problem?
We don't have such a problem. We are all brothers, we are all Jews,
we are all equal, all of us. . . . The principal commander in the districts was a Yemenite Jew, Uzi was a Sephardic Jew, Gidi, who did
the historic operation at the King David Hotel, was a Sephardic Jew,
the commander of the prisoners in Latrun was a Yemenite Jew, and
all our young men stood at attention before him. What problem? We
had no such problem. We are all Jews. All brothers. All fighters."

But listen, when that fellow, what's-his-name, Du-Du To-Paz, said
that wretched word, that vain language and empty wind of his, the
whole crowd that was here last night cheered. Now I will tell Dudu
Topaz who he had in mind. The Oriental Jews among us were brave
fighters, in the underground, too. There are among them those who
ascended the gallows, who until the last moment of their lives sang
[the Zionist anthem] "HaTikva" and made the whole world stand astonished before their extraordinary bravery. And they went to prison, to
concentration camps, they fought and they did not break, they shouted
before the British judges these words: "We do not recognize your
rule at all, you must leave here, leave the Land of Israel." Feinstein
was of European origin, how do you say it, "an Ashkenazi"; Moshe
Barazani was a Sephardic Jew from Iraq. On the night after, [Fein-
stein and Barazani] were sentenced to death, and early in the morning they would be brought down from hanging, and the rabbi was an
old man, he said that he would come to take their bodies down, they
didn't want to cause harm to the rabbi, so they took to their hearts a

hand grenade, they released the trigger. Ashkenazim? Iraqis? Jews. Brothers. Fighters!

Shall every hired actor of the Alignment rant and blaspheme God's name? Oriental Jews are among the best fighters in the IDF [Israel Defense Force]. Together with Arik Sharon, they crossed the Suez Canal and passed to the other side. He commanded them, among the best of Israel's fighters. And you stand before the nation, and the people, and before the wild crowd of the Alignment shouting cries, what did he say there? Tzach-tzachim, tzach-tzachim, that is what he called them—those tzach-tzachim are fit only to be battalion MPs. Battalion MP, that's like a "jobnik" [i.e., a poorly esteemed noncombat position]? "Jobniks" don't fight at all. Blasphemy. And the whole crowd cheered! Where was Mrs. Shoshana Arbeli, who stands in the second spot on the Alignment list? And where were the others? Why didn't they leave that demonstration in protest? Never has a man blasphemed to that extent, never has a man so wounded the honor of an entire tribe in Israel, as the Alignment did last night here on this very spot.

What I request of you, tomorrow, from morning 'til night—do a coordinated telephone operation. What has to be done, what is important that be done, is call all your acquaintances in Jerusalem and in Haifa and in Rishon Letzion and Nes Tziona and Rehovoth and Be'er Sheva. Just tell them what Dudu Topaz said here. The whole people of Israel have to know this. It is one sentence, that's all: "The tzach-tzachim are all in Metzudat Ze'ev." And we are happy that they are all in Metzudat Ze'ev![56]

Begin's conclusion is effective rhetoric because it is factual, concrete, and direct. It is little more than a string of anecdotes and a recitation of names, intended to demonstrate to his audience that at crucial moments in the history of Israel those whom Begin's opponents labeled as Oriental Jews served their country by serving under Begin. But precisely because it was effective rhetoric, the speech and its factual style are transparent, and thus the actual words are forgotten: here too, Israelis recall falsely that Begin swayed the crowd *because* he indulged his taste for loaded adjectives and overblown comparisons. But the end of the speech works, as the beginning does not, because Begin avoids the turns we usually think of as "rhetorical."

56. Menachem Begin, "Speech at Malkhei Yisrael Square" (1981), in *Speeches for All Occasions* [in Hebrew], ed. Tamar Brush (Tel Aviv: Yediot Aharonot and Open University Press, 1993), 201–2 (all translations of extracts from *Speeches for All Occasions* are mine).

The Manipulation of Concreteness

Persuasiveness frequently comes from the power of assertion, which is generally more convincing than actual proof.[57] The factual style can, therefore, take advantage of our tendency to accept what people say, if they say something at all, without demanding that they offer additional reasons why we should accept what they say. Garry Wills describes the stratagem thus: "Hal Evry says that the most specific thing to say about one's own candidate is 'Three cheers for Joe Smith,' while the approach to one's adversary should be 'End the parking meter racket!' (Let the other fellow explain, in ridiculous detail, that there is no such thing as a parking meter racket. Everyone will suspect him of a cover-up.)"[58] As Kenneth Burke has said, the power of reason in speech is revealed in negation, in being able to deny, in contradicting or besmirching, what has already been posited. What is negative actuates our critical faculties in a way that what is positive does not. One can use concrete assertion not to invite the audience to reason about one's assertions but in order to lull the audience into nodding agreement with a drone of irrelevant detail. Therefore, those with positive messages can get away with more shading of the truth—Kathleen Hall Jamieson has found that in American political advertisements, positive ads are more inaccurate than negative ones.[59]

This inference from the specificity of an assertion to its truth has some ground in that liars tend to speak less specifically, concretely, or directly than persons telling the truth.[60] As Quintilian suggests: "We shall secure the vividness we seek if only our descriptions give the impression of truth; nay, we may even add fictitious incidents of the type that commonly occur. He who desires to obscure the situation will state what is false instead of the truth, but he must still strive to secure an appearance of greatest evidence for what he relates."[61] The big lie is therefore a lie in the style of truth, with all the specificity of detail we expect in the truth. Aeschines accuses

57. Quintilian, *Institutio oratoria* 11.3.154.

58. Garry Wills, *Nixon Agonistes: The Crisis of the Self-Made Man* (1970; repr., New York: New American Library, 1979), 81–82.

59. Kenneth Burke, "A Dramatistic View of the Origins of Language" in *Language as Symbolic Action: Essays on Life, Literature and Method* (Berkeley and Los Angeles: University of California Press, 1966). Kathleen Hall Jamieson, *Everything You Think You Know About Politics . . . and Why You're Wrong* (New York: Basic Books, 2000), 97–110.

60. Hart, *Modern Rhetorical Criticism*, 164–65; see the studies Hart cites there (Mark L. Knapp et al., "Exploring Deception as a Communication Construct," *Human Communication Research* 1, no. 1 [1974]: 15–29; Charles E. Osgood and Evelyn G. Walker, "Motivation and Language Behavior: A Content Analysis of Suicide Notes," *Journal of Abnormal and Social Psychology* 59, no. 1 [1959]: 58–67).

61. Quintilian, *Institutio oratoria* 4.2.65, trans. Butler (translation modified).

Demosthenes of lying in concrete detail: "And on this account, too, he is greatly worthy of being hated, that he is such a wicked man as to destroy the signs of honesty."[62]

Although one's assertions should be as specific, concrete, and detailed as possible, they should not necessarily be put forward with supporting arguments. Indeed, one who would persuade ought generally to elaborate the assertion rather than elaborate the argument. This is because the constraints on public debate (including the time constraint) are such as to make the fullest disclosure of reasons impossible. If the arguments used in deliberation "happen not to be entirely plain and conclusive, it is the business of the orator to make them appear so," Adam Smith advises.[63] Yet if reasons can only be partially disclosed or clarified, the reasons that are disclosed will always be insufficient. If the audience can spot the insufficiencies but cannot fill the gaps on their own, giving reasons may make one's claims less persuasive.[64] As Nietzsche counsels: "Assertion safer than proof.—An assertion produces a stronger effect than an argument, at least among the majority of mankind; for argument arouses mistrust. This is why public speakers seek to hammer home their party's arguments with assertions."[65]

Nietzsche here is faithful to the rhetorical tradition he knew better, perhaps, than any other classicist of his time. Quintilian writes: "In speaking there are certain things that have to be concealed, either because they ought not to be disclosed or because they cannot be expressed as they deserve."[66] Quintilian's first category is just a special case of the second: you should not give an explanation if the explanation will just become one more action that has to be explained.[67] Kathleen Hall Jamieson has noted that network coverage of speeches tends to edit out the evidence and leave the assertions.[68]

---

62. Aeschines, *Against Ctesiphon* §99; Jon Hesk, *Deception and Democracy in Classical Athens* (Cambridge: Cambridge University Press, 2000), 232–33. G. B. Stiff and J. R. Miller ("'Come. to Think of It . . .': Interrogative Probes, Deceptive Communication, and Deception Detection," *Human Communications Research* 12, no. 3 [1986]: 339–57) showed that lying statements are shorter and refer more often to the speaker than true statements; see also W. Peter Robinson, *Deceit, Delusion, and Detection* (Thousand Oaks, Calif.: Sage, 1996), 118.

63. Adam Smith, *Lectures on Rhetoric and Belles Lettres*, ed. J. C. Bryce (Oxford: Oxford University Press, 1985), 145.

64. See Perelman and Olbrechts-Tyteca, *The New Rhetoric* §101, "The Dangers of Amplitude," 480–81.

65. Friedrich Nietzsche, "Assorted Opinions and Maxims," no. 295, in *Human, All Too Human*, trans. R. J. Hollingdale (Cambridge: Cambridge University Press, 1996), 280–81.

66. Quintilian, *Institutio oratoria* 2.13.12, trans. Butler (translation slightly modified).

67. For a case study of how in politics winners tell stories while losers explain, see Graetz and Shapiro, *Death by a Thousand Cuts*, 45, 50–61.

68. Jamieson, *Everything You Think You Know About Politics*, 42–43, 52.

This may very well have the effect of making the politicians into more effective speakers!

Sometimes, too, one uses factuality not as a substitute for the supporting reasons one prefers not to proffer but as a distraction from vagueness. Saying nothing, as chapter 4 suggests, is an important weapon in the politician's arsenal: it is one way of "not activating your opponents' potential supporters."[69] But saying nothing is not always enough. In particular, it cannot get you a hearing; rather it is intended to avoid the consequence of a hearing you would prefer not to take place. If you must have something that looks as if it supports your case to put forward but cannot afford to say anything relevant, you better say something irrelevant. This is what Bernays called "the technique of presenting favorable facts" or what Quintilian describes as supporting "a bad case . . . by matters foreign to the case."[70] Advertising copywriters describe the features of their products in detail in order to conceal from us their refusal to promise any particular benefit from using them.[71] When this technique is used, as Walter Lippmann notes, "on the noncontentious record, the detail is overwhelming; on the issue everything is cloudy."[72] "The job of political discourse is to open up the mind to new thoughts and to fully occupy the mind with those thoughts," Roderick Hart writes. "Rhetoric gives us something to think about as well as something not to think about."[73]

Menachem Begin's 1948 speech providing his version of the sinking of the *Altalena*, the Irgun arms-running ship, by the newborn Israel Defense Force is a masterful example of the manipulation of concreteness.[74] Begin's speech gives the listener or reader a sense of place: everything is situated carefully in space. Begin speaks of the land of Israel as opposed to the lands of exile, the homeland as against the prison camps in Cyprus and Eritrea where the British sent political prisoners and security detainees. No place in the speech is referred to by pronouns; instead, all are particularized. Begin

69. Stephen K. Medvic, *Political Consultants in U.S. Congressional Elections* (Columbus: Ohio State University Press, 2001), 15.

70. Edward L. Bernays, *Public Relations* (Norman: University of Oklahoma Press, 1952), 64; Quintilian, *Institutio oratoria* 5.13.35, trans. Butler.

71. Sugarman, *Advertising Secrets*, 173.

72. Lippmann, *Public Opinion* (1922; repr., New York: The Free Press, 1965), 131. Lippmann's whole analysis of Charles Evans Hughes's speech accepting the Republican nomination in 1916 (129–31) is worthy of study.

73. Roderick P. Hart, *The Sound of Leadership: Presidential Communication in the Modern Age* (Chicago: University of Chicago Press, 1987), 69.

74. Menachem Begin, "Speech of the Commander of the National Military Organization [Irgun] after the Shelling of the *Altalena*" (1948), in *Speeches for All Occasions*, 153–62.

gives a roll call of the towns and settlements the Irgun is trying desperately to defend from the Arab enemy and describes the final journey of the *Altalena*, under fire from shore, in complete detail.

Begin speaks of the pier at which the ship initially dropped anchor, the sandbank where the unloading of the *Altalena* began. The sandbank is both literal and metaphorical: the Hagana, like a sandbank, obstruct the national purpose just as they send their boats to blockade the *Altalena* and use their men to obstruct, rather than assist, the unloading.[75] Begin speaks of the voyage under fire from the sandbank near Herziliya to Tel Aviv. It was not in the port, however, Begin tells his radio audience, but opposite Frishman Street that the *Altalena* finally sank, burning. Even the *Altalena* has parts, a deck, a belly, a door, an anchor, and a mast.[76]

The factuality of Begin's speech, to which he himself alludes, is made possible by this list of places. One could say that Begin demonstrates his superior patriotism by speaking of all of the places in the Jewish motherland. The sense of time is much looser: the speech has very few dates, and the passage of time during the last voyage is noted in relative terms rather than by clock time. Keeping the time references vague serves Begin's purpose; it enables him to downplay and even blur the issue of the cease-fire with the Arabs, whose clauses the landing and unloading of the *Altalena* violated. Begin reminds us of these places and thereby makes us put out of mind or forget that the cease-fire had already commenced.[77] Begin manipulates what we keep in mind in order to persuade us to approve of the actions of his organization and thus to condemn Ben-Gurion. Begin nonetheless has the chutzpah to use "cease-fire" as a key term in the speech, when he asserts that Ben-Gurion's forces had a cease-fire with the Arab enemy but not with Begin's Irgun.[78]

Sometimes a speaker will use this device of "displaced concreteness" when the nature of one's point is such that specificity is impossible. In the address to the protesters attending the 1963 march on Washington, Martin Luther King is specific about the unjust constraints on African American

75. Begin, "Speech of the Commander of the National Military Organization," 157.

76. Begin, "Speech of the Commander of the National Military Organization," 161.

77. "'Forgetfulness,'" as Stanley Fish reminds us, "in the sense of not keeping everything in mind at once, is a condition of action, and the difference between activities . . . is a difference between differing species of forgetfulness" (*Doing What Comes Naturally: Change, Rhetoric, and the Practice of Theory in Literary and Legal Studies* [Durham: Duke University Press, 1989], 397; see also Fish, *There's No Such Thing as Free Speech, and It's a Good Thing, Too* [Oxford: Oxford University Press, 1994], 176).

78. Begin, "Speech of the Commander of the National Military Organization," 161.

citizens, but at the high point of the speech, he indicates the locations of freedom instead of the content of freedom, playing on the well-known line from the patriotic hymn "My Country 'Tis of Thee": "From every mountainside, let freedom ring."

> Let freedom ring from the prodigious hilltops of New Hampshire.
> Let freedom ring from the mighty mountains of New York.
> Let freedom ring from the heightening Alleghenies of Pennsylvania.
> Let freedom ring from the snowcapped Rockies of Colorado.
> Let freedom ring from the curvaceous slopes of California.
> But not only that: Let freedom ring from Stone Mountain of Georgia.
> Let freedom ring from Lookout Mountain of Tennessee.
> Let freedom ring from every from every hill and molehill of Mississippi.
> From every mountainside, let freedom ring.

Martin Luther King's address to the march on Washington is a call to struggle to realize freedom for all. Yet the idea of freedom is hard to get across because it cannot in its essence be pinned down to this or that activity, this or that achievement. Freedom is a relation to possibilities rather than to actualities, but it includes the possibility of reconceiving our possibilities.[79] That is to say, with J. M. Coetzee, "Freedom is another name for the unimaginable," the unrepresentable.[80] "There is nothing to be said about freedom, except that within its space we construct our ethics and our lives."[81] King chose to specify the places where blacks and whites would live free lives rather than attempt the impossible task of making concrete the content of free lives.

The Art of Letting the Facts Speak for Themselves

The whole work of persuasion is done if we can get the facts or things to speak for themselves. To quote Gerald Rafshoon, Jimmy Carter's principal

79. Philip Pettit, "Two Neglected Aspects of Deliberation," paper presented to the 2003 annual meeting of the American Political Science Association, Philadelphia, Penn., August 31, 2003.

80. J. M. Coetzee, *Doubling the Point: Essays and Interviews*, ed. David Attwell (Cambridge, Mass.: Harvard University Press, 2002), 341.

81. Ian Hacking, *Historical Ontology* (Cambridge, Mass.: Harvard University Press, 2002), 120; cf. Henri Bergson, *Time and Free Will: An Essay on the Immediate Data of Consciousness*, trans. F. L. Pogson (London: Allen and Unwin, 1910), 230: "All determinism will thus be refuted by experience, but every attempt to define freedom will open the way to determinism."

advertising man in Carter's 1980 presidential reelection campaign: "If we had to do it all over again, we would take the 30 million dollars we spent in the campaign and get three more helicopters for the Iran rescue mission."[82] One could claim, with Samuel Popkin, that Rafshoon's statement shows the limits of image-making when one is confronted by political reality. But we will better understand the gravity of Carter's and Rafshoon's problem if we remind ourselves that the most effective image of President Carter would have been his receiving the freed hostages. Rafshoon is saying, only half in jest, that the "permanent campaign" for Carter's reelection should have invested in creating that image.

It takes a lot of work, of course, to get things to speak for themselves, and no one has expounded the ways in which that work is accomplished better than the sociologist of science Bruno Latour: "There is only one way in which an actor can prove its power. It has to make those in whose names it spoke speak and show that they all say the same thing." Through graphs and charts the facts themselves speak in a presentation or article. To make things have a stable existence requires getting people together on what these things should be like, and conversely it is only what exists that can stabilize viewpoints. Science works, says Latour, because we invest in making it work. "It is pointless to claim that Pasteur's discoveries were believed because they were convincing. They ended up being convincing because the hygienists believed and forced everybody else to put them into practice."[83]

Science is effective at persuasion because since we value science, we are willing to indulge the scientist in experimentation. As Latour and his collaborators have shown, the scientist works on the things in private, in the laboratory, until he or she can get them to work so that the public demonstration goes without a hitch. It is the very distance between the laboratory, where the facts are produced, and the outside, where they are applied, that gives the impression of a miraculous correspondence between science and the world, Latour has shown. "The impression disappears . . . if one considers the long,

82. Quoted in Samuel Popkin, *The Reasoning Voter: Communication and Persuasion in Presidential Campaigns* (Chicago: University of Chicago Press, 1994), 4. Rafshoon makes a similar claim in his December 1980 interview with Patrick Devlin, "I don't see where anything that happened . . . except for the hostages and the aftermath of the hostage crisis really had much to do with the way the vote turned out" ("Reagan and Carter's Ad Men Review the 1980 Television Campaigns," *Communication Quarterly* 30, no. 1 [1981]: 3–12, 8).

83. Bruno Latour, *The Pasteurization of France*, trans. Alan Sheridan and John Law (Cambridge, Mass.: Harvard University Press, 1988), 54, 196; Bruno Latour, *Science in Action: How to Follow Scientists and Engineers Through Society* (Cambridge, Mass.: Harvard University Press, 1987), 46–47; Bruno Latour, *Aramis, or, The Love of Technology*, trans. Catherine Porter (Cambridge, Mass.: Harvard University Press, 1996), 48–49, 77.

continuous sequence of experiments." Public experiment is the scientific version of the trial lawyers' advice never to ask a witness a question in court to which you do not already know the answer, that is to say, in which you have not already invested time and resources to discover what the witness is going to say. Even Richard Feynman "cheated," trying out the famous O-ring and ice water experiment in his hotel room, before he faced the media and gave his explanation of the space shuttle *Challenger* disaster.[84]

The surprising result of Latour's analysis is that the distinction between the craftwork of the scientific laboratory and political action turns out to be quantitative rather than qualitative, because the scientist gets many tries to get things right, whereas the politician gets only one: "The respected expert is indistinguishable from the politician who is scorned by everyone. The expert makes large numbers of secret small-scale mistakes and confidently emerges from hiding at the end of the day. The politician makes really grand mistakes and has to perform in front of everyone. Here the decisions are made—before the mistakes."[85] The politician "is limited to a single shot and has to shoot in public," and if he or she shoots and misses, the failure is as public as the effort that failed.[86] Publicity makes it easier to spot failures; further, the very size and diversity of your audience it makes it more difficult to escape the consequences of failure for your reputation: as Elizabeth Noelle-Neumann points out, "There is . . . no way to explain or excuse one's actions, when an anonymous public is involved."[87]

The culture of experiment and the theatricality of public scientific demonstration indicate the work required to let things speak for themselves. Yet sometimes that work must be negative: to persuade, you must let things go the way they are going until they make your point. In this way the speaker lets the narrowing of possibilities take place in the world, rather than in his or her speech, and then speaks to present how these circumstances make clear that his or her preferred alternative is the necessary one—that is to say, the only reasonable one. As governor of Massachusetts, faced with the Boston police strike, Calvin Coolidge refused to commit troops until rioting

84. Latour, *Pasteurization*, 88; Richard Feynman as told to Ralph Leighton, *What Do You Care What Other People Think? Further Adventures of a Curious Character* (New York: Norton, 1988), 146–53.

85. Latour, "Irreductions," 4.5.3, in *Pasteurization*, 225.

86. Latour, "Irreductions," 3.6.3, in *Pasteurization*, 210. "Failed rhetoric does not leave its context quietly," as Thomas B. Farrell emphasizes. "It crashes and burns with the weight of the event, in full public light" (*Norms of Rhetorical Culture* [New Haven: Yale University Press, 1993], 241).

87. Elisabeth Noelle-Neumann, *Spiral of Silence: Public Opinion, Our Social Skin*, 2nd ed. (Chicago: University of Chicago Press, 1993), 215.

had begun. Before order had begun to fray, Coolidge writes, explaining his seeming inactivity, "the issue was not understood, and the disorder focused public attention on it, and showed just what it meant to have a police force that did not obey orders."[88] Coolidge needed actual violence in order to persuade, he needed to let the facts speak for themselves, in their own time. As Thomas Silver has observed, Coolidge's exemplar could well have been Lincoln's passivity between the time of his election and his inauguration, during which he allowed the war to come by waiting for the South to strike the first blow.[89]

Still controversial is Eisenhower's decision to wait on events in implementing the judicial order for school desegregation at Little Rock. Eisenhower did nothing until the city had shown that it was unable to enforce the desegregation order and the state, under Governor Faubus, had shown that it was unwilling to enforce it. By letting things take their course, Eisenhower could claim "the law and the national interest demanded that the President take action."[90]

But perhaps the most arresting example of waiting on events is Franklin Delano Roosevelt's conduct regarding the banking crisis in the four-month "interregnum" between his election in November of 1932 and his inauguration in March of 1933. Roosevelt refused to make any statements on his policies or appointments in order to avoid responsibility for the crisis while taking all the credit for its solution. By allowing tension to build as the inauguration came closer and the runs and panics continued, Roosevelt prepared both Congress and the country to accept the necessity of the measures he was to propose, thus building decisive momentum for their emergency adoption.[91] "Selling a cure is a lot easier than selling a preventative," advises Joseph Sugarman.[92]

Fenno summarizes the matter thus in his book in praise of New Mexico senator Pete Domenici: "Leadership involves both waiting on events and

88. Calvin Coolidge, *The Autobiography of Calvin Coolidge* (New York: Cosmopolitan Book Corporation, 1929), 131; Thomas B. Silver, *Coolidge and the Historians* (Durham, N.C.: Carolina Academic Press for the Claremont Institute, 1982), 56–57. For a general analysis of strategies for waiting on events, see François Jullien, *A Treatise on Efficacy: Between Western and Chinese Thinking*, trans. Janet Lloyd (Honolulu: University of Hawai'i Press, 2004).

89. Silver, *Coolidge and the Historians*, 57. For a compelling interpretation of Lincoln's policy during this period, see Harry V. Jaffa, *A New Birth of Freedom: Abraham Lincoln and the Coming of the Civil War* (Lanham, Md.: Rowman and Littlefield, 2000), 240–46.

90. See Martin J. Medhurst, "Eisenhower, Little Rock, and the Rhetoric of Crisis," in *The Modern Presidency and Crisis Rhetoric*, ed. Amos Kiewe , esp. 32–33, 35–36.

91. Davis W. Houck, *Rhetoric as Currency: Hoover, Roosevelt, and the Great Depression* (College Station: Texas A&M University Press, 2001), 172–75.

92. Sugarman, *Advertising Secrets*, 182–83.

seizing the day. Domenici demonstrated skill in both respects. And that added to his influence, his reputation, and his independence."[93] The power of letting things take their course is the source of the persuasive power of the suppressed premise: by omitting what everyone can fill out for themselves you let the facts speak for themselves in the minds of the listeners, without ever making your strongest claim yourself. A 1980 Reagan advertisement on Carter's foreign policy failures doesn't even mention Iran, "so that the most damaging indictments are invited from but not forced on the audience."[94]

Character, Action, Things, Nothing

We come to the facts through the knowledge we gain from others and of others via their actions. We saw in chapter 2 that we judge acts by their orientation toward things, but it is through human actions that we get to things. "Fact," Yaron Ezrahi reminds us, comes from the Latin word "factum" denoting a deed or an act.[95]

In the practice of modern science the way to the things is brightly illuminated in the demodalizing of scientific statements. From "Crick and Watson say that DNA has two strands" we move to "DNA has two strands (Crick and Watson 1953)," to "DNA has two strands," that is, to common knowledge that no longer requires citation and that need not even be asserted explicitly in order to be assumed. The facts speak for themselves when they no longer need the authority of individual scientists to authorize them: as Carolyn R. Miller writes, "This rhetorical style of impersonality, in which facts 'speak for themselves,' is itself an appeal that universalizes results originating in particularity: the scientist must seem fungible, so that her results could have been—and might be—achievable by anybody."[96] Conversely, to question facts is to move back along the chain, remodalizing statements by questioning the trustworthiness of those who have supplied them.[97]

93. Richard F. Fenno Jr., *The Emergence of a Senate Leader: Pete Domenici and the Reagan Budget* (Washington, D.C.: Congressional Quarterly Press, 1991), 127.

94. Kathleen Hall Jamieson, *Packaging the Presidency*, 3rd ed. (New York: Oxford University Press, 1996), 438–39; see also Quintilian, *Institutio oratoria* 9.2.71, cited in Brian Vickers, *In Defence of Rhetoric* (Oxford: Oxford University Press, 1989), 318.

95. Yaron Ezrahi, *Descent of Icarus* (Cambridge, Mass.: Harvard University Press, 1990), 62.

96. Carolyn R. Miller, "Expertise and Agency: Transformations of *Ethos* in Human-Computer Interaction," in *The* Ethos *of Rhetoric*, ed. Michael J. Hyde (Columbia: University of South Carolina Press, 2004), 203.

97. Wayne Booth writes that "most authors in the hard sciences . . . are suspicious of historians' assumption that quotation and citations provide adequate evidence for any conclusion"

As Latour and his collaborators have emphasized, this is how facts come to have existence apart from human beings. Nature is the product of the demodalization of scientists' claims.[98] To coin a phrase from Habermas's exposition of George Herbert Mead, "The concept of an objective world is formed via a desocialization of the perception of things." Facts are the constituent parts of the world: "The world is everything that is the case," writes Wittgenstein in proposition 1 of the *Tractatus*. Less gnomically, Latour and Woolgar write: "It is a small wonder that the statements appear to match external entities exactly: they are the same thing."[99]

We are persuaded by what lets the facts speak for themselves, and we are persuaded to trust the person who has something to say over the one who can present only himself, if we don't know who he is. Nixon gave sound advice to a friend in college who was running for student office: "You've got to find an issue and concentrate on it, not on yourself."[100] We are unpersuaded to the extent that we ask, who are you to speak for these things, to represent these things to us, to tell us about these things? To contest an assertion we personalize it. One might call this the rule of "Says who?"

Self-reference is thus the last refuge of the floundering. Lyndon Johnson, Gerald Ford, and Richard Nixon all personalized. "The superpersonalization of presidential speech did not take hold until Lyndon Johnson's administration and even he could be considered modest when compared to Richard Nixon and Gerald Ford. Truman and Eisenhower, in contrast, spoke as if they thought it presumptuous or dangerous to attach themselves to the policies they endorsed."[101] Reagan, writes Kathleen Hall Jamieson, "is not asking us to believe in him, as Carter, Johnson, and Nixon often did, but to believe in ourselves and in the country. . . . Reagan's rhetoric is self-effacing;

(*The Rhetoric of Rhetoric: The Quest for Effective Communication* [Oxford: Basil Blackwell, 2004], 19). But if we have learned anything from post-Kuhnian work on structures of authority in science, it is that scientists are no exception to our general reliance on the statements of others in investigating things ourselves.

98. Bruno Latour and Steve Woolgar, *Laboratory Life: The Construction of Scientific Facts* (1979; repr., Princeton: Princeton University Press, 1986), 75–86; Latour, *Science in Action*, 14–15, 22ff., 94–100. On demodalization used to resolve disputes with the laboratory, see Karin Knorr-Cetina, *Epistemic Cultures: How the Sciences Make Knowledge* (Cambridge, Mass.: Harvard University Press, 1999), 200–201. Compare Fish's account of legal principle, where legal doctrine is not what resolves legal contests—rather, legal doctrine is the result of legal contests; Stanley Fish, *The Trouble with Principle* (Cambridge, Mass.: Harvard University Press, 1999).

99. Jürgen Habermas, *Theory of Communicative Action*, trans. Thomas McCarthy, 2 vols. (Boston: Beacon Press, 1984–89), 2:71; Latour and Woolgar, *Laboratory Life*, 177.

100. Wills, *Nixon Agonistes*, 154.

101. Roderick P. Hart, *Verbal Style and the Presidency: A Computer-Based Analysis* (Orlando, Fla.: Academic Press, 1984), 87.

the rhetoric of Carter, Nixon, and Johnson often bordered on self-promotion or self-indulgence."[102]

To know we must trust. Yet we trust those who refrain from asking us to trust them but instead invite us to judge for ourselves. The most persuasive argument is the one that the audience cannot help but make in response to the things the speaker has presented.

To speak vividly, to have something to say, is to challenge the way things are going on, whether from a position of power or from a position of relative weakness. Those who have credible reputations rely on these reputations to persuade, while those who lack reputation must have something to say; as the communications researchers Charles Larson and Robert Sanders put it, "Evidence is, in effect, a 'substitute' for credibility."[103] In American elections, challengers favor advertisements laden with policy content and factual assertions, while incumbents favor advertisements that focus on their life stories or their records of achievement.[104] Parliamentary majorities vote and decide, and their backbenchers are supposed to stay quiet in the House of Commons so that work can be done. Parliamentary minorities, by contrast, talk, and in particular, the opposition has to try to talk its way into power by being as specific and concrete as possible.[105] One sees this even in the U.S. House of Representatives, where the cable telecast of House proceedings on c-span and "special orders" (speeches that do not require a pending motion, made "for the record" or, these days, for broadcast) were first used almost solely by House Republicans in their drive to become the majority party by turning a congressional election into a nationwide plebiscite on the parties' platforms and records. In the years from 1994 to 2006, as House Democrats suffered through six terms in the minority, they continually

102. Kathleen Hall Jamieson, *Eloquence in an Electronic Age* (Oxford: Oxford University Press, 1988), 157.

103. Charles Larson and Robert Sanders, "Faith, Mystery, and Data: An Analysis of 'Scientific' Studies of Persuasion," *Quarterly Journal of Speech* 61, no. 2 (1975): 178–94, 187. Larson and Sanders are restating the principal finding in James C. McCroskey, "A Summary of Experimental Research on the Effects of Evidence in Persuasive Communication," *Quarterly Journal of Speech* 55, no. 2 (1969): 169–76.

104. Linda Lee Kaid and Anne Johnston, *Videostyle in Presidential Campaigns* (Westport, Conn.: Praeger, 2001), 79, 81.

105. See George Orwell on the early twentieth-century British Left: "The greatest of all the disadvantages under which the left-wing movement suffers: that being a newcomer to the political scene, & having to build itself up out of nothing, it had to create a following by telling lies" ("Extracts from a Manuscript Notebook," entry of 17 March 1949, in *In Front of Your Nose, 1945–1950*, vol. 4 of *Collected Essays, Journalism, and Letters of George Orwell*, ed. Sonia Orwell and Ian Angus [London: Penguin, 1970], 578–79).

increased the number and the vigor of their "special order" attacks on the Republican majority.[106]

Every speech is given in the knowledge of the possibility that it could change everything, for good or for ill.[107] To say something clear and unequivocal draws attention.[108] But to draw attention, to be seen, is to take the risk of being seen to get things wrong and thus "to be wrong."[109] "He is wrong" is not merely shorthand for "He is wrong about Iraq." Audiences always apply their views of what one has said to the speaker himself or herself.[110] It is all very well to say with Karl Popper and Steve Fuller that we want "our ideas to die in our stead."[111] The plural pronoun "our" is crucial; we want ideas to die in our stead, but for that to work someone has to risk her reputation and thus risk professional or literal death for her own ideas. If you speak without hedging, you run risk of forfeiting the audience's good opinion if you fail to persuade. Sometimes, it is better not to take the chance.[112] As we shall see in the next chapter, this is often enough reason to say nothing, especially for speakers with reputations to protect.

106. On the Democrats' use of special orders during their first term in the minority, see Stephen Frantzich and John Sullivan, *The C-SPAN Revolution* (Norman: University of Oklahoma Press, 1996), 39–40, 336–37, 341–42.

107. Hart, *Sound of Leadership*, 88–89.

108. Although communications experiments have had little success at showing the persuasive impact of vivid speech, they have demonstrated its attention-getting effect, as even the vividness skeptics Taylor and Thompson admit ("Stalking the Elusive Vividness Effect"; see also Collins, Taylor, Wood, and Thompson, "The Vividness Effect: Elusive or Illusory?").

109. See Lawrence A. Hosman's summary of the experimental studies by M. Lee Williams in "Language and Persuasion," in *The Persuasion Handbook: Developments in Theory and Practice*, ed. James Price Dillard and Michael Pfau (Thousand Oaks, Calif.: Sage, 2002), 375–76.

110. On this point, see Russell Bentley, "Rhetorical Democracy," in *Talking Democracy: Historical Perspectives on Rhetoric and Democracy*, ed. Benedetto Fontana, Cary J. Nederman, and Gary Remer (University Park: Pennsylvania State University Press, 2004), 126, 128–34. Bentley rightly rejects the claim by Gutmann and Thompson (*Deliberative Democracy* [Cambridge, Mass.: Harvard University Press, 1996], 87) that one ought not to judge one's fellow citizens' views on an issue by their views on an unrelated issue. What I have tried to do in these first three chapters is to show, following Aristotle, the nature of such inferences from what is said to the character of the speaker.

111. See, for example, Steve Fuller, *Knowledge Management Foundations* (Woburn, Mass.: Butterworth-Heinemann, 2002); Steve Fuller, *Kuhn vs. Popper: The Struggle for the Soul of Science* (Cambridge, U.K.: Icon, 2003), 40.

112. See Francis-Noël Thomas and Mark Turner, *Clear and Simple as the Truth: Writing Classic Prose* (Princeton: Princeton University Press, 1994), 60. On science as an evolutionary process, driven by differential rates of professional extinction, see David L. Hull, *Science as a Process* (Chicago: University of Chicago Press, 1988). On the consequences for science of the fear of professional death, see Fuller, *Kuhn vs. Popper*, 108–9.

4

NOTHING

[PRESIDENT GEORGE W. BUSH]: *I need some ribs.*

Q: *Mr. President, how are you?*

THE PRESIDENT: *I'm hungry and I'm going to order some ribs.*

Q: *What would you like?*

THE PRESIDENT: *Whatever you think I'd like.*

Q: *Sir, on homeland security, critics would say you simply haven't spent enough to keep the country secure.*

THE PRESIDENT: *My job is to secure the homeland and that's exactly what we're going to do. But I'm here to take somebody's order. That would be you, Stretch—what would you like? Put some of your high-priced money right here to try to help the local economy. You get paid a lot of money, you ought to be buying some food here. It's part of how the economy grows. You've got plenty of money in your pocket, and when you spend it, it drives the economy forward. So what would you like to eat?*

Q: *Right behind you, whatever you order.*

THE PRESIDENT: *I'm ordering ribs. David, do you need a rib?*

Q: *But Mr. President—*

THE PRESIDENT: *Stretch, thank you, this is not a press conference. This is my chance to help this lady put some money in her pocket. Let me explain how the economy works. When you spend money to buy food it helps this lady's business. It makes it more likely somebody is going to find work. So instead of asking questions, answer mine: are you going to buy some food?*

Q: *Yes.*

THE PRESIDENT: *Okay, good. What would you like?*

Q: *Ribs.*

THE PRESIDENT: *Ribs? Good. Let's order up some ribs.*

Q: *What do you think of the [D]emocratic field, sir?*

THE PRESIDENT: *See, his job is to ask questions, he thinks my job is to answer every question he asks. I'm here to help this restaurant by buying some food. Terry, would you like something?*

Q: *An answer.*

Q: *Can we buy some questions?*

THE PRESIDENT: *Obviously these people—they make a lot of money and they're not going to spend much. I'm not saying they're overpaid, they're just not spending any money.*

Brought up in Tammany Hall, [the Tammany leader] has learned how to reach the hearts of the great mass of voters. He does not bother about reaching their heads. It is his belief that arguments and campaign literature have never gained votes. He seeks direct contact with the people, does them good turns when he can, and relies on their not forgetting him on election day. His heart is in his work, too, for his subsistence depends on its results.

One method of minimizing the risk of saying something wrong is by not speaking, as in the oft-quoted line from Calvin Coolidge: "You don't have to explain something you haven't said," which Sam Rayburn used to call "the smartest thing he'd heard outside of the Bible." Or, as Coolidge put it in a statement more reliably attributable to him, "I don't recall any candidate for president that ever injured himself very much by not talking."[1] Especially in dealing without what are generally perceived as "special interests," Popkin correctly observes that "tamales may be better than promises": it is less risky to demonstrate your identification with a group by showing that you understand its ways, by showing that you know how to eat a tamale, in Popkin's example, than to promise it specific benefits. To deliver on the promises may force you to renege on promises to other groups, while to fail to deliver on the promises may cause the speaker to be discredited before all.[2]

Yet sometimes the situation is such that it calls for a speech, demands that one say something, anything, that responds to and takes us through

---

The epigraphs for chapter 4 come from "Remarks by the President to the Press Pool, Nothin' Fancy Café, Roswell, New Mexico," 22 January 2004, available at http://www.whitehouse.gov/news/releases/2004/01/20040122-5.html (accessed February 2004), and William Riordan, *Plunkitt of Tammany Hall* (New York: E. P. Dutton, 1963), 91.

1. Robert A. Caro, *The Path to Power*, vol. 1 of *The Years of Lyndon Johnson* (New York: Vintage, 1990), 319; Robert Sobel, *Coolidge: An American Enigma* (Washington, D.C.: Regnery, 1998), 304.

2. Samuel Popkin, *The Reasoning Voter: Communication and Persuasion in Presidential Campaigns* (Chicago: University of Chicago Press, 1994), 230; for a typically biting formulation, see Kenneth Hudson, *The Language of Modern Politics* (London: Macmillan, 1978), 42.

the situation even if it provides nothing new to resolve it.[3] The alternative to not saying anything at all is to speak and say nothing. We usually think of speaking and saying nothing as a sign of stupidity or ignorance, as in the maxim of La Rochefoucauld: "As it is the character of great minds to make many things understood with few words, so small minds, to the contrary, have the gift of talking a lot and saying nothing."[4] Worse, with Peter Levine, we may find saying nothing a sign of political corruption: "After [political consultants] have identified a divisive 'wedge issue' on which their candidate happens to agree with the majority, they often want to *prevent* any shift in public opinion. Thus they are adept at using rhetorical formulas that freeze public opinion in place, and that polarize and inflame voters."[5]

In any event, saying nothing takes more work than La Rochefoucauld realizes. We owe to Kenneth Thompson's Miller Center of Public Affairs the following illuminating exchange between two former Republican presidential speechwriters:

WILLIAM BRAGG EWALD [former Eisenhower speechwriter]: I think the likelihood that the president will say something of substance in the Rose Garden or anywhere else is far greater if you don't give him a script and simply send him out there.

LANDON PARVIN [former Reagan speechwriter]: That's why he's given a script.[6]

---

3. Lloyd Bitzer in his oft-cited paper "The Rhetorical Situation" claims not only that the rhetorical situation can demand a speech and constrain the form of what is said but also that it determines the content ("The Rhetorical Situation," *Philosophy and Rhetoric* 1, no. 1 [1968]: 1–14). There are two problems with this argument, one that is the focus of subsequent comment on Bitzer, and one that has been ignored. First, it is not always the case that the situation to which a speaker responds was manifest to his or her audience before that audience heard the speech. Sometimes there is a common sense of an exigency, and sometimes we only see the exigency after the speaker has presented and clarified it for us; on this point, see Scott Consigny, "Rhetoric and Its Situations," *Philosophy and Rhetoric* 7, no. 3 (1974): 175–86, 178. In that sense the rhetorical situation can be produced and not merely responded to by the speaker. Second, since one always has the option to speak but to say nothing in the speech, it is hard to see how the situation can actually control content. Lincoln had to give a speech at Gettysburg, but it is unclear why he had to give a memorable speech.

4. François La Rochefoucauld, maxim 142, in *Maxims*, trans. Stuart D. Warner and Stéphane Douard (South Bend, Ind.: St. Augustine's Press, 2001).

5. Peter Levine, "Consultants and American Political Culture," *Report from the Institute for Philosophy and Public Policy* 14, nos. 3/4 (1994), 1–6, 2, quoted by Stephen K. Medvic, *Political Consultants in U.S. Congressional Elections* (Columbus: Ohio State University Press, 2001), 153.

6. C. Landon Parvin and William Bragg Ewald Jr., "The Role of Presidential Speech Writers," in *Institutions and Issues,* ed. Kenneth W. Thompson (Lanham, Md.: University Press of America; Charlottesville, Va.: Miller Center of Public Affairs, 1994), 66.

As Garry Wills wrote of a Nixon campaign speech: "It is a speech that could not be given without notes—all *studied* clusters of cliché."[7]

Generally, if one has something to say one can get it across somehow without conscious reflection on the available means of persuasion. Saying nothing—that is to say, talking and saying nothing—requires much more care: "It is said that during a campaign in the forties, [Alben] Barkley was interrupted in the middle of a magnificent town square speech in eastern Kentucky when someone yelled, 'How do you stand on FEPC? [the Fair Employment Practices Commission].' Barkley surveyed the crowd. Eastern Kentucky, like eastern Tennessee, had long been divided on the racial issue. There were the grandchildren of Unionists and of Confederates and copperheads in that audience; no one knew how many of each. At last Barkley quietly replied, 'I'm all right on FEPC.' And went on with his speech."[8] To take a stand there and then would be to alienate some of the crowd from Barkley and his party, the Democrats, and to alienate some of the crowd from each other. Barkley maintains support by saying nothing and letting each hear what he or she wants to hear.

"Societies are active, and their activity is to produce themselves."[9] Our life together has a direction given to it by the unreflective and imperfect reproduction of practices and institutions through time.[10] We can therefore analyze any effort at communication as a combination of an attempt to communicate something, and get us to change our direction accordingly, and an attempt to preserve a relation from the threat of communication, thereby keeping things going in the direction they were already going or keeping the relation from degenerating through neglect. "It is not enough for the survival of a community that memories come randomly," Clarke Cochran points out. "Rather, the remembering on which a community's life and identity depend are intentional; they depend on acts of willed remembrance."[11] This willed remembrance must be evoked in speech.

The need to maintain the community limits our powers to communicate

7. Garry Wills, *Nixon Agonistes: The Crisis of the Self-Made Man* (1970; repr., New York: New American Library, 1979), 23.

8. Harry McPherson, *A Political Education* (Boston: Little, Brown, 1972), 66.

9. Gerard Hauser, *Vernacular Voices: The Rhetoric of Publics and Public Spheres* (Columbia: University of South Carolina Press, 1999), 114, citing Alan Touraine, *The Self-Production of Society*, trans. Derek Coltman (Chicago: University of Chicago Press, 1977).

10. On the process of imperfect reproduction, which Anthony Giddens calls "structuration," see Giddens, *Central Problems in Social Theory: Action, Structure, and Contradiction in Social Analysis* (London: Macmillan, 1979).

11. Clarke E. Cochran, "Joseph and the Politics of Memory," *Review of Politics* 64, no. 3 (2002): 421–44, 436.

things and therefore limits the art of rhetoric as an art of communicating things. Yet these limits themselves are maintained in time through the power of speech. This process of maintaining the ties of community in speech is itself amenable, to some extent, to a conscious art of persuasion. What we need to understand is how rhetoric can be both an art of saying something and an art of saying nothing.

Saying nothing is tolerable when we accept that politics, and especially elections, are about men rather than measures. Harry McPherson writes of some of the more liberal southern senators of the 1950s: "It would have done the country no ultimate good to know their precise views on birth control, intermarriage, or relations with Eastern Europe, if the consequence would have been their defeat and replacement by lesser men."[12] It is also acceptable in those circumstances where doing nothing is the best policy alternative, as in this tale told by William Safire from his period as a Nixon speechwriter: "The President said he would look over the speech a little while longer by himself, and as I was on my way out the door he wondered what I thought its impact would be. 'No news in it,' I said. 'Frankly, it's not going to set the world on fire.' 'That's the whole object of our foreign policy,' Nixon said, almost to himself, 'not to set the world on fire.'"[13]

Eisenhower was a master of saying nothing to back up a policy of doing nothing. During the Cold War, U.S. deterrence of Communist expansion depended on a complicated and highly ambiguous policy about whether such an attack would be stopped, if necessary, by the use of nuclear weapons, even if that put the U.S. homeland at the risk of Soviet nuclear retaliation. Preparing for a press conference in which the press would demand clarification of the willingness of the United States to defend the Chinese Nationalists on the Formosa Straits islands of Quemoy and Matsu, and by extension on Taiwan, Eisenhower reassured his press secretary Jim Hagerty that the country had nothing to fear from an outburst of sincerity. As Eisenhower relates the story in his memoir:

> As I was about to cross West Executive Avenue to the Executive Office Building for my press conference. . . . Jim Haggerty reported a frantic plea he had just received.
>
> "Mr. President," he said, "some of the people in the State Department say that the Formosa Strait situation is so delicate that no

12. McPherson, *Political Education*, 67.

13. William Safire, *Before the Fall: An Inside View of the Pre-Watergate White House* (New York: Belmont Tower Books, 1975), 397.

matter what question you get on it, you shouldn't say anything at all."

I could see the point of this advice. But I didn't take it.

"Don't worry, Jim," I told him as we went out the door of my office, "if that question comes up, I'll just confuse them."[14]

And that Eisenhower did. Joseph Harsch of the *Christian Science Monitor* asked:

> If we got into an issue with the Chinese, say, over Matsu and Quemoy, that we wanted to keep limited, do you conceive of using this specific kind of atomic weapon in that situation or not?

Eisenhower's answer:

> Well, Mr. Harsch, I must confess I cannot answer that question in advance. The only thing I know about war are two things: the most changeable factor in war is human nature in its day-by-day manifestation; but the only unchanging factor in war is human nature. And the next thing is that every war is going to astonish you in the way it occurred, and in the way it is carried out. So that for a man to predict, particularly if he had the responsibility for making the decision, to predict what he is going to use, how he is going to do it, would I think exhibit his ignorance of war; that is what I believe. So I think you just have to wait, and that is the kind of prayerful decision that may some day face a President.[15]

As Fred Greenstein writes: "Neither pride in his ability nor his natural predilection for clarity kept [Eisenhower] from deliberately turning to language that was emotive and inspirational or purposely ambiguous. Verbal expression was his instrument; he refused to indulge his obvious pleasure in analytic thought and clear expression as an end in itself."[16] To quote Ike himself, "It is far better to stumble or speak guardedly than to move ahead smoothly and risk imperiling the country."[17]

14. Dwight D. Eisenhower, *Mandate for Change: 1953–1956* (London: Heinemann, 1963), 478.
15. Dwight D. Eisenhower, "The President's News Conference of March 23rd, 1955," available at http://www.presidency.ucsb.edu/ws/print.php?pid=10437 (accessed 24 October 2007); see also Stephen E. Ambrose, *The President*, vol. 2 of *Eisenhower* (New York: Simon and Schuster, 1984), 240.
16. Fred I. Greenstein, *The Hidden-Hand Presidency: Eisenhower as Leader* (New York: Basic Books, 1982), 66.
17. Greenstein, *Hidden-Hand Presidency*, 19.

Speaking in a deliberately confusing manner is, however, not the most common way to speak and say nothing. More typically, one speaks and says nothing by presenting one's relation to the audience, the experiences, locations, and affiliations one shares with one's audience, instead of the things to which one is calling the audience to respond. Writing of Georgia congressman Jack Flynt, Richard Fenno relates that "Flynt's public speeches revealed more interest in community maintenance than in public policy. His purpose was to talk about the many things that linked him to his white constituents and to present himself as a maintainer of, and spokesman for, their common interests. He was a master of binds, links, ties, and memories."[18]

Jack Flynt had a long history of relations with his constituents that he could recount to avoid speaking on the issues. Where such a shared history is not available to the speaker, as was the case for Eisenhower, who identified publicly with the Republican party only in the run-up to the 1952 campaign, then speaking about somebody else's time-tested bonds may do instead. Consider this passage from Eisenhower's 1956 speech to the Republican Convention accepting the party's nomination for reelection:

> Ladies and gentlemen, when Abraham Lincoln was nominated in 1860, and a committee brought the news to him at his home in Springfield, Illinois, his reply was two sentences long. Then, while his friends and neighbors waited in the street, and while bonfires lit up the May evening, he said simply, "And now I will not longer defer the pleasure of taking you, and each of you, by the hand." I wish I could do the same—speak two sentences, and then take each one of you by the hand, all of you who are in the sound of my voice. If I could do so, I would first thank you individually for your confidence and your trust. Then, as I am sure Lincoln did as he moved among his friends in the light of the bonfires, we could pause and talk awhile about the questions that are uppermost in your mind.[19]

Only the accidents of circumstances, Eisenhower says, keep him from relating personally to each of the members of his audience as Lincoln did to the

---

18. Richard F. Fenno Jr., *Congress at the Grassroots: Representational Change in the South, 1970–1998* (Chapel Hill: University of North Carolina Press, 2000), 37.

19. Dwight D. Eisenhower, "Address at the Cow Palace on Accepting the Nomination of the Republican National Convention," San Francisco, Calif., 1956, cited in Roderick P. Hart, *Campaign Talk: Why Elections Are Good for Us* (Princeton: Princeton University Press, 2000), 78–79, available at http://www.presidency.ucsb.edu/ws/index.php?pid=10583 (accessed 15 October 2007).

committee offering him the 1860 Republican nomination. Eisenhower maintains his relation with Republican partisans by using a Lincoln anecdote to talk about his own relation rather than by making promises about what he is going to use their support to accomplish. Eisenhower invokes Abraham Lincoln in order to strengthen his own relation as candidate to the party faithful by linking it to the tradition of relations between the Republican standard-bearer and his supporters.

Eisenhower uses the Lincoln story to introduce a long speech that offers "five reasons why the Republican party is the party of the future." The reasons offered seem vague in expression, to the point where meditating on them initially results in bringing thought to a halt, though with redoubled concentration the listener or reader can see how Eisenhower's "five reasons" imply significant differences with the Democratic alternative:

> Because it is the Party of long-range principle, not short-term expediency.
>
> It is the Party which concentrates on the facts and issues of today and tomorrow, not the facts and issues of yesterday.
>
> The Republican Party is the Party of the Future because it is the party that draws people together, not drives them apart.
>
> The Republican Party is the Party of the Future because it is the party through which the many things that still need doing will soonest be done—and will be done by enlisting the fullest energies of free, creative, individual people.
>
> Finally, a Party of the Future must be completely dedicated to peace, as indeed must all Americans. For without peace there is no future.

In sum, the Republican party is, Eisenhower claimed in 1956, the party of the American consensus: "We want them all! Republicans, independents, discerning Democrats—come on in and help!" With four successful years behind him and an overwhelming lead over his Democratic challenger, nothing Eisenhower could say in his acceptance speech could increase his splendid chances of reelection. Much better for the candidate to speak of his ties to the party and to praise the party he would lead through another campaign in such a way as to avoid alienating the Democrats or independents who might vote for him. Maddening this speech no doubt was to those of Adlai Stevenson's partisans with a thirst for ideas—they forgot that no one promised them that politics had to be interesting.

Speaking to Reweave

כָּל אַהֲבָה שֶׁתְּלוּיָה בְדָבָר בָּטֵל דָּבָר בְּטֵלָה אַהֲבָה. וְשֶׁאֵינָהּ תְּלוּיָה בְדָבָר,
אֵינָהּ בְּטֵלָה לְעוֹלָם. אֵי זוֹ הִיא אַהֲבָה שֶׁהִיא תְּלוּיָה בְדָבָר, זוֹ אַהֲבַת
אַמְנוֹן וְתָמָר. וְשֶׁאֵינָהּ תְּלוּיָה בְדָבָר, זוֹ אַהֲבַת דָּוִד וִיהוֹנָתָן (אבות ת:טו).

All love that is dependent on something [davar], when the thing is
annulled the love is annulled. And love that is not dependent on a
thing will never ("in this world") be annulled. What is love that is
dependent on something? This is the love of Amnon and Tamar. What
is the love that is not dependent on anything? This is the love of David
and Jonathan. (Ethics of the Fathers 5:15)

This passage from the Mishnah is a rejection of the Platonic formula that
all love is love of something: according to the Rabbis of the Mishnah, love
must somehow be independent of things in order to be sustained. "Why do
you love me?" she asks. Woe, woe, to the man who knows why.[20]

The Platonists are convinced that eternal love is based on shared love of
eternal things. The Platonists have their say in Maimonides' commentary
on this very Mishnah as well as in Augustine's famous account in *The City
of God* of how all human communities are held together by love of the same
things. Any attempt to explain the power of community in terms of shared
"values" is likewise Platonizing dressed up in Nietzschean vocabulary. Our
communities and their institutions are in fact far more lasting than our
transient value commitments.[21]

The Platonizers, no matter the stripe, fail to respect a fundamental distinction between types of human relations: relations whose existence depends
on the reasons of the participants and relations in which reasons serve only
to alter the expression or conduct of the relation without being able to alter
the fact of there being a relation. To quote the examples offered by Talcott
Parsons: "A patient's claim on his doctor's time is primarily a matter of the
objective features of the 'case' regardless of who the patient is, while a wife's
claim on her husband's time is a matter of the fact that she is his wife, regardless, within limits, of what the occasion is." Evaluations or values should

20. I owe this illustration to a sermon preached by Rabbi Shmuel Krauthammer, rabbi of
Young Israel of Petah Tiqwa, Israel, on the fifth Sabbath after Passover 5761, the Sabbath when
the fifth chapter of Aboth is customarily studied.

21. See J. Enoch Powell and Keith Wallis, *The House of Lords in the Middle Ages: A History
of the English House of Lords to 1540* (London: Weidenfeld and Nicholson, 1968), xi.

be considered as reasons for action within a framework of human relations. This is not to say that these frameworks are immutable, but it is to say that the activity of giving reasons, of reasoning together in speech, cannot explain or justify the alteration of these frameworks.[22]

The power of reason to persuade must somehow be tempered by human relations, if speech is to be kept within its humane bounds. "What we find words for is that for which we no longer have use in our own hearts. There is always a kind of contempt in the act of speaking."[23] This is the objection to rationalism in the name of human nature: the existence of the community cannot be dependent just on shared things or judgments. Insofar as that community requires certain opinions of us, our opinions about things depend to that extent on our relations with others.

My point is but an abstract version of the German public opinion researcher Elisabeth Noelle-Neumann's claim about the "spiral of silence." Noelle-Neumann has shown that people are silenced by what they perceive as public disapproval of their opinions, and they tend to adjust their opinion to conform to what they perceive as the climate of opinion. The quantitative result is that popular perception of the majority opinion leads the majority opinion, because the perception of opinion depends on expression of opinion. A tiny shift in expressions of support for one of the two major parties produces a large shift in the number of people who say that most people will support the party.[24] The spiral-of-silence effect thus favors the vocal, the activists, or those who have the favor of the media.

The conformative power of public opinion, was, of course, not discovered by Noelle-Neumann. Katz and Lazarfeld, who studied opinion formation in a medium-sized American town just before the age of television, write that "to the extent that a group is attractive for an individual, and to the extent that he desires acceptance as a member of that group, he will be motivated—whether he is aware of it or not—to accept that group's outlook." It is enough to hope to join a group to feel pressured to conform to group opinions, so "an individual's opinions will be substantially affected

22. Talcott Parsons, "The Professions and Social Structure," in *Essays in Sociological Theory*, rev. ed. (Glencoe, Ill.: The Free Press, 1954), 41. Consider here Socrates' claim in Plato's *Protagoras* that the virtuous man often compels himself to praise an unjust parent or fatherland (345d–347a).

23. Friedrich Nietzsche, *Twilight of the Idols*, "Expeditions of an Untimely Man," aphorism 26, as translated by Kenneth Burke in *Counter-Statement*, 2nd ed. (Berkeley and Los Angeles: University of California Press, 1968), 62.

24. Elisabeth Noelle-Neumann, *Spiral of Silence: Public Opinion, Our Social Skin*, 2nd ed. (Chicago: University of Chicago Press, 1993), 13, fig. 4.

by the opinions of others whose company he keeps, or whose company he aspires to keep."[25] The phenomenon is by no means confined to the sublime expressions of it in love and friendship; it occurs whenever we bandwagon with the winning side in order to be on the winning side, whenever "the mere pleasure of being the friend of the man who was going to make the speech that secured the most votes . . . [is] enough to crystallize an organization of insiders around him."[26]

Through our perception of public opinion we are oriented as to how to conduct ourselves. Perceptions of the climate of opinion are more widely shared across the whole population than are the opinions themselves.[27] We orient ourselves by the climate of opinion within a group so as to preserve our connection, as in Solomon Asch's famous experiment where the subjects were persuaded to deny their own perceptions about which of two lines was longer by the expressions of the investigator's stooges. The typical group response to deviance is not logical. It does not take the rational form of contradiction or argument; rather it takes the social form of ostracism: "The disapproval that punishes someone who strays from the majority view does not have the rational character of the disapproval that arises from 'an incorrect logical conclusion, a mistake in solving an arithmetic problem, or an unsuccessful work of art; rather it is expressed as the conscious or unconscious practical reaction of the community to injury of its interests, a defense for the purposes of common security.'" It is this individual shame at deviance that makes it possible for there to be communities at all.[28]

It is well known that after an election more people remember having voted for the winner than actually did so because most people do not adhere to their views for reasons but in order to conform to their milieu or "reference group," to conform with the views of the group to which they belong. In 1980s Germany, old people moved right while young people moved left; in the America of the first decade of the twenty-first century, old people move left while young people move right. This conformative power can be manipulated by the vocal, or by party activists organizing people to speak out, so that when different camps are integrated, the resulting integration favors the most vocal.[29]

25. Elihu Katz and Paul Lazarfeld, *Personal Influence* (Glencoe, Ill.: The Free Press, 1955), 50–51, 53.

26. Walter Lippmann, *Public Opinion* (1922; repr., New York: The Free Press, 1965), 145.

27. Noelle-Neumann, *Spiral of Silence*, 14.

28. Noelle-Neumann, *Spiral of Silence*, 57, 238–39; the words in quotation marks are from Rudolph von Ihering.

29. Noelle-Neumann, *Spiral of Silence*, 33, 124–25.

As Noelle-Neumann points out, the conformative power of public opinion must be taken into account in attempting to analyze it. We should not be misled by the rationalism of normative democratic theory that focuses on critical judgment or treat public opinion as strictly informative rather than conformative. Noelle-Neumann sees social control as something exercised on the individual but not by the individual, but it is the power of social control as exercised by the individual on other individuals that constrains both private individuals and those individuals in public office who make up our governments. In this process of the reproduction of social norms, it is we who reproduce our norms.[30]

Noelle-Neumann defines public opinion thus: "Public opinions are attitudes or behaviors one *must* express in public if one is not to isolate oneself; in areas of controversy or change, public opinions are those attitudes one can express without running the danger of isolating oneself." It might be better, however, not to define public opinion but to analyze it as a concept in public opinion. Noelle-Neumann has shown that we often have a sense of how other people think: we understand when we are asked what the public opinion about something is. The fact that the phenomenon of public opinion is a phenomenon of the public world means that the external validity of laboratory studies of public opinion is dubious: the public is precisely what is excluded in the lab.[31] Unlike Noelle-Neumann, I am interested both in the informative and in the conformative powers of public opinion.

Sweet Nothings

The Platonist is also right to an extent: some love is contingent on qualities, facts, or things. This is why communities defend themselves against changes in opinion, lest their own ties of affection be overcome by newly presented facts.[32] Speech and writing can be used not only to change opinions about things but also to protect human relations from things, dependence on which threatens them. A story that speaks to this point is retold by

30. Noelle-Neumann, *Spiral of Silence,* chaps. 4 and 62, 93–94, 96; cf. Anthony Giddens, *Central Problems in Social Theory.*

31. Noelle-Neumann, *Spiral of Silence,* 178, 42; cf. Roderick P. Hart, *Seducing America: How Television Charms the Modern Voter,* rev. ed. (Thousand Oaks, Calif.: Sage, 1999), 73 n. 35.

32. This is the central tenet of "cultural theory" as developed by the anthropologist Mary Douglas and her collaborators: "A way of life will remain viable only if it inculcates in its constituent individuals the cultural bias that justifies it" (Michael Thompson, Richard Ellis, and Aaron Wildavsky, *Cultural Theory* [Boulder, Colo.: Westview, 1990], 2).

Stendhal: "Everyone in France knows the anecdote of Mademoiselle de Som-
mery, who, surprised in the very act by her lover, denied the fact brazenly
and, when he protested, exclaimed: 'Ah! How well I see you don't love me
any more; you believe what you see sooner than what I tell you.'"[33] Or as
Groucho Marx put it, "Who you gonna believe, me or your own eyes?"

It is by means of speech that human relations are maintained through
time and changing circumstances. But not all human relations are dependent on the content of what is said. Don't think of this kind of talk as aimless
just because its aim is to maintain a relation through time rather than to
communicate facts.[34] To quote Kenneth Burke: "Malinowski has a term,
'phatic communion,' to designate the exchanging of words not for explicit
informative purposes, but as an easy way of establishing a bond. Stereotyped
greetings, comments on the weather, polite inquiries about health, are examples. A subtle variant would be gossip, where people malign an absent friend,
not so much because of a vindictive attitude toward the absent, but as an
easy way of making allies for the moment."[35] We sway one another not just
through the content of communication but also through the activity of communicating.[36] Here is another description of Congressman Jack Flynt that
shows him seeking to maintain his relation to his constituents:

> [Flynt] is protective of his existing constituency relations and will not
> want to risk alienating any of his support by introducing or escalat-
> ing controversy of any kind. He is a stabilizer, a maintainer. And so,
> when asked to speak formally, he often responds with communitar-
> ian homilies: "I believe that if ever there was a promised land, that
> land is America, and if ever there was a chosen people, those people
> are Americans." "If a man isn't proud of his heritage, he won't leave
> a heritage to be proud of. And that goes for his family, his community,
> and his country." These utterances are not the secret of his success.
> But they do testify, again, to his continuing efforts to articulate a sense
> of community, to construct and reconstruct a web of enduring per-
> sonal relationships and to present himself as totally a part of that web.[37]

33. Stendhal, On Love, trans. H. B. V. (1927; repr. New York: Da Capo, 1983), 125.

34. Contrast H. Paul Grice, Studies in the Way of Words (Cambridge, Mass.: Harvard University Press, 1989), 370.

35. Kenneth Burke, Attitudes Toward History, 3rd ed. (Berkeley and Los Angeles: University of California Press, 1984), 235.

36. See Katz and Lazarfeld, Personal Influence, 185.

37. Richard F. Fenno Jr., Home Style: House Members in Their Districts (1978; repr., New York:
Longman, 2003), 69; on the identity of the speaker, see Fenno, Congress at the Grassroots.

Note that it is this ever rewoven web that allows members of Congress "some freedom of maneuver on Capitol Hill": "So long as members can successfully explain a vote afterward, their constituent depends—except for one or two issues—more on what they do at home than on what they do in Washington.[38] Members of Congress thus empower themselves to act as trustees and not just delegates. It is a job requirement for a representative or senator to sometimes vote his or her conscience rather than his or her constituency: "So powerful is independence as a political value in contemporary politics that every politician is constrained to signal his or her independence at some point in a career."[39]

The web of constituent relations is rewoven by personal contact since most people will not vote against someone they know personally, no matter how great their political differences.[40] The web of constituent relations is rewoven by constituency service, as in Burke's letter to the electors of Bristol, where he attempts to balance his disagreements with his constituents over Britain's American policy by detailing his energetic attention to their particular grievances.[41] By connecting personally with some at, for example, town meetings, Fenno's members of Congress let others know that personal connection is possible: "About forty people come [to a town meeting], but several thousand know we have been around and know they could see me if they wished. Politically, that's more important than the forty." As Fenno himself says, "access and assurance of access, communication and the assurance of communication—these are the irreducible underpinnings of representation."[42]

Talking to maintain a connection is both part of the motherly love expressed by patient lullabies and nonsense songs and of the seduction a lover engages in when he or she tirelessly whispers sweet nothings to the beloved. Roderick Hart lists as one offensive mode of "seducing America" the fact that "it is often possible in politics to give the rhetoric to one disputant and the decision to the other," as when a judge expounds on the gravity of

38. Fenno, *Home Style*, 157, 231–32.

39. Richard F. Fenno Jr., *Senators on the Campaign Trail: The Politics of Representation* (Norman: University of Oklahoma Press, 1996), 251.

40. See, for example, Roderick P. Hart, *The Sound of Leadership: Presidential Communication in the Modern Age* (Chicago: University of Chicago Press, 1987), 45; Richard F. Fenno Jr., *When Incumbency Fails: The Senate Career of Mark Andrews* (Washington, D.C.: Congressional Quarterly Press, 1992), 6–11.

41. Edmund Burke, "A Letter to John Farr and John Harris, Esqrs., Sheriffs of the City of Bristol, on the Affairs Of America" (1777) available at http://tinyurl.com/2a5ak2 (accessed 15 October 2007).

42. *Home Style*, 239, 240.

a crime before acquitting the defendant on a procedural violation by the police.[43] Giving the rhetoric to one side shows, at least, that the losing disputant deserves an explanation as to why the decision went against him or her that takes his or her grievances seriously; in that way he or she is woven back into the community to whom justification is necessary.[44] "The fact of the attempt to communicate," writes William Safire, can be "more important than success or failure."[45] Discussing the crisis in Britain's American colonies in the 1770s, William H. Nelson writes that Loyalists and Patriots "do not truly argue with each other; had they done so, they probably would not have fought."[46] The racial liberal Calvin Coolidge spoke of "the progress of a people" in a speech at Howard University but promised no concrete measures to hasten that progress. Yet one cannot imagine Woodrow Wilson speaking there, at the federally sponsored black university whose very name conjures up the ghosts of Reconstruction that Wilson had worked so hard to bury.[47]

To the extent that what we want to achieve through speech requires reorientation, there is an incentive to mitigate that reorientation by adding platitudinous nothings. The more we have to say, the more platitudes we must add on to what we want to communicate. "When the action is hot, keep the rhetoric cool," Richard Nixon advised his speechwriters.[48] As Roderick Hart disapprovingly describes this approach, "the more radical my policy, the

43. Hart, *Seducing America*, 137, quoting Murray Edelman, *Political Language: Words That Succeed and Policies That Fail* (New York: Academic Press, 1977).

44. Compare Jack Orr's observation that "when the literal content of reporters' words explicitly confront the President with criticism, reporters present themselves and question the President in a style consistent with deference to a Chief of State; but when their words are literally informative and only implicitly critical, reporters assume a style of self-presentation and questioning consistent with an interpretive assembly." In Orr's example of the presidential press conference, the tie between president and reporter is hierarchal, and the reporter labors to maintain the structure that subordinates him or her to the chief of state to the extent that the content of the reporter's question undermines the president's authority ("Reporters Confront the President: Sustaining a Counterpoised Situation," *Quarterly Journal of Speech* 62, no. 1 [1980]: 17–32, 31). See also Richard A. Joslyn, "Keeping Politics in the Study of Political Discourse," in *Form, Genre, and the Study of Political Discourse,* ed. Herbert W. Simons and Aram A. Aghazarian (Columbia: University of South Carolina Press, 1986), 332–33, on the presidential inaugural addresses as efforts to reconcile those who lost the election to the new administration. On the general principle that there are some to whom we owe at least lies, see F. G. Bailey, *The Prevalence of Deceit* (Ithaca, N.Y.: Cornell University Press, 1991), 7.

45. Safire, *Before the Fall*, 472.

46. William H. Nelson, *The American Tory* (1961; repr., Boston, Beacon Press, 1964), 170.

47. Coolidge, "The Progress of a People," in *Foundations of the Republic* (1926; repr., Freeport, N.Y.: Books for Libraries Press, 1968), 29–36. Howard is named for Union general Oliver O. Howard, head of the Freedmen's Bureau, during the era of Reconstruction.

48. Safire, *Before the Fall*, 194.

more I will claim it is moderate, to appease the moderate or stand-pat who I must disappoint. The more moderate my policy, the more radically I will speak to appease frustrated radicals." Coolidge no doubt would not have disagreed with Goldwater's platitudinous quotation from Cicero, "Extremism in the defense of liberty is no vice; . . . moderation in the pursuit of justice is no virtue."[49] Yet where his policy was genuinely moderate, as on civil rights, Coolidge gave his hopes for racial equality free rein.[50] Where his policy was radical, as on immigration restriction, Coolidge found the moderate words with which to sweeten the medicine.[51]

The Objects of Public Opinion

Rhetoric is informative about things because public opinion is informative, not just conformative.[52] That public opinion can be informative is a myth, according to Elisabeth Noelle-Neumann: "Must we create a fiction of public opinion based on critical judgment because to acknowledge the real forces that keep human society together would not be compatible with our ego ideal?" It is the illusion, Noelle-Neumann claims, that we ourselves are rational. Yet the classical political thinkers Noelle-Neumann delights in citing—Locke, Rousseau, the Federalists, even Plato—all recognize the duality of public opinion as informative and conformative. Even Noelle-Neumann recognizes that public opinion can be more than a force compelling us to conform: "The rational exchange of arguments," she writes, "unquestionably plays some role in the process of public opinion."[53]

Opinion is not simply locked in a cave of its own making: opinions are formed about something—about the world, and in particular, about the future of things in the world. The Greek Sophist Protagoras famously taught that "Man is the measure of all things." Socrates in Plato's *Theaetetus*

49. Hart, *Seducing America,* 137. See Richard N. Goodwin, *Remembering America: A Voice from the Sixties* (New York: HarperCollins, 1995), on the remarks as a platitude.

50. Coolidge, "Equality of Rights," in *Foundations of the Republic,* 69–72; Sobel, *Coolidge,* 249–50.

51. Contrast Coolidge's speech at the laying of the cornerstone for the Jewish Community Center in Washington, D.C., May 3, 1925 ("The Spiritual Unification of America") with the passage on immigration restriction in his 1924 Labor Day address ("The High Place of Labor"), both in *Foundations of the Republic: Speeches and Addresses,* 209–20; 75–88.

52. Noelle-Neumann's claim that rhetoric is merely conformative is at the center of Jacob Shamir and Michal Shamir's attack on her argument (*The Anatomy of Public Opinion* [Ann Arbor: University of Michigan Press, 2000]).

53. Noelle-Neumann, *Spiral of Silence,* 100, 232.

expounds Protagoras as driving at what we would call relativism, the view that things truly are for each human being as they seem to be to him or her. Socrates then goes on to show that it is the fact that practical judgment concerns the future that refutes this relativistic doctrine, since it is absurd to suppose that things will *in fact* turn out for each individual as that individual currently *supposes* that things will turn out. We do not wish for things to seem to turn out well for us, but actually to turn out well for us. Moreover, contemporary public opinion analysts have shown that prospective judgments of future opinion reflect current opinion better than judgments of present opinion: we not only wish to judge correctly concerning the future, but, as Socrates hints, our practical judgments become more accurate when we focus on the future rather than the present.[54]

The crucial test of public opinion as informative comes when we see that opinions are changed in the proper direction by events. Consider an example used by Noelle-Neumann: German public opinion about the safety and hence the desirability of nuclear generation of electric power. Noelle-Neumann claims that mass opinion about nuclear power shifted because of a change in the climate of opinion that activists and the media effected. But Shamir and Shamir reply that public opinion about nuclear power shifted in response to the 1986 fire at the Chernobyl nuclear plant in the Ukraine, that is, because of a change in the world to which public opinion responded by taking account of the new information.

It is a platitude that public opinion does not always respond rationally to salient events: Germany's nuclear reactors were of a type that made a Chernobyl-type accident impossible. But elites are often no better: the drug thalidomide was universally banned, even though it had ill effects only on fetuses and so was "contraindicated," as the doctors say, only for pregnant women. The rationality of public processes is limited not primarily because individuals are irrational but because they are many, plural, with diverse opinions and interests, and therefore to mobilize them for collective action would-be leaders must compromise or motivate.

A challenge to the way things are presently ordered will be effective to the extent it can reorganize the way we live.[55] Rachel Carson's *Silent Spring* was hardly the first conservationist tract, but the civil rights movement had made shown that it was possible to mobilize a mass issue movement, and so

54. Plato, *Theaetetus* 172a–b, 177c–179b; Shamir and Shamir, *Anatomy of Public Opinion*, chap. 6, "Public Opinion Expectations."

55. See Katz and Lazarfeld, *Personal Influence*, 29.

beginning in the late 1960s we see an environmental movement emerging with something like its present scope and organization.[56] The American conservative movement went from a collection of tiny quarreling sects to a mass movement in mobilizing for Goldwater in 1964, and though Goldwater lost, the organizational ties remained to make possible the "Reagan Revolution" of the 1980s.[57] Goldwater himself made the connection between the organizational success of the movement and the success of its ideology in speaking to a group of "Youth for Goldwater": "Turn your group into a permanent organization of young conservatives. The man is not important. The principles you espouse are."[58] Though the principles matter more than the man, Goldwater claims, he hastens to remind his audience that the principles cannot be left to sell themselves. One needs an organization of men and women mobilized behind the principles. "The British people," George Orwell wrote in a 1948 fund-raising letter for a civil liberties group, "accept freedom as a matter of course and tend to forget that its price is 'eternal vigilance.' Even if they remember that famous saying, they do not seem to realize that vigilance is an activity involving time, energy, and money."[59]

To persuade is to organize. And "when the best leader's work is done, the people say, 'We did it ourselves.'"[60]

56. On the relation between organizational structure and aspirations in the environmental movement, see Mary Douglas and Aaron Wildavsky, *Risk and Culture: An Essay on the Selection of Technical and Environmental Dangers* (Berkeley and Los Angeles: University of California Press, 1982), esp. chap. 7.

57. Rick Perlstein, *Before the Storm: Barry Goldwater and the Unmaking of the American Consensus* (New York: Hill and Wang, 2001).

58. Perlstein, *Before the Storm*, 92.

59. George Orwell, "The Freedom Defence Committee," in *In Front of Your Nose, 1945–1950*, vol. 4 of *Collected Essays, Journalism, and Letters of George Orwell*, ed. Sonia Orwell and Ian Angus (New York: Harcourt, Brace, Jovanovich, 1970), 505.

60. Attributed to Lao Tzu in Tony Benn, *Arguments for Democracy* (London: Jonathan Cape, 1981), quoted in David Powell, *Tony Benn: A Political Life* (London: Continuum, 2001), 77. D. C. Lau's translation reads, "When his task is accomplished and his work done / The people all say, "'It happened to us naturally'" (Lao Tzu, *Tao Te Ching*, trans. D. C. Lau, ed. Sarah Allen [New York: Everyman's Library, 1994], §61); for what is at stake in the difference between Lau's translation and Tony Benn's democratic paraphrase, see François Jullien, *Treatise on Efficacy: Between Western and Chinese Thinking*, trans. Janet Lloyd (Honolulu: University of Hawai'i Press, 2004), 166–69.

5

ART

William Jennings Bryan, no slouch at oratory, claimed about his campaign for the presidency in 1896 that "Men who had never spoken before in public have gone forth in this campaign because their hearts were so full of the truth that they could not keep silent. If they had taken from us every man who had made a public speech before, we would have had sufficiency of public speaking from these new men who have demonstrated that eloquence is the speech of one who knows what he is talking about and believes what he says."[1] Yet if a speaker needs only knowledge and sincerity in order to persuade, as Bryan claims, who needs rhetoric, who needs a conscious art of persuasion? "Why spend so much labor over our studies if naked and unornamented things [*res nudas atque inornatas*] are sufficiently expressive?" we should ask with Quintilian.[2]

We need a conscious art of persuasion, I argue in this chapter, precisely because naked and unornamented things don't necessarily come naturally. Naked facts are more like naked pieces of furniture, or rather, like pieces of furniture that have been "stripped" and then carefully polished to reveal the grain, the "natural" grain. Trees, of course, do not have grain; only wood as a material does. To show naked and unornamented things requires its own art. The phrase "letting the facts speak for themselves" is an example of the phenomenon it describes. It speaks passively of something that always requires us to be active, concealing the work we do to make the truth credible so as to move others to act on it.[3] In the wake of modern philosophers

---

1. Quoted by Barnet Baskerville, *The People's Voice: The Orator in American Society* (Lexington: University Press of Kentucky, 1979), 132; cf. Michel de Montaigne, "On Educating Children," in *The Complete Essays*, trans. and ed. M. A. Screech (London: Penguin, 1991), 190–94.

2. Quintilian, *Institutio oratoria* 2.4.3.

3. See Quintilian, *Institutio oratoria* 4.2.34.

such as Descartes, Hobbes, and Kant, rhetoric has come to be understood as an art of moving the emotions through style, ornamentation, or adornment rather than an art of laying bare and revealing the facts.[4] Yet if we want to understand the power of rhetoric as a conscious art of persuasion, the art of clarification is the right place to start.

To show the power of the art of persuasion we must also show its limits. We must therefore contend with those who claim that rhetoric is all powerful: not merely capable of presenting or clarifying things or of adorning things so as to make them seem other than they are but capable of making things up, of inventing worlds. "Regimes and interest groups," Murray Edelman claims, "have learned that in practice they can use the media to place mass audiences in invented worlds that justify the outcomes of any policies at all."[5] Edelman's words slide between the platitude that there is always something to be said for any position (what the Greeks reviled as making the worse speech seem the better) and the grandiose claim that there it is always possible to persuade others of the truth of any position. Harry Reichenbach, in his compendium of semibelievable tales of his prowess as a press agent, tells us of his success at overthrowing the junta in Uruguay at the behest of a local leader named Crispo. Crispo, in power thanks to Reichenbach, now expels him from Uruguay, explaining, "If you could take a government that was intrenched for more than two decades and overthrow it with a coupon, I don't want you around here. Next week, the opposition may hire you."[6] Yet if the public relations man, or the rhetorician, is so powerful, we should wonder how he can be cast off so easily by those who hired him.

Because we suspect orators, they strive to conceal their art—in public speaking, "rhetoric" is a dirty word.[7] Even a Cicero feels compelled in a forensic speech to delimit the power of oratory to win a case: "For everything does not depend, as you two think it does, on eloquence. There is still some truth so manifest that nothing can weaken it."[8] Yet if the artful rhetoricians

4. For a compelling presentation and critique of the views of Hobbes and Kant on rhetoric, see Bryan Garsten, *Saving Persuasion: A Defense of Rhetoric and Judgment* (Cambridge: Harvard University Press, 2006).

5. Murray Edelman, *From Art to Politics: How Artistic Creations Shape Political Conceptions* (Chicago: University of Chicago Press, 1995), 129.

6. Harry Reichenbach, *Phantom Fame: The Zany World of Press Agentry* (New York: Simon and Schuster, 1931), 122.

7. See Jon Hesk, *Deception and Democracy in Classical Athena* (Cambridge: Cambridge University Press, 2000), and, most famously, Socrates' disavowal of rhetoric at the beginning of Plato's *Apology* (17a–b).

8. Cicero, *Pro publio Quinctio* §80.

were truly skilled, could they not put their deceptions on us without our noticing?

In order to answer the question formulated by Quintilian, namely, why study rhetoric, there are three views of the art of rhetoric we will need to consider: rhetoric as crafter of all-powerful speeches, rhetoric as mere ornament or adornment, and rhetoric as the art of clarification. Strangely enough, it will turn out that the view of rhetoric as adornment is but a modification of the claim that rhetoric is all-powerful: omnicompetent rhetoric claims to be able to make all things, or at least to be able to make all things appear to the audience, while ornamental rhetoric claims to make some things, namely ornaments or appearances. For that reason, we can clarify the reality of rhetoric by exploring the historical origin of the adornment view of rhetoric in the encounter between Gorgias the Sophist, Socrates, and Plato.

Gorgias provides the starkest account of the power of the rhetorician to make things up so as to manipulate the listener. In *On What Is Not* and in the *Encomium of Helen,* Gorgias professes an art that purports to be a trick for the few to retain their control over the masses, or at least the few so hope. Gorgias's tools are not so much manipulative as demobilizing: Gorgias wants to break our faith in speech as persuasion and convince us that all human relations are relations of physical violence, sometimes with fists and swords, whose material existence we readily acknowledge, sometimes with speeches, for whose material existence Gorgias argues. After expounding Gorgias's own account of the material being of speeches and his consequent picture of rhetoric, I explore the arguments and the action of Plato's *Gorgias* as a response to the project of the historical Gorgias in the *Encomium of Helen* and *On What Is Not.*[9] Both the historical Gorgias and Plato's Gorgias see the justification of the profession of the rhetorical master as grounded in the ontological claim that speeches (*logoi*) exist as a distinct class of things. In order to show the true powers and limitations of a conscious art of persuasion we must show that rhetoric is or comprehends the art of making things clear in speech. We must refute Gorgias's claim to an omnipotent

9. The fragments and biographical statements pertaining to the historical Gorgias are conveniently collected in *Gorgias von Leontinoi: Reden, Fragmente und Testimonien,* ed. and trans. Thomas Buchheim (Hamburg: Felix Meiner, 1989). In this chapter, I return to the "Gorgias/Gorgias" problematic addressed by Robert Wardy, *The Birth of Rhetoric: Gorgias, Plato, and Their Successors* (London: Routledge, 1996). My approach differs from Wardy's in three respects: I situate Gorgias's arguments as appeals to the class interest of the Athenian elite; I stress the coherence of Gorgias's ontological views notwithstanding their expression in paradoxes; and I explore the parallels between these views and the ontological claims put forward by Plato's Socrates.

art of rhetoric, and we must also refute Plato's claim that that there is a separate realm of things, a realm of "appearances" that rhetoric constitutes and over which rhetoric holds sway.

Gorgianic Omnipotence

Gorgias of Leontini (c. 490–c. 380 B . C . E .; ancient sources indeed attest that he lived to be over a hundred) was a Sicilian but made his fame in Athens when he came in 427 on an embassy. Gorgias professed the art of speaking well or perhaps the art of rhetoric, *rhetorikē*.[10] We have inherited the Platonic problematic of defining Gorgias's profession in relation to clearly conceived notions of the orator and the philosopher. Whether this problematic is based on a genuinely adequate account of rhetoric is another matter.

Whatever Gorgias's profession was, he was enormously successful at it. He charged high fees, and a golden statue was erected to him at in the sanctuary of the Pythian Apollo at Delphi, where it would have been seen by all the Greeks.[11] Of his writings very little survives: two more-or-less complete display speeches (that is, speeches that exhibit one's talents), the *Encomium of Helen* and the *Defense of Palamedes;* a text called *On What Is Not; or, On Nature* that survives paraphrased in two different presentations; and scattered fragments of other speeches and pronouncements. Gorgias was notorious in antiquity for his style, which readers of Plato can sample in pastiche in Polus's answer to Chaerophon.[12] The style is homophonic, jingly, with balanced sentences, and often seems to sacrifice meaning to the effect of sound.

---

10. It is true, however, that the word "rhetorikē" does not appear in any of the fragments of Gorgias's writings that have come down to us and that it appears for the first time in extant Greek literature, recent scholars have shown, when Plato's Gorgias is asked about his profession; see Thomas Cole, *The Origins of Rhetoric in Ancient Greece* (Baltimore: Johns Hopkins University Press, 1991), and Edward Schiappa, *The Beginnings of Rhetorical Theory in Classical Greece* (New Haven: Yale University Press, 1999). Yet since even those scholars such as Cole and Schiappa who assert that the term is a Platonic coinage agree that the historical Gorgias professed an art of speaking well, that he claimed that this art was teachable, and that he distinguished this art from philosophy (Gorgias, *Encomium of Helen*, trans. and ed. D. M. McDowell [Bristol, U.K.: Bristol Classical Press, 1982], §13), it seems fair to describe Gorgias in twenty-first-century English as a rhetorician and his art as the art of rhetoric; on this point, see Scott Consigny, *Gorgias: Sophist and Artist* (Columbia: University of South Carolina Press, 2001), 12–13.

11. *Gorgias von Leontinoi*, testimonium 1.4 = Philostratus, *Lives of the Sophists* 1.9. A statue was also dedicated to him at Olympia by his great-nephew Eumpolus, the inscription of which survives (*Gorgias von Leontinoi*, testimonium 8).

12. Plato, *Gorgias* 448c.

It is enchanting, magical, bewitching.[13] Though we contemporaries, "nattering nabobs of negativism" all, affect to despise the Gorgianic style, his style was in fact enormously influential on later Greek prose and on English in the Elizabethan age of "euphuism."[14] One can hear echoes of Gorgias even in the highest moment of American political rhetoric, Lincoln's second inaugural address: "Fondly do we hope, fervently do we pray, that this mighty scourge of war shall speedily pass away."[15]

The *Encomium of Helen*, is, as Gorgias puts it, a plaything (*paignion*), whose purpose is pleasure (*terpsis*), and yet it is relentlessly and exhaustively logical.[16] Gorgias moves systematically through four possible explanations for why Helen abandoned her husband and went to Troy with Paris. Helen either did what she did because the gods wished it and necessity decreed it, because she was seized by force (*bia*), because she was persuaded by speech (the explanation to which Gorgias devotes the most attention), or because she acted out of love for Paris (that is, she was stimulated erotically by the beautiful body of Paris Alexandros). Gorgias then works through each possible explanation to show that Helen herself, if any of these explanations holds, was not the true cause (*aitia*) of her going to Troy with Paris.

In the *Encomium of Helen* Gorgias presents a doctrine of speech as material object, albeit with the smallest, least manifest embodiment (*smikrotatōi sōmati kai aphanestatōi*).[17] Robert Wardy writes that according to Gorgias a speech "is, or is like, a unique physical object incapable of bilocation or

13. Charles Segal, "Gorgias and the Psychology of the Logos," *Harvard Studies in Classical Philology* 66 (1962): 99–155, 127; Jacqueline de Romilly, *Magic and Rhetoric in Ancient Greece* (Cambridge, Mass.: Harvard University Press, 1975).

14. See Bromley Smith, "Gorgias: A Study of Oratorical Style," *Quarterly Journal of Speech Education* 7, no. 1 (1921): 335–59, 348.

15. On the legacy of Gorgias, see Garry Wills, *Lincoln and Gettysburg: The Words That Remade America* (New York: Simon and Schuster, 1992), 212; for a sample of Gorgianic tropes in Lincoln's rhetoric, see Charles N. Smiley, "Lincoln and Gorgias," *Classical Journal* 13, no. 2 (1917): 124–28. Lincoln's successful uses of Gorgianic style seems to me sufficient refutation of James J. Porter, who reads the *Encomium of Helen* on the assumption that the *Helen* is not merely unpersuasive but self-consciously unpersuasive ("The Seductions of Gorgias," *Classical Antiquity* 12, no. 2 [1993]: 267–99); similar in approach to Porter is Richard A. Lanham, "The Rhetorical Ideal of Life," in *The Motives of Eloquence* (New Haven: Yale University Press, 1976).

16. Gorgias, *Encomium of Helen*, §§21, 5. On Gorgias's "passion for antithetical argument, trading mercilessly on the law of the excluded middle," see A. A. Long, "Methods of Argument in Gorgias, *Palamedes*," in *The Sophistic Movement: Papers Read at the First International Symposium on the Sophistic Movement Organized by the Greek Philosophical Society, 27–29 September 1982* (Athens: Athenian Library of Philosophy, 1984), 233–41.

17. Gorgias, *Encomium of Helen*, §8.

cloning"—but Wardy's "is like" simply shows the difficulty most of us have in digesting such a materialist account of language.[18]

To overcome our dyspepsia, it is useful to look at the doctrine regarding perception of Empedocles (also attributed to Gorgias by Socrates in the *Meno*[19]). On that account images are effluvia (*aporroai*) produced by things. These flows are of the same material composition as the things that produce them, and they are also of the same material composition as the organs of sense and thought by which we perceive them. As Empedocles himself put it, "By earth we see earth; by water, water; by aither, shining aither; by fire, too, blazing fire; love by love and strife by blazing strife."[20] These material effluvia act on the materially similar parts of our eyes, causing visual perceptions.

Gorgias's doctrine regarding speeches appears to be modeled after Empedocles' doctrine regarding perception and thought.[21] Empedocles, like Gorgias writing of Helen and Paris, gives the example of sexual arousal, which comes through the desiring person's sight of the desirable person: "Upon him comes also, through sight, desire for sexual intercourse."[22] According to the *Encomium of Helen,* speeches (*logoi*) are material objects that move from the speaker to the listener and thereby alter the judgments (*doxai*) of the

18. Wardy, *Birth of Rhetoric*, 20. Charles Segal similarly writes of "the almost physical dynamis of logos and persuasion" or the "almost physical impingement on the psyche" ("Gorgias and the Psychology of the Logos," 106, 142–43 n. 44). Segal cannot bring himself to write "the literally physical dynamis of logos and persuasion." Segal subsequently attributes to Gorgias the notion of "a reciprocal relationship between the psychic and the physical worlds" (142). For Gorgias there is in fact only one world, in which speech is a material element. Our resistance to Gorgias's linguistic materialism is justified inasmuch as his account denies our experience that speech can successfully present things. The most useful commentary on *On What Is Not* is G. B. Kerferd, "Meaning and Reference: Gorgias and the Relation Between Language and Reality," in *The Sophistic Movement*, 215–22.

19. Plato, *Meno* 76c–e.

20. Empedocles, frag. 17/109, in *The Poem of Empedocles*, ed. and trans. Brad Inwood, rev. ed. (Toronto: University of Toronto Press, 2001) (translation slightly modified); cf. frag. 16/110. For a broader picture of the Empedoclean doctrine, with its consequences for thought as well as perception, see *Gorgias von Leontinoi*, testimonium A86 = Theophrastus *De sensibus* 1–2, 7–24. *Meno* 76c–e is discussed by John M. Robinson, "On Gorgias," in *Exegesis and Argument: Studies in Greek Philosophy Presented to Gregory Vlastos*, ed. Edward N. Lee, Alexander P. D. Mourelatos, and Richard M. Rorty (New York: Humanities Press, 1973), 53–54. Robinson does not connect this perceptual materialism with the linguistic materialism of Gorgias's own writings. See also the account of perception as the reception of material films (*membranae*) in the only surviving ancient systematic presentation of materialism, Lucretius's *de rerum natura* (4.26ff).

21. See, for example, Mario Untersteiner, *The Sophists*, trans. Kathleen Freeman (Oxford: Basil Blackwell, 1954), 158. On Gorgias as a student of his fellow Sicilian Empedocles—according to the doxographical tradition, at any rate—see *Gorgias von Leontinoi*, testimonia 2, 3, 10.

22. Empedocles frag. 68/64.

listener's soul, which is likewise material.[23] Speech, Gorgias writes in the *Encomium of Helen,* impacts through the sense of hearing to produce changes in the souls of the listeners: for speech "is able to stop fear and remove pain and to work up joy and make pity grow."[24] Gorgias shows the material effect of speech through the examples of the effects of poetry and sorcerous incantations. Poetry inspires fear, pity, and longing not though its meaning but through its meters, through the material effect of metrical rhythms, while soothing incantations work as charms to produce pleasure in the bodies of their hearers or ease their sorrows.[25] Gorgias compares speech working on the soul to a drug working on the body: "Just as different drugs expel different humors from the body, and some stop it from being ill but others stop it from living, so too some speeches cause sorrow, some cause pleasure, some cause fear, some give the hearers confidence, some drug and bewitch the soul with some base persuasion."[26] Gorgias's psycho-logical materialism, as Charles Segal has written, "treats the psyche as a tangible reality and places its functions on a level of reasonable explicability coordinate with other physical phenomena."[27]

Gorgias (like the more recent cultural materialists of the Frankfurt School) denies that opening ourselves to the influence of those speaking can make us free. Speech is just another means of bodily, somatic—or as we would say, physical—compulsion. Speech is compulsion (*anankē*), even as the force of a forcible rapist is compulsion.[28] "All who persuade anybody mold a false

23. Gorgias's claims for power of *logoi* over judgments, perceptions, and opinions are expounded usefully by Untersteiner, *The Sophists,* 117–18.

24. Gorgias, *Encomium of Helen* §8. See also Thomas G. Rosenmeyer, "Gorgias, Aeschylus, and *Apate,*" *American Journal of Philology* 76, no. 3 (1955): 225–60, 231; Empedocles, by contrast, teaches that although his true tales, like any thought, work by their material impact, they do not work easily: "Very troublesome indeed it makes / men, and harshly resented, the impulse of persuasion into their thought organ [epi phrena hormē pistios]" (frag. 2/114 [translation modified]).

25. Gorgias, *Encomium of Helen* §§9, 10. On meter as a corporeal cause of a corporeal effect, see Bruce McComiskey, *Gorgias and the New Sophistic Rhetoric* (Carbondale: Southern Illinois University Press, 2002), 42–43; cf. Plato, *Republic* 398c–403c, Plato, *Laws* 790c–791b, and Allan Bloom, *The Closing of the American Mind* (New York: Simon and Schuster, 1987), 73–75.

26. Gorgias, *Encomium of Helen* §14 (translation slightly modified).

27. Segal, "Gorgias and the Psychology of the Logos."

28. Gorgias, *Encomium of Helen* §28. On this point, see John R. Wallach, *The Platonic Political Art: A Study of Critical Reason and Democracy* (University Park: Pennsylvania State University Press, 2001), 183. It is difficult to reconcile the claim in the *Encomium of Helen* that persuasive speech is compelling with Protarchus's statement at Plato, *Philebus* 58a–b, that according to Gorgias, the art of persuasion "makes all things slaves to itself, through their being willing [*dia hekontōn*], not by force"; see Brian Vickers, *In Defence of Rhetoric* (Oxford: Oxford University Press, 1989), 147.

speech [*logos*]"; that is to say, they use a speech that alters the soul's judgments but reveals nothing of what is.[29] The effect of speech on the soul is molding like the effect of sight on the soul. Hearing frightful speeches is like seeing frightful sights, not because the speeches represent frightful things or communicate them but because the speeches are themselves frightful.[30] Speech operates on the soul without being understood or interpreted.

The reader of the *Encomium* is thus liberated from the dichotomy between force and persuasion that he had previously taken for granted.[31] In the hands of a skilled rhetorician, logos can form the soul as it wishes: no judgment or opinion can remain standing before it, as can be seen from the effects of philosophic disputes.[32] Charles Segal correctly points out that rhetoric, the art of speech, is therefore revealed in Gorgias's *Encomium* as an art that "can directly touch the psyche through a process of aesthetic and emotional excitation, and hence guide or control human action."[33] Segal's words "directly touch" are, once again, for Gorgias not a metaphor but a description. Speech is a material thing that impacts on the soul, another material thing, and artful speech or rhetoric moves the judgments of the target soul or souls as the master of the art wishes. That Gorgias calls *Encomium* a plaything (*paignion*) might be read as him reassuring us that he is not trying to bewitch, or move, our embodied souls for his own purposes. But we have been beguiled, of course, if we are so reassured.[34]

Gorgias's *On What Is Not; or, On Nature* is a response—a parodic response, it seems safe to say—to Parmenidean and later Eleatic treatises on being. *On What Is Not* has come down to us in two later texts: in Sextus Empiricus's *Against the Logicians* and in the treatise *On Melissus, Xenophanes, Gorgias* in the received corpus of the works of Aristotle.[35] Gorgias's original text

29. Gorgias, *Encomium of Helen* §11.

30. Cf. Gorgias, *Encomium of Helen* §§15, 17.

31. Schiappa, *Beginnings of Rhetorical Theory*, 128; Guido Calogero, "Gorgias and the Socratic Principle *nemo sua sponte peccat*," *Journal of the Hellenic Society* 77, no. 1 (1957): 12–17, 13.

32. Gorgias, *Encomium of Helen* §13.

33. Segal, "Gorgias and the Psychology of the Logos," 133.

34. Wardy, *Birth of Rhetoric*, 51.

35. Jonathan Barnes classifies *On Melissus, Xenophanes, Gorgias* among the works "whose spuriousness has never seriously been contested" in his revision of the Oxford translation of Aristotle, *The Complete Works of Aristotle*, 2 vols. (Princeton: Princeton University Press, 1984). Diogenes Laertius lists in his catalog of the works of Aristotle (5.25) a book *Against Melissus*, a book *Against Gorgias*, and a book *Against Xenophanes*. The most thorough recent treatment in English of *On Melissus, Xenophanes, Gorgias* begins with the statement that "no agreement as to the nature, the quality, or the date of the pseudo-Aristotelian treatise *On Melissus, Xenophanes, Gorgias* has yet been reached" (Jaap Mansfeld, "*De Melisso Xenophane*

apparently contended that we cannot say, know, or communicate anything by showing that we cannot say, know, or communicate that anything is. Nothing exists—existence cannot truthfully be predicated of anything.[36] If something exists, its existence cannot be thought. If something's existence can be thought, its existence cannot be communicated.

Things, on Gorgias's account, cannot be communicated because things are not speeches. I cannot communicate what I see or hear, because I must speak speeches, not colors or sounds. We therefore cannot say what is, because what we say exists in a different way from what is. *Logos* is a type of thing alongside the other beings, brought into being by the impression of external things on the speaker. Perceptions cause speeches: a speech that predicates color is caused by the color perception, but the speech does not reveal or signify the color.[37] That claim that perceptions cause speeches is simply the converse of the claim of the *Helen* that speeches alter judgments and perceptions.

Thoughts and perceptions cannot therefore be shared. I cannot communicate my thoughts, because my thoughts and your thoughts are two different material things. My thoughts are located in me and your thoughts are located in you, but to communicate a thought would require that the same thought could be made present simultaneously in two different people.[38] Even if, counterfactually, the same thought were copresent in two thinkers, that thought would be thought differently by the two people thinking it. One cannot communicate perceptions because perceptions are not even shared by the same person across time, much less by different people at different times.[39]

The doctrine concerning speeches that we learn from *On What Is Not*

Gorgia: Pyrrhonizing Aristotelianism," *Rheinisches Museum für Philologie* 131, nos. 3–4 [1988]: 239–76). I am not persuaded, however, by Mansfeld's own thesis that the treatise reflects Pyrrhonist influence. The greatest interpreter of Aristotle since Aquinas, Martin Heidegger, implies that the treatise is authentically Aristotelian when he writes that "Aristotle wrote *Pros ta Gorgiou,* and we can assume Aristotle would not do battle against a mere babbler" (*Basic Concepts of Ancient Philosophy,* trans. Richard Rojcewicz [Bloomington: Indiana University Press, 2008], 71).

36. Sextus Empiricus, *Against the Logicians* 1.65–76; *On Melissus, Xenophanes, Gorgias* 979a10–33. I thus follow the predicative interpretation of the paradoxes in *On What Is Not,* after G. B. Kerferd, "Gorgias on Nature or That Which is Not," *Phronesis* 1, no. 1 (1955): 3–25, and Kerferd, "Meaning and Reference: Gorgias and the Relation Between Language and Reality." For a presentation of the two distinctive families of interpretation of *On What is Not,* the existential and predicative, see Edward Schiappa, "Interpreting Gorgias's 'Being' in *On Not-Being or On Nature,*" *Philosophy and Rhetoric* 30, no. 1 (1997): 13–30.

37. Sextus Empiricus, *Against the Logicians* 1.85–86.

38. Sextus Empiricus, *Against the Logicians* 1.83–84; *On Melissus, Xenophanes, Gorgias* 980b5–10.

39. *On Melissus, Xenophanes, Gorgias* 980b10–17.

and the *Encomium of Helen* is that a speech manipulates corporeally the same way that garlicky breath manipulates corporeally—by pushing on the sense organs of the one breathed on. Language cannot communicate anything. Speeches are false; speeches are unrevealing of what is and in that sense are deceptive, but these deceptions are not caused by the necessary imperfections of language.[40] According to Gorgias's doctrine, language is not a sometimes imperfect medium of communication but a field of moving, material, rhythmically pulsating speeches that effect change when they impact receptive bodies. Speech is effective but not because it represents things. Speech cannot represent sensible things—speech simply is another kind of sensible thing, perceived through the appropriate sense.[41]

The art of speaking well, what we would call rhetoric, teaches one to manipulate others proficiently. The art of medicine teaches what foods to eat or liquids to drink and what drugs to administer so as to alter the body, while the art of speaking well teaches how to alter the judgments of the soul, the soul that is a material part of the self, using speeches that are themselves material and that materially impact the sense organs.[42] Rhetoric, according to Gorgias, is a conscious art of manipulating others through speeches that corporeally overpower the judgments and perceptions of the listeners and leave the speaker supreme.

The doctrine of Gorgias would obviously have great appeal to the few who would rule the many. The Gorgianic doctrine appeals to the few not just because of its positive promise of an all-powerful art of manipulation, but because in its negative aspect, the doctrine denies the idea of the common, the idea that we can reason together about things through speeches. If Gorgias is correct, speech, which for Aristotle we supposedly possess as animals that live together in a multitude, is in fact the exertion of the will of one alone.[43] Conversation is only a charade. We can act on each other through speeches, but being persuaded is to suffer passively the manipulation of others. "The aim of [Gorgias's] rhetoric is to influence action, nothing more," Paul Woodruff writes.[44] One should say, rather, that for Gorgias the aim of

40. Pace Bruce E. Gronbeck's pioneering effort, "Gorgias on Rhetoric and Poetic: A Rehabilitation," *Southern Speech Communication Journal* 38, no. 1 (1972): 27–38, 35.

41. Sextus Empiricus, *Against the Logicians* 1.86.

42. Segal, "Gorgias and the Psychology of the Logos," 128.

43. See Aristotle, *Politics* 1.1.10–11, 1253a7–18, 2.1.3–7, 1261a10–b15, 2.2.9–10, 1263b30–37.

44. Paul Woodruff, "Rhetoric and Relativism: Protagoras and Gorgias," in *The Cambridge Companion to Early Greek Philosophy*, ed. A. A. Long (Cambridge: Cambridge University Press, 1999), 308.

all production of speeches is to provoke reaction, nothing more. To be per-suaded is neither to be free nor to be rational—Gorgias thus abolishes the distinction between rule and domination, or subjugation. Gorgias's doctrine is therefore a potent attack on the vaunted superiority of democracy—the notion that through institutions and practices human beings can speak and reason together as equals about common concerns and thus come to decide well about these concerns.

Gorgias's doctrine is easily appropriated as a defense of privilege, the priv-ilege of those, to appropriate the phrases of a contemporary rhetorical critic, whose power "is not rhetorical in any public sense. . . . When they think of power they rarely think of words, and when they think of the mass media they think of an enemy, not of a friend."[45] Like Strepsiades in Aristophanes' *Clouds*, these few desire the power to manipulate words freely, that is, to make free use of their material and familial resources. The few do not see them-selves as threatened by the Gorgianic attack on the notion of a common good because their own shared good, their family interest, does not require deliberation in order to be constituted.[46] This is what Andrew Sabl, follow-ing Tocqueville, calls the isolation of the rich: the rich do not need the force of the public in order to have power over their own lives and the lives of others.[47] It is not surprising, therefore, that the elite opponents of the Athe-nian democracy had a particular interest in Gorgias's professed art of verbal manipulation, an art that could dissolve the domination of the people, who can be constituted as a demos, as a body politic, only through language.[48] Gorgias denies the rational authority of language, and "anything tending to undermine language itself as a political tool will have distributive biases: it will work in favour of established elites, who have plenty of other ways of getting what they want; and it will work against oppressed groups enjoying few if any other opportunities."[49]

Gorgias's rhetoric is to be used within "democratic" institutions, but it is intended to serve those whose capacity for violence does not depend on speech but rather on familial wealth and on familial relations. The many

45. Roderick P. Hart, *Seducing America: How Television Charms the Modern Voter*, rev. ed. (Thousand Oaks, Calif.: Sage, 1999), 142–43.

46. See Marvin Meyers's discussion of Martin van Buren's defense of political parties as a barrier to the spontaneously united special interests of the privileged in *The Jacksonian Per-suasion: Politics and Belief* (Stanford: Stanford University Press, 1957), 281.

47. Andrew Sabl, *Ruling Passions: Political Offices and Democratic Ethics* (Princeton: Princeton University Press, 2002), 251–52.

48. Schiappa, *Beginnings of Rhetorical Theory*, 55–56.

49. Robert E. Goodin, *Manipulatory Politics* (New Haven: Yale University Press, 1980), 116.

can only exercise violence to impose their decrees on the few if the many can be joined together by common deliberation. Gorgias argues that a sharing of things through common deliberation is in fact impossible: what seems like agreement is in fact simply the imposition by one alone of his speech as a master speech, a speech that one body among other bodies uses to master the bodies (including the souls) of his audience.[50] The rule of one is always and everywhere the case, Gorgias claims, but that rule can be more effective if the one who rules has mastered the art of verbal manipulation that Gorgias professes and offers to teach—to those wealthy young men who can afford his substantial fees. The rule of many, especially the rule of an equal many, the regime first known as *isonomia* and later as *demokratia,* cannot exist. The few, therefore, need not and ought not submit to the claim that the people rule. Turning from the surviving Gorgianic texts to Plato's dialogue *Gorgias,* we see that Socrates tries to drive a wedge between the master Gorgias and his would-be student Callicles by calling into question the aspirations that Gorgias's art of rhetoric purports to serve.[51]

50. Eric Havelock's claim that the sophists in general and Gorgias in particular accepted the notion of a "common mind" and therefore strove to support rather than subvert democratic practices is hardly grounded in the sources, as he himself virtually admits. Havelock's contention is contradicted explicitly by Gorgias in *On What is Not* and implicitly in the *Encomium of Helen.* For Havelock's very influential view, see *The Liberal Temper in Greek Politics* (New Haven: Yale University Press, 1957), 201, 247–48.

51. On the "oligarchism" of Gorgias and professionalized *paideia* in general, see Kenneth Freeman, *Schools of Hellas,* 2nd ed. (London: Macmillan, 1912), 177; cited in Consigny, *Gorgias: Sophist and Artist,* 118, 220 n. 10; Thomas Conley, *Rhetoric in the European Tradition* (Chicago: University of Chicago Press, 1994), 5. Cf. also Gorgias, *Apology of Palamedes* §33, with Plato, *Gorgias* 454e, and Untersteiner, *The Sophists,* 139 n. 12. While the claim is frequently made that there is a connection between Gorgianic rhetoric and democratic institutions, partisans of a prodemocratic Gorgias do not ask which interest, faction, or class would have been in a position to learn and use Gorgias's professed art within democratic institutions; see e.g. Vickers, *In Defence of Rhetoric,* 6–7, and Richard Leo Enos, "Why Gorgias of Leontini Traveled to Athens: A Study of Recent Epigraphic Evidence," *Rhetoric Review* 11, no. 1 (1992): 1–15. After pointing out that the sophists' pupils must generally have come from the wealthy, Susan Jarratt claims that the very fact that they offered political education for pay was itself a democratic move, since "the shift from birth to wealth as a criterion of rule was a major step on the way to democracy" (*Rereading the Sophists: Classical Rhetoric Reconfigured* [Carbondale: Southern Illinois University Press, 1991], 82–84). Jarratt here is following Havelock, *The Liberal Temper in Greek Politics,* 162. The weight of the evidence (admittedly, our evidence overwhelmingly comes from the fourth century, well after Gorgias's flourishing) is that the Athenian demos did not deny that good birth was a merit but claimed the right to participate in government on the basis of its own sufficiently good birth as free Athenians; see, for example, Aristotle, *Politics* 1280a, John Hart, "The Athenian Nobility," in *Herodotus and Greek History* (Beckenham, U.K.: Croom Helm, 1982), 1, and Cynthia Farrar, *The Origins of Democratic Thinking: The Invention of Politics in Classical Athens* (Cambridge: Cambridge University Press, 1988), 22. There is no evidence, however, that Athenian democrats at any period saw in the accumulation of wealth outside of the traditional aristocracy a development favorable to popular power. The spread of wealth undoubtedly fosters social pluralism, which

What Does Callicles Want?

Among the many riches of Plato's own, hardly prodemocratic, presentation of Gorgias, I concern myself with Socrates' confrontation with Gorgianic rhetoric in his conversations with all three of the dialogue's antagonists, Gorgias, Polus, and Callicles. I also try to decode the place of Callicles' hopes for Gorgias within Callicles' own Typhonic soul, the Calliclean bog of contradictory desires.[52]

What is it, Socrates asks, that the man Gorgias teaches?[53] In answer Polus and Gorgias state the thesis of the omnicompetence of rhetoric, the claim that the art of rhetoric grants its master the power to manipulate matters through speech, forcing his listeners to respond completely to his own will. This is illustrated by the example of the arts, and in particular by the contest between the rhetorician and the physician and by the contest between

---

social theorists since Benjamin Constant and Alexis de Tocqueville have seen as favorable to modern representative democracy, but as Constant points out, and as Jarratt herself admits (87–88, 91), ancient direct democracy was solidaristically hostile to pluralism (see Constant, *The Spirit of Conquest and Usurpation and Their Relation to European Civilization* and *The Liberty of the Ancients Contrasted with That of the Moderns,* both in *Political Writings,* trans. and ed. Biancamaria Fontana [Cambridge: Cambridge University Press, 1988]). Jarratt argues that Sophistic pedagogy was critical of the hegemonic ideas of its time (104), forgetting that in democratic Athens it was democratic ideas that were hegemonic, and, as we see from Plato's Callicles, the elites subjected to popular hegemony looked to sophistic pedagogy for the critical tools they might use to liberate themselves from enslavement to the people. Jeffrey Walker therefore rightly speaks of "privilege" in ascribing to the age of Gorgias and his pupils "an increasing trend toward individualistic self-assertion (at least among those privileged enough to participate in politics or to come into contact with the new philosophies)" (*Rhetoric and Poetics in Antiquity* [Oxford: Oxford University Press, 2000], 17). On the tension between democracy and professionalized education, see also Leo Strauss, "The Liberalism of Classical Political Philosophy," in *Liberalism Ancient and Modern* (1968; repr., Chicago: University of Chicago Press, 1995), 54–56, and George Steiner, "The Archives of Eden," in *No Passion Spent: Essays, 1978–1996* (London: Faber and Faber, 1996), 283–303.

52. Socrates in the *Gorgias* "draws attention much more frequently than in any other dialogue to the personal shortcomings of his young antagonist" (George Kimball Plochmann and Franklin E. Robinson, *A Friendly Companion to Plato's* Gorgias [Carbondale: Southern Illinois University Press, 1988], 106). Thematic treatments of the encounter between Socrates and Callicles abound; the most useful are the chapter in Josiah Ober, *Political Dissent in Democratic Athens: Intellectual Critics of Popular Rule* (Princeton: Princeton University Press, 1999), and the series of papers stressing Callicles' hidden and incoherent moralism (he thinks in justice he deserves to rule because he knows that justice is but appearance) including Thomas Pangle, "Plato's *Gorgias* as a Vindication of Socratic Education," *Polis* 10, nos. 1/2 (1991): 3–21, and Devin Stauffer, "Socrates and Callicles: A Reading of Plato's *Gorgias,*" *Review of Politics* 64, no. 4 (2002): 627–57. Here I wish to situate the Callicles/Socrates encounter within the framing encounter between Socrates and Gorgias in the text of the *Gorgias* as well as within the intertextual encounter between Plato and the historical Gorgias.

53. Plato, *Gorgias* 447c.

the rhetorician and the hypothetical possessor of a political art.[54] Omnicompetence would alienate the artful speaker from the normal run of human things in that it would give him complete autonomy from the world of appearances and thereby free him from the rule of shared opinion (*doxa*). His alienation from human things as they show themselves would be that of the wearer of the ring of Gyges in the *Republic*. Rhetoric would be the art that enables the unjust man to appear perfectly just.[55]

Yet Socrates expresses doubt that the posited art of rhetoric can be separated from the other arts. After all, nearly all human activities use speech at least to some extent.[56] Rhetoric's peculiar product, Socrates claims, is persuasion (*peithō*) about justice or injustice that produces belief, opinion, or trust (*pistis*) rather than persuasion that produces knowledge.[57] Gorgias seems to confirm this ontological differentiation of belief-producing-persuasion from knowledge-producing-persuasion with his example of the rhetorician outdoing the doctor at persuading the sick. Persuasion in the courts and assemblies where the just and unjust things are considered, Socrates easily gets Gorgias to admit, is the implanting of belief rather than knowledge in the hearers.[58]

Rhetoric is sovereign over persuasions that produce belief, and, in particular, rhetoric is sovereign over the imitation in speeches of what is.[59] In that sense Socrates endorses Gorgias's claim in *On What Is Not* that we cannot communicate *things*. Socrates asserts with no uncertainty that we cannot communicate things when the occasion of communication is public and subject to limitations of time.[60] In any human communicative context the best we can do, Socrates suggests elsewhere, is to communicate speeches that while distinct from the things they imitate or represent, are as similar as possible to those things.[61] Rhetoric is the cosmetic knack of adorning the appearances or imitations of things in speech so as to produce belief in the listeners.[62]

Socrates' separation of persuasive speeches that produce belief from other entities serves Gorgias's interest as a professional teacher of rhetoric. Gorgias's problem, on Plato's presentation—the need that brings Gorgias to

---

54. Plato, *Gorgias* 456–457.
55. See Seth Benardete, *The Rhetoric of Morality and Philosophy: Plato's Gorgias and Phaedrus* (Chicago: University of Chicago Press, 1991).
56. Plato, *Gorgias* 449eff.
57. Plato, *Gorgias* 454b–d.
58. Plato, *Gorgias* 459a–b.
59. Cf. Plato, *Gorgias* 453b, 463c–e, and 465a–b with Plato, *Cratylus* 423cff., 430a–e.
60. Plato, *Gorgias* 454e–455a; cf. *Gorgias* 522b–c and Plato, *Cratylus* 408c.
61. Plato, *Cratylus* 435c.
62. Plato, *Gorgias* 454e–455a.

hope for something from his conversation with Socrates—is that Gorgias must have something teachable to profess in order to justify his practice of teaching and underwrite the cash value of that teaching. If Gorgias doesn't have an art among the arts, how can he have something to teach others for pay? The mere fact that Gorgias is frightfully good at making brief or long speeches on any subject is irrelevant to Gorgias's capacity to teach, because that ability could be natural talent, mere unteachable eloquence, or the product of his personal and thus incommunicable or unteachable experience.[63]

Socrates and Gorgias can agree on a distinction between belief and knowledge as traits in the soul, on the notion that speeches are images or imitations of things, and on the notion that there are rhetorical tools peculiar to lying or deception.[64] Gorgias can then be the professor of that highly valuable art (or, at least, knack) of deception. Socrates thus concedes to Gorgias an entire ontological realm, the realm of belief-producing-speeches, as his personal—and lucrative—province.[65] This is not a realm of things, but a realm of appearances.

The ontological separation of speeches that produce belief from speeches that produce knowledge requires that there be some marks of knowledge-directed speech, either marks within the soul of the listener and speaker or marks within the speech itself. The being of speech in itself (when separated in thought from what the speech is about) is syntax or grammar: only if there are syntactic or grammatical marks of knowledge-directed speech can there be a internal or grammatical distinction between arguments that aim toward truth and arguments that aim toward opinion, a differentiation in the sorts of things that these two kinds of arguments are. Socrates gives an example of such a syntactic or grammatical distinction when he asserts that arguments based on the authority of witnesses cannot aim at the truth but only at making things *seem* to the jury as they *seemed* to the witnesses.[66]

Plato is principally interested in exploring the possibility of marks of correct speech in the soul of the listener or in the speech itself. If there can be

63. Plato, *Gorgias* 449b–d.
64. Plato, *Gorgias* 454e, 459c–e.
65. Plato, *Gorgias* 454e–455a.
66. Plato, *Gorgias* 471e–472a. Every scientific paper with footnotes is a refutation of this, as we saw in chapter 1. An alternative approach would be to treat the distinction between true and false speech as one between saying things as they are and saying them as they are not. True and false speech would not be different from things in themselves, nor would true speech be a different kind of thing from false speech. True and false speech would not be things at all but rather the ways things are presented to us. Good arguments would be better than bad arguments because they would come closer to stating things as they are. The logical connections of good arguments would then present the real relations between facts.

marks of correct speech in the soul of the listener or the speech, then there must be a separation between knower and known. How, Plato then asks, can this gap be bridged? One wonders if this Platonic project should be replaced with a project that does not assume that there are self-subsisting marks that distinguish true knowledge from false opinion, whether in the soul or in the *logoi* themselves, but that instead understands knowing as a relation between knower and known and true statements as those statements we can utter that state things as they are.

Rhetoric, Socrates claims, is but a phantom of politics, a crafting of imitations of knowledge of what is good for the city.[67] Rhetoric does not educate the multitude but rather creates images of the truth, even as the wants of the multitude are but images of the truth of their needs. By presenting these images the artful rhetorician flatters the multitude into pursuing the pleasant rather than the good. Rhetoric is a kind of sweet-sauce cookery for the soul, and the masses who are the audiences for rhetorical performances are childlike in their ignorance of their own real interests.[68] The speaker flatters them in part by claiming that they know their own good and are capable of acting to get it. The judgment of the many as to their own needs and wants cannot stand in for the true needs of the many as the standard for correctness in speeches about the public good, Socrates claims.

Note that at this point in the dialogue Socrates' arguments still have to be seen in the context of Gorgias's professional needs—or, rather, Gorgias's need to have a defined profession in which he can sell instruction. Socrates does not yet dispute (though he will later in the dialogue, in the conversations with Polus and Callicles) that the flatterer's seeming prosperity counts as success. As Bruno Latour writes, "The most moving feature . . . is that even in this famous coup de grâce Socrates is still complimenting rhetoric. How can we not consider as positive qualities being 'good at guessing,' 'having courage,' 'knowing how to interact with people'? . . . For that matter, what is so bad about being talented as a cook? I myself prefer a good chef to many bad leaders."[69] This convenient correspondence between Gorgias's professional aspirations and Socrates' ontology puts that ontology into question.[70]

67. Plato, *Gorgias* 463d.
68. Plato, *Gorgias* 463, 500e–501a, 521e–522a.
69. Bruno Latour, *Pandora's Hope: Essays on the Reality of Science Studies* (Cambridge, Mass.: Harvard University Press, 1999), 233.
70. Consigny claims that Gorgias "would adamantly dispute Plato's foundationalist conclusion[] . . . that our distinction between knowledge and opinion in any way suggests that there are two distinct ontological domains of, say, Being and Non-Being, to which are terms

The ontological status of the productions of rhetoric is determined by the relation between rhetoric and justice. The crucial issue is whether rhetoric must be used justly, that is, used to present only the truly just things.[71] Gorgias readily admits that rhetoric can be used justly or unjustly, but he contradicts himself on the claim as to whether knowledge of rhetoric is different from knowledge of justice.[72] For the rhetorician to be unjust while seeming just there must be more to justice than the mere appearance of justice, although nearly all the Athenians, including Pericles and other famed and glorious statesmen, would seem to agree that justice is only a matter of appearances.[73] Socrates tells Polus that nearly all Athenians and foreigners would agree with what he says about justice. The few pride themselves on their cynicism, but their cynicism is in fact shared, and even heightened, among the demotic mob, whose cynical opinions, the aristocratic Plato might add, are untempered by extensive experience of the beautiful.

If justice is only a matter of appearances, freely manipulable, as Gorgias professes, by the rhetorician skilled in speeches, we cannot inquire about justice in order to find out how we truly want to be. Some truth about what

---

ultimately refer" (*Gorgias: Sophist and Artist*, 81); see also Bruce McComiskey, *Gorgias and the New Sophistic Rhetoric* (Carbondale: Southern Illinois University Press, 2002), chap. 1. Yet Consigny himself recognizes that for Gorgias, *logos* "is ontologically different from the objects it purports to communicate" (71). It is precisely because the historical Gorgias admits that there are two ontological domains, and by claiming that he possesses an art of rhetoric claims knowledge and not mere opinion of what ought to persuade, that Plato found it plausible that Gorgias would have accepted Socrates' distinction between ontological domains of reality and appearance *as long as that ontological distinction offered support for Gorgias's profession to be a knower of the art of rhetoric*. Relativist or antifoundationalist accounts of Gorgias's teaching (such as those of Consigny and McComiskey) run aground on the difficulty of explaining what makes Gorgias's professed art uniquely valuable when compared with ordinary, untutored, ways of going on speaking within social conventions—in much the way that the most celebrated contemporary defender of professional conventions, the self-proclaimed "sophist" Stanley Fish, repeatedly ran aground as dean of the College of Arts and Sciences at the University of Illinois, Chicago, in trying to justify higher salaries for humanities professors to Illinois citizens and legislators. If "reality is rhetorical," as McComiskey puts it (88), then what distinctive hold on reality is given to us by professors of rhetoric? Plato seems to have thought that forced to choose between foundationalism and undermining his ability to make a living by charging tuition for teaching his professed art, Gorgias would have preferred foundationalism (compare Plato, *Theaetetus* 161c–162a, where Socrates makes a similar point about Gorgias's rival teacher, Protagoras, and Plato, *Republic* 339b–341a, where a profession of realism as against conventionalism is extracted from Thrasymachus). Or to put it in a way Fish might like, there are foundations and Foundations, and deconstructing one might lead to being cut off from the other.

71. Plato, *Gorgias* 459–460.

72. Plato, *Gorgias* 457, 460a.

73. Plato, *Gorgias* 472a–b; on the critique of Pericles in the *Gorgias*, see Plochmann and Robinson, *Friendly Companion to Plato's* Gorgias, xxiii–xxiv.

is humanly desirable would have to stand behind rhetoric, telling us how to use it. As Seth Benardete has written, the reality of the good would dominate the shadow of justice.[74] If we lack the knowledge of the things that are truly good but possess an art of rhetoric that enables us to evade the weight of appearances by allowing us to mold others' opinions of us and our actions, we simply drift, in putting that art of rhetoric to use, further from what we ought to want. This problem dominates the conversation with Polus.[75]

Callicles enters the conversation by contending that Socrates has defeated Polus and Gorgias by equivocating on the fine or noble (*to kalon*), ignoring the distinction between those things that are fine by nature and those things that are fine by convention. To benefit from doing wrong to others is fine by nature but wrong by convention, while to suffer wrong is foul by nature. It is better by nature to do wrong than to suffer it and better by convention to suffer wrong than to do it. This natural right, the sovereignty of the strong over the weak, Callicles claims, is the right that the Persians invoked against the Greeks and Darius against Scythia. Callicles thus ignores the small problem that the Persians lost these wars.[76] If might truly maketh right, than the Persian claim to rule was unjustified, just as the mightiest refutation of Hitler's National Socialist ideology was the conquest of Berlin by the Red Army.

The few, Callicles wants to argue, are by nature strong but weak by the convention or law (*nomos*) that makes the many strong. The doctrine of Callicles is apparently what one learns from taking in a moderate amount of philosophy. Callicles' doctrine is what many have learned from the nature philosophers, whom we call the pre-Socratics. Among those whose view of

74. Benardete, *Rhetoric of Morality and Philosophy*, 21, 29–30.

75. Plato, *Gorgias* 466bff. Alternatively, one could suggest that the human world is merely a product of the human will. Socrates discusses this claim in the *Protagoras* and, principally, in the *Theaetetus*, where he argues persuasively that our acknowledgment of the reality of a common future shows that the world is given to us in some way and not merely constructed by us (Plato, *Theaetetus* 172a–b, 178b–179b). Socrates' answer here in the *Gorgias* is that rhetoric is communicative and that it conceals a truth about just and unjust things that is not constructed but that exists in itself. In particular we should like to use rhetoric to communicate our own injustices to the proper authorities (480), perhaps even to the Demos whom his elite interlocutors resent, whose power they hope to escape by learning from Gorgias his professedly all-powerful art of rhetoric. This is, of course, a deliberately bizarre claim.

76. Plato, *Gorgias* 483d–e. See R. B. Rutherford, "The Gorgias," in *The Art of Plato: Ten Essays in Platonic Interpretation* (Cambridge, Mass.: Harvard University Press, 1995), 163; Alessandra Fussi, "Callicles' Examples of *nomos tēs phuseōs* in Plato's *Gorgias*," *Graduate Faculty Philosophy Journal* 19, no. 1 (1996): 119–49. As Seth Benardete has pointed out, these are examples of the universal rule that everyone seeks to have more, not the rule that the right to have more belongs to the stronger (*Rhetoric of Morality and Philosophy*, 66–67).

nature comes from the materialists among the nature philosophers is the historical Gorgias. The real personage Gorgias is thus split among the personae of Plato's dialogue: Plato's Gorgias and Polus have the commitment to a profession and the style, or in Polus's case a pallid imitation of the style, while Plato's Callicles takes in Gorgias's naturalism. Callicles' materialist form of naturalism would seem to be what Socrates calls, in irony, the "greater mysteries."[77]

The result, then, is that Callicles' claim to be superior is a claim to superiority in knowledge, that is to say, knowledge of the truth about justice. The superior should have more, that is to say, more of what the many value, not what the discerning few value. Crucially, rhetoric can only help Callicles do what the many want because his notion of his own superiority amounts to the idea that he possesses superiority in the goods the many value.[78] Callicles is well educated, as many of the Athenians say, that is, Callicles is well steeped in the opinions of the many about the good and the bad, the fine and the foul, the just and the unjust.[79] At bottom, the elite too subscribe to the thesis of the wisdom of the many—this is unsurprising, inasmuch as the elite act as individuals according to the views that Athens adopts, say, in her conduct toward her empire, as one can see in Thucydides' account of the Mytilinean debate and the dialogue on Melos.[80]

The Demos thus shows its power to mold the few, to do violence to the most just (biaiōn to dikaotaton), as Callicles in the heat of his passion misquotes Pindar, to tame the young lions.[81] Callicles even forgets himself and speaks of "we" enslavers of the best men.[82] This is a truth that the few with whom Socrates is speaking do their best to avoid confronting, for they might then have to confront the question as to whether the superiority of the many in number over the few in number is in fact grounded in nature. Better simply to repeat to oneself the Gorgianic doctrine that what looks like many

77. Plato, Gorgias 497c.

78. Plato, Gorgias 489e, 490, 491e–92c.

79. Plato, Gorgias 487b; Ober, Political Dissent, 202–3.

80. Plato, Gorgias 503c–d; Thucydides, History of the Peloponnesian War 3.36–50, 5.84–116.

81. Plato, Gorgias 484b4–5, accepting the reading of the manuscripts. On Plato's text and its relation to Pindar, see Giorgio Agamben, Homo Sacer: Sovereign Power and Bare Life, trans. Daniel Heller-Roazen (Stanford: Stanford University Press, 1998), 30–34, whose argument, citing an expression of Hippias's that is similar to Callicles' at Protagoras 337c, is more persuasive than E. R. Dodds in Plato: Gorgias, ed. E. R. Dodds (Oxford: Oxford University Press, 1959), 270–72.

82. Plato, Gorgias 488c–489b, 483e–484a4; Benardete, Rhetoric and Morality of Philosophy, 65.

joined together to hold the few in bondage is in fact many embodied souls manipulated artfully through the speeches of one alone.[83]

In the soul of Callicles, as Socrates exposes it, there is a fundamental ambivalence about the many.[84] At one moment Callicles wishes to express his love for the Demos, and another moment he wishes to turn the tables and escape his love enslavement. Callicles hates his rivals in love, the demagogues, and yet disparages his beloved Demos. Callicles resents his erotic subjugation by the Demos, for he regards the people as uneducated, boorish, and ugly. He resents even more the prospect that the Demos would abandon him and subjugate somebody else.

Callicles thinks that, in natural justice, he deserves something for being, as he believes, superior to his beloved mob in knowledge of the conventionality of justice, and he consorts with Gorgias because he thinks that Gorgias's professed art will help him to get what he deserves. What Callicles wants from Gorgias is what young male readers hope for from books with titles like *How to Get Any Woman You Want:* an all-powerful rhetorical prescription that will permit them to have their way with those whom they desire. Gorgias has proclaimed that his art "is both the cause of freedom for persons for themselves, and for each to rule others in his own city."[85] Callicles hopes that Gorgias's rhetoric will free him by helping him to manipulate commonplace opinions freely and thus enable him to rule in democratic Athens without having either to betray his beloved Demos by seizing power by force or having to enslave himself wholly to these demotic opinions.[86]

Callicles wishes to manipulate the democratic regime, not destroy it. After all, Callicles distinguishes himself from the antidemocratic lovers of things Spartan—for example, Plato's relatives.[87] He is a neo-Periclean, it would seem: he is a great admirer of the old statesmen of the democracy, and he is careful to distance himself from Socrates' attack on Pericles.[88] It would seem that what Callicles wants to know is if the art of Gorgias will make him a new Pericles, a free but unchallenged leader of a free people.[89] It is this aspiration that Socrates is determined to purge.

If rhetoric is not an art but merely an effective mode of flattering and

83. Cf. Plato, *Gorgias* 452e.
84. Plato, *Gorgias* 481c–482a.
85. Plato, *Gorgias* 452d.
86. Cf. Plato, *Philebus* 58a–b; Consigny, *Gorgias: Sophist and Artist,* 178.
87. Plato, *Gorgias* 515e.
88. Plato, *Gorgias* 516d, 517a–b.
89. Plochmann and Robinson, *Friendly Companion to Plato's* Gorgias, xxiii–xxiv.

courting the Demos, the fact that the elite seek training in rhetoric is the triumph of the Demos. One could even say that assuming that the claim of the many to rule is just, rhetoric could then only be employed justly, that is to say, in submission to the just rule of the many.[90] Something like this is, of course, suggested by the images of the beast and the cave in the *Republic*. We tend to think that the few corrupt the many, but Socrates speaks of the many corrupting the few. The people, he says, are like a great beast, and the pretended art of sophistry is skill in anticipating its whims rather than in guiding it. All the sophists do is teach how to guess the whims of the many in regard to the good or the bad, the beautiful or the ugly, the just or the unjust. Moreover, as one devotes oneself to this practice of anticipatory flattery, one's own standards of the beautiful and just are inevitably assimilated to these ignorant whims, Socrates argues.[91] Political reputation is simply based on flattering the beast. It is not an activity suitable for refined, "beautiful people" or for real men.[92]

Socrates offers a twofold refutation of the possibility that Gorgias can teach Callicles what Callicles wants to know. First, Pericles and Themistocles did not study rhetoric. Second, at best learning rhetoric will only help the exceptional man do what the Demos wants, tempting him away from acting in his own interest.[93] Being a Pericles was not good for Pericles himself; the Demos, when it is done with a would-be statesman, beats him, fines him, exiles, or even sentences him to death, according to its whims.[94] Socrates is astonished, or affects to be astonished, that Callicles has foresworn the life of philosophy, the life that is devoted to doing your own thing, in order to enter a life of service to the very Demos Callicles affects to despise. Callicles, to speak in the image of the *Republic*, returns to the cave, after only a little venture into the sun, and Socrates is determined to drag him out of the cave again.

To Callicles, Socrates offers the choice between public rhetorical life as it currently is lived and a life of public speaking that aims only at the good

90. See on this point Josiah Ober, *Mass and Elite in Democratic Athens: Rhetoric, Ideology and the Power of the People* (Princeton: Princeton University Press, 1989). As Consigny writes, turning Socrates' indictment of Gorgias into an apology, Gorgias's "rhetorical education promotes socialization, encouraging people to become active members of the community by learning its discourses and participating in its agons" (*Gorgias: Sophist and Artist*, 202).

91. Plato, *Republic* 493; cf. Plato, *Gorgias* 510a–511b, 512e–513e. See also my "Academic Politics Between Democracy and Aristocracy," available at http://www.politicalontology.com.

92. Plato, *Gorgias* 512d–513c.

93. Plato, *Gorgias* 525d.

94. Plato, *Gorgias* 515c–516e. This is the claim of the personified Demos in Aristophanes' *Knights* (1121–50).

of the audience, not at pleasing them by flattering their false sense of their own goodness.[95] It is the second form of public speaking that Socrates, both here and in Plato's *Apology,* claims to practice.[96] Socrates therefore speaks only when speaking can contribute to the realization of the good, and public speaking can contribute to the public good, Socrates claims, only very rarely indeed.[97] But at least to the extent that such opportunities arise to intervene for the sake of the true good of the public, philosophy itself is a kind of governance or a kind of political life, and we should note of Socrates that, as Bruno Latour has put it, "no tyranny has been more lasting than that by this sacrificed, dead man, over the living, no power more absolute, no reign more undisputed."[98] The fact that the historical record shows no trace of a Callicles as an active politician suggests that Socrates' refutation was successful, that Callicles eventually returned to the life of philosophy.[99]

Add (Rhetoric) Sauce and Serve

Pace Plato, one cannot separate the essential from the inessential in speech, nor the supposed adornment provided by rhetoric from the content of the speeches. The ornamentation or "sauce" view of rhetoric originates here, in Plato's *Gorgias,* and it will subsequently be retained even by those like Hobbes and Locke, who understand themselves to be rebels against the old philosophy.[100] Notwithstanding the antiquity and authority of the sauce view

95. Plato, *Gorgias* 500c–d, 503a–b.
96. Plato, *Apology* 29d–33b, 36b–37a; Plato, *Gorgias* 521d.
97. Plato, *Gorgias* 503a–b.
98. Latour, *Pandora's Hope,* 234.
99. Plato, *Gorgias* 527e. On the historicity of Callicles, see Dodds, *Plato: Gorgias,* 12–13, and W. K. C. Guthrie, *The Sophists* (Cambridge: Cambridge University Press, 1971), 102 and n. 1. In seeing the silence of the historical record as evidence that Callicles abandoned a political career I follow Ober, *Political Dissent,* 208–9 and n. 94; for contrasting speculations on the fate of Callicles, cf. Dodds with Rutherford, *The Art of Plato,* 168 and n. 47.
100. On rhetoric as sauce or ornamentation, see, for example, Thomas Hobbes: "For wheresoever there is place for adorning and preferring of error, there is much more place for adorning and preferring of truth, if they have it to adorn" (*Leviathan,* ed. Edwin Curley [Indianapolis, Ind.: Hackett, 1994], 489); see also Locke, *Essay Concerning Human Understanding,* bk. 3, chap. 10. Instead of "sauce," Wayne Booth speaks of the mistaken view that rhetoric is but "icing to a cake that is produced by real thought"; Booth, *Rhetoric of Rhetoric,* ix; Booth discusses Locke on 6–7. Yet even Booth himself falls prey to the "sauce" or "icing" conception of rhetoric in that *The Rhetoric of Rhetoric* attempts to distinguish between salutary and pernicious rhetorical tools (rhetoric vs. what he calls "rhetrickery") instead of distinguishing between salutary and pernicious speech simply. I take my stand with the Wayne Booth who writes in *The Rhetoric of Fiction* ([Chicago: University of Chicago Press, 1961], 388) that "a well-made phrase can serve the rhetorical purposes of a Hitler as well as the literary purposes of a Zola."

of rhetoric, rhetoric is not separate from the substance of governing—rhetoric is indispensable for governing many through speech. Nothing has failed more consistently in practice than the view of rhetoric that treats the manufacture of policy as distinct from its marketing. Nixon, his former speechwriter William Safire has argued, thought that he had to control his image in order to control his "place in history." Nixon did not realize that, whatever attacks partisan Democrats and Nixon enemies such as Arthur Schlesinger might write while he was alive, his true place in history would be determined by less partisan historians based on their assessments of his policy actions.[101]

You sell yourself by selling what you have to say: "measures not men" merely means judge the men by the measures they propose. For that reason, as Peggy Noonan has written, great speeches come from great policy.[102] In Eisenhower's case there was a "deliberate integration of speechwriting and policy-making activities as [the 1954 State of the Union address] progressed."[103] When speechwriting and policy are integrated, speechwriting can drive policy constructively, as when Theodore Sorensen catalyzed the Kennedy administration's response to the deployment of missiles in Cuba by beginning to draft the president's remarks on the situation.[104]

The key negative example may well be Gerald Ford, who gave more speeches a week, an average of ten a week, than any previous president.[105] Jack Casserly, who wrote some of those speeches, records observations such as the one that Ford was "talking the country's ears off" and that "for several months now, the speechwriters keep asking themselves this question: Why is he giving so many speeches?" Ford's speeches, read today, range from the banal to the terrible. Casserly contends, and no one disputes, that Ford's speechwriters were not integrated into the policy process: "We are actually writing the policy of the United States with little or no guidance

101. Safire, *Before the Fall*, 546, 604.

102. This argument comes in two flavors, Republican and Democratic: for a Republican version, see two books by Peggy Noonan, *What I Saw at the Revolution* (New York: Random House, 1990) and *On Speaking Well;* for a Democratic version, see Carol Gelderman, *All the President's Words* (New York: Walker, 1997).

103. Charles J. G. Griffin, "Dwight D. Eisenhower," in *Presidential Speechwriting: From the New Deal to the Reagan Revolution and Beyond,* ed. Kurt Ritter and Martin J. Medhurst (College Station: Texas A&M University Press, 2003), 74.

104. Theodore O. Windt Jr., "John F. Kennedy: Presidential Speechwriting as Rhetorical Collaboration," in *Presidential Speechwriting,* ed. Ritter and Medhurst, 103.

105. Roderick P. Hart, *Verbal Style and the Presidency: A Computer-Based Analysis* (Orlando, Fla.: Academic Press, 1984); Gelderman, *All the President's Words,* 116–17.

from the top."[106] Speeches always make policy, but they make policy successfully only if speechwriting is integrated with the rest of the policy process.
Decisions are made to meet deadlines, and sometimes the speechwriter is
the "3am President."[107] We should not be shocked: the speechwriters' decisions matter because many if not most presidential decisions are expressed
for the first time in a presidential speech.[108] Moreover, every successful decision maker delegates some decisions, and the president has more control over those decisions made by his speechwriters, who are protected by
"executive privilege" from congressional scrutiny and interference, than he
does over decisions made by his cabinet members, who must answer not
just to the president but to the relevant House and Senate committees.

Why, then, do some politicians fail to integrate speechwriting and policy?
Largely, it would seem, because they fail to grasp that the most effective
language is not generally "the most rhetorical," when rhetoric is understood
as sauce for substance. The style that most effectively persuades is not the
most heavily ornamented, high-falutin', jingly, or poetic. The style that persuades, we have seen, the style that presents clearly and transparently the
course of action proposed, gives the audience the sense that the speaker
has balanced and mastered the reasons behind the action and the sense
that the reasons that favor his or her proposed course outweigh the reasons
for alternative courses. Reagan and Eisenhower, the "Great Communicator"
and the "Strategic Communicator," were effective without generally being
quotable: Reagan was "as good a speaker as one can be without eloquence,"
and "one is hard pressed to recite a single ringing phrase from the Eisenhower rhetorical corpus."[109] As Nixon speechwriter Raymond Price wrote
in the heat of the 1968 campaign about Lyndon Johnson, "LBJ was successful once he came across on TV as caring only about what he said and
not about the way he said it. He gave the impression of being no longer self-
conscious about his *manner* of expression, but rather seemed to have his
mind fixed on what he was talking *about*."[110] When "rhetoric" is disparaged
in public discourse, it is artfully whipped-up word-sauce that is usually

106. John J. Casserly, *The Ford White House: The Diary of a Speechwriter* (1977, repr., Back-
inprint.com, 2001), 68, 73, 32, 41, 65.

107. James C. Humes, *Confessions of a White House Ghostwriter: Five Presidents and Other
Political Adventures* (Washington, D.C.: Regnery, 1997), 12–13.

108. Arthur Larson, *Eisenhower: The President Nobody Knew* (New York: Charles Scribner's
Sons, 1968), 153.

109. Harvey C. Mansfield Jr., *America's Constitutional Soul* (Baltimore, Md.: Johns Hopkins
University Press, 1991), 23; Hart, *Verbal Style and the Presidency*, 79–80.

110. Ray Price, memorandum, quoted in Joe McGinniss, *The Selling of the President, 1968*
(1969; repr., New York, Penguin, 1988), 196.

meant. The need to avoid ornate language, as Marshall McLuhan pointed out, is exacerbated by television: on television, "the harder a man tries, the better he must hide it."[111]

Contemporary observers who claim that an all-powerful and manipulative art of rhetoric exists may have more democratic intentions than did Gorgias. Who has not read the endless complaints by intellectuals about the American system of political campaigning, where money in the form of campaign contributions supposedly rules all? These writers claim that capitalist society is peopled by one-dimensional men whose lives are ruled by manipulated passions and desires. The only problem is that no such all-powerful art of rhetoric exists, and not only because, as J. L. Austin wrote, "you cannot fool all of the people all of the time" is an analytic truth.[112] If the product is lousy, the best advertising campaign in the world will only ensure that people never forget who sold them that junk.[113]

Moreover, in politics, advertising gimmicks don't usually work because it is not enough to get attention to appeal to the tastes or vulnerabilities of a minority: "You can't sell the candidate like a product," says Nixon aide Jim Howard in Joe McGinniss's *The Selling of the President:* "A product, all you want to do is get attention. You only need two percent additional buyers to make the campaign worthwhile. In politics you need a flat fifty-one percent of the market and you can't get that through gimmicks."[114]

There are, Socrates and Gorgias notwithstanding, no tools peculiar to deception or lying. This is the main difficulty with the claim that rhetoric is just adornment. All the alleged tools of adornment are in fact used as tools of communication and can be found in scientific and philosophic texts.[115]

111. McGinniss, *The Selling of the President, 1968,* 30.

112. J. L. Austin, *Philosophical Papers,* 3rd edition (Oxford: Oxford University Press, 1979), 113 n. 1.

113. Jerry Della Femina, *From Those Wonderful Folks Who Gave You Pearl Harbor: Front-Line Dispatches from the Advertising War,* ed. Charles Sopkin (New York: Pocket Books, 1971), 141–43.

114. Jim Howard, quoted in McGinniss, *The Selling of the President, 1968,* 47. Joe Trippi's account of Howard Dean's campaign for the 2004 Democratic presidential nomination shows from an insider's perspective how the cleverest Internet-based viral marketing techniques were not enough to overcome Dean's weak background in national affairs (*The Revolution Will Not Be Televised: Democracy, the Internet, and the Overthrow of Everything* [New York: HarperCollins, 2004]).

115. The clearest demonstrations of the philosophers' employment of the full range of rhetorical devices can be found in Michèle Le Dœuff, *The Philosophical Imaginary,* ed. Colin Gordon (Stanford: Stanford University Press, 1989). Once we recognize that the difference between the philosopher and the sophist is a matter of fundamental orientation, or in Platonic language, of choice of lives, not of choice of words or even of choice of dogmas, we can look past our dismay at Socrates' employment of so-called sophistic tactics and read his

Rhetoric cannot be said to operate only when there is a disparity between the form of a statement and the substance of a statement, since a statement does not have a substance that can be separated from its form.[116]

The sauce view of rhetoric is a distorted image of the true view. Yet it is this image that Plato's Socrates expresses in the *Gorgias*. Socrates claims to Polus and Gorgias that rhetoric is deception—or, in any event, that it is the inculcating of images of things that are not as true as the things imaged. He claims to Callicles that rhetoric is an expression of the speaker's love of the people. We have seen that rhetoric is the art that shows one how to present things as they are but that also offers instruction in how to use speech and writing to maintain ties to the audience one addresses.

Rhetoric as an Art of Clarification

There is, on the one hand, an art of persuasive communication that aims to present things clearly and, on the other, a defensive art whose aim is to disparage the authority of speech and thereby preserve the existing fabric of human relations from the corrosive power of things.[117] By the latter art the speaker tries to draw attention to himself or herself: to seduce, to emphasize our relation to himself or herself rather than to the things of which he or she is speaking. Gorgias is the great theorist of this second, defensive art, even if his claims of the comprehensiveness of his own peculiar contribution to rhetoric must be rejected.

The first type of rhetoric, the art of persuasive communication that aims to present things clearly, has not yet found its expository master, and perhaps it cannot: "It is hard to describe a centrist style because it is a style that does not distract."[118] "Ugliness is describable," says Roland Barthes, but

---

strictures on the orators and the rhetorical masters as more of that habitual Socratic irony. Contrast on this point Jyl Gentzler, "The Sophistic Cross-Examination of Callicles in the *Gorgias*," *Ancient Philosophy* 15, no. 1 (1995): 17–43, with Martin Heidegger, *Plato's Sophist*, trans. Richard Rojcewicz and André Schuwer (Bloomington: Indiana University Press, 1997), §§30–31, 34.

116. Contrast Edwin Black, *Rhetorical Questions: Studies of Public Discourse* (Chicago: University of Chicago Press, 1992), 10, 16.

117. Socrates, one might say, presents a distorted but still recognizable image of rhetoric in the *Gorgias*. There is rhetoric as deception, as the inculcating of images of things, images that although imperfect nonetheless are connected by the relation of imaging to the things they image; this is a distorted image of rhetoric as communicative of things. Second, there is rhetoric as the expression of the speaker's love of the people; this a distorted image of the rhetoric that defends human relations from the threat of communicated things.

118. Roderick P. Hart, *Campaign Talk: Why Elections Are Good for Us* (Princeton: Princeton University Press, 2000), 99.

"beauty is stated." It is rather through a conscious looseness of style, a relaxation of the conscious control of style, that one shows that one is paying more attention to things than to words.[119]

The great trick of persuasion is to stand back and let the facts speak for themselves, that is to say, let the reader be moved inexorably to the conclusion by the weight of the evidence you have piled up, once you have cleared the obstacles to securing the reader's assent. As Charles Bazerman has shown, Newton spent years in revising his second great scientific treatise, *Optics,* so that the reasoning and the reported experiments would have unimpeded persuasive effect: "By allying itself more closely to the available empirical evidence, the improved claim is actively relying on passive constraints for its force."[120] The great appeal of the passive voice is that it turns statements about human agency into statements about the circumstances that justify a particular action.

In letting the facts speak for themselves, that is, in presenting the facts forthrightly and in removing the obstacles to these facts being heard, one accomplishes "a complete regeneration of the audience" and thereby succeeds in "adjusting . . . people to ideas"; that is to say, one presents them with a new mode of getting along that puts the ideas to work.[121]

Would-be advertising writers are taught to present the product, not to speak to the audience: don't tell them why they should be attracted to your product but rather show them something attractive. "Describing the audience to itself directly doesn't work: if you were trying to talk fish onto a lure, you would describe the bait, not recite 'you're swimmin' upstream, you're breathin' underwater. This is your kind of lure, isn't it, fish boy?'"[122] Don't tell the audience why they should agree with your proposal; rather, tell them who they are and what they have done, just as Pericles shows the Athenians to themselves by praising what they have done, and then show how your proposal is the only one that permits them to go on as they have been going

119. Roland Barthes, *Sade, Fourier, Loyola,* trans. Richard Miller (New York: Hill and Wang, 1976), 22, and see Cicero, *Orator,* trans. H. M. Hubbell, in Cicero, *Brutus, Orator* (Cambridge: Harvard University Press, 1962), xxiii.77.

120. Charles Bazerman, *Shaping Written Knowledge: The Genre and Activity of the Experimental Article in Science* (Madison: University of Wisconsin Press, 1988), 108, 121.

121. Donald C. Bryant, "Rhetoric: Its Functions and Scope," *Quarterly Journal of Speech* 39, no. 4 (1953): 401–24, 413. As Charles Larson and Robert Sanders put it, responding to Bryant, "rhetoric adjusts people to each other; ideas serve as mediators between them" ("Faith, Mystery, and Data: An Analysis of 'Scientific' Studies of Persuasion," *Quarterly Journal of Speech* 61, no. 2 [1975]: 178–94, 193).

122. Luke Sullivan, *Hey, Whipple, Squeeze This! A Guide to Creating Great Ads* (New York: John Wiley, 1998), 201–2.

on. On the other hand, if you want your listeners to change the way they do things, it is not enough merely to reaffirm what brings them together as an audience. Rhetoric can reweave community, but it can also reconfigure the possibilities for action we see in the world.[123]

The principal part of the art of rhetoric does not lie in the manufacture of apparent goods but rather in their arrangement and presentation as reasons in the speech. Rhetorical invention is the composition of sentences that make the reasons or facts relevant to the action being urged present to the attention of the audience.[124] Here is this advice, expressed by a master, Adolf Hitler: "The function of propaganda does not lie in the scientific training of the individual, but in calling the masses' attention to certain facts, processes, necessities, etc., whose significance is thus for the first time placed within their field of vision."[125] As Hitler's great opponent Churchill put it, "Leave a picture in the listener's mind."[126]

"Specificity," as Ronald Reagan said, "is the soul of credibility."[127] Roderick Hart's stylistic analysis shows that the Reagan speechwriters practiced what their boss preached: "[Reagan's] remarks carry punch because his nouns and verbs stand alone, making his style almost aphoristic. This makes Ronald Reagan the sort of American whom Tocqueville wrote about, a person whose faith in certain simple values was so strong that his words needed no adornment."[128] Powerful style, the style that has the power to move and the style that belongs to the powerful, goes unmarked by its audience. When listening to the direct, clear speech affected by powerful speakers, listeners attend only to what speaker wants or argues—when listening to the hedging, qualified style of the powerless, listeners attend to the very features that mark that speaking style as weak and unpersuasive.[129]

To seek to communicate things is to rely on things rather than qualifiers, nouns and verbs rather than adjectives and adverbs. "Express main characters as subjects. Express their actions as verbs." The fact that these

123. See Steve Fuller, *Philosophy, Rhetoric, and the End of Knowledge: The Coming of Science and Technology Studies* (Madison: University of Wisconsin Press, 1993), 18.

124. See Chaïm Perelman and Lucie Olbrechts-Tyteca, *The New Rhetoric*, trans. John Wilkinson and Purcell Weaver (Notre Dame, Ind.: University of Notre Dame Press, 1969), §29; Richard McKeon, "Character and the Arts and Disciplines," *Ethics* 78, no. 2 (1968): 117.

125. Hitler, *Mein Kampf*, trans. Ralph Mannheim (Boston: Houghton Mifflin, 1971), 179.

126. Sullivan, *Hey, Whipple*, 85–87.

127. Gelderman, *All the President's Words*, 105–6.

128. Hart, *Verbal Style*, 220–21; Kathleen Hall Jamieson, *Eloquence in an Electronic Age* (Oxford: Oxford University Press, 1988), 169.

129. Ng and Bradac, *Power in Language: Verbal Communication and Social Influence* (Newbury Park, Calif.: Sage, 1993), 18–22, 33–34.

kinds of rules can be easily stated does not make them easy to keep—"It is not just hard to be clear, it is close to an unnatural act."[130] The same people speak simpler prose as presidents than before they ascended, no doubt because they have more help in crafting plain talk.[131] Clarity is as unnatural an achievement as the vaunted realism of David Mamet's dialogue. Nothing is more difficult in oratory, Quintilian reminds us, than to say that which, once heard, all think they would have said.[132]

To eliminate the ornament from language requires training and practice. Listen to those who have not benefited from either and you will discover that to be the case. As Adam Smith puts it, "There is nowhere more use made of [rhetorical] figures than in the lowest and most vulgar conversation."[133] Here is an example from Boswell's *Life of Johnson:*

> When I rose to go to church in the afternoon, I was informed that there had been an earthquake, of which, it seems the shock had been felt in some degree at Ashbourne. JOHNSON: "Sir, it will be much exaggerated in public talk: for, in the first place, the common people do not accurately adapt their thoughts to the objects; nor, secondly, do they accurately adapt their words to their thoughts: they do not mean to lie; but taking no pains to be exact, they give you very false accounts. A great part of their language is proverbial. If any thing rocks at all, they say it rocks like a cradle; and in this way they go on."[134]

Allegory and hyperbole, Quintilian reminds us, are frequently used by men of little ability and in the conversation of everyday life, but as he goes on to say, these rhetorical figures escape our attention precisely because they are clichéd.[135] "When you hear grammatical terms such as metonymy, metaphor,

---

130. Joseph M. Williams, *Style: Ten Lessons in Clarity and Grace,* 6th ed. (New York: Longman, 2000), 44, 232.

131. Hart, *Verbal Style,* 39, 42, 72; the last quoting Robert Underhill, *Truman Persuasions* (Ames: Iowa State University Press, 1981), 196.

132. We see Lincoln, Lord Charnwood writes, "watching and waiting while blood flows, suspending judgment, temporising, making trial of this expedient and of that, adopting in the end, quite unthanked, the measure of which most men will say, when it succeeds, 'That is what we always said should be done'" (*Abraham Lincoln* [1916; repr., New York: Pocket Books, 1943], 165).

133. Adam Smith, *Lectures on Rhetoric and Belles Lettres,* ed. J. C. Bryce (Oxford: Oxford University Press, 1985), 34.

134. James Boswell, *The Life of Samuel Johnson,* 2 vols. (1906; repr., London: Everyman's Library, 1973), 2:102.

135. Quintilian, *Institutio oratoria* 8.6.51, 8.6.75; cf. Perelman and Olbrechts-Tyteca, *The New Rhetoric* §88.

and allegory do they not seem to refer to some rare exotic tongue?" asks Montaigne. Not so, he answers: "They are categories which apply to the chatter of your chambermaid."[136]

The orator's goal, when he or she wishes to say something, is not to speak the mother tongue but to achieve the extraordinary effect of moving the audience to action or persuading it to refrain from action. This requires not so much the application of the devices carefully classified in the rhetorical handbooks as their elimination; Nixon, writes Safire, was "so practiced an orator that [he] knew when not to orate."[137] As George Bernard Shaw said, "In literature the ambition of the amateur is to acquire the literary language; the struggle of the adept is to get rid of it." One can apply to speaking what the Japanese master Kageyama wrote of Go: "Go is the kind of game in which you are an expert if you can just keep on making ordinary moves. You need not play any especially brilliant moves at all."[138]

Thus Frank Kermode points out that simplicity and clarity are the distinguishing marks of educated prose, not of the authentic proletarian voice. As James Fennimore Cooper says in *The American Democrat,* "One of the most certain evidences of a man of high breeding, is his simplicity of speech."[139] Any style that is learned belongs to a learned elite, and those who are learning to express themselves have not mastered it.[140] Yet because the clear style is learned, the realm of the elite is accessible to anyone who masters it.[141] Clear writing and clear speaking are peculiar to the educated— that is to say, perspicuity can be taught. Clarity is thus the principal supplement that the conscious art of rhetoric offers to natural eloquence.

To learn to be clear is to learn to mobilize one's audience for action by presenting to it the things that justify action. Ornate prose expresses the feelings of the speaker, but its effect on its audience is cathartic: to the extent that the members of the audience recognize those feelings in themselves, the act of listening to another express those feelings distances them from those feelings and thereby diminishes them. "Upon the audience," writes Winston Churchill, "the effect is to reduce pressure as when a safety valve

---

136. Montaigne, "On the Vanity of Words," in *The Complete Essays,* trans. Screech, 343.

137. Safire, *Before the Fall,* 537.

138. Shaw quoted by Williams, *Style,* 152; Toshiro Kageyama, *Lessons in the Fundamentals of Go,* trans. James Davies (Tokyo: Ishi Press, 1978), 56.

139. Frank Kermode, *History and Value* (Oxford: Oxford University Press, 1989), 89; James Fenimore Cooper, *The American Democrat* (1838; Indianapolis: Liberty Fund, n.d.), 153; quoted by Joseph Williams, *Style,* 7–8.

140. See Quintilian, *Institutio oratoria* 2.4.6–8.

141. Francis-Noël Thomas and Mark Turner, *Clear and Simple as the Truth: Writing Classic Prose* (Princeton: Princeton University Press, 1994), 49.

is opened. Their feelings are more than adequately expressed. Their enthusiasm has boiled over."[142]

Clear prose, by contrast, makes shared the things that will arouse and channel a response in the audience. To strip prose down is therefore to transform that text from subjective and cathartic to objective and therefore energizing. To quote Frantz Fanon:

> It is as if a kind of internal organization or law of expression existed which wills that poetic expression become less frequent in proportion as the objectives and the methods of the struggle for liberation become more precise. Themes are completely altered; in fact, we find less and less of bitter, hopeless recrimination and less also of that violent, resounding, florid writing which on the whole serves to reassure the occupying power. . . . Stinging denunciations, the exposing of distressing conditions and passions which find their outlet in expression are in fact assimilated by the occupying power in a cathartic process. To aid such processes is in a certain sense to avoid their dramatization and to clear the atmosphere.
>
> But such a situation can only be transitory. In fact, the progress of national consciousness among the people modifies and gives precision to the literary utterances of the native intellectual. The continued cohesion of the people constitutes for the intellectual an invitation to go further than his cry of protest. The lament first makes the indictment; then it makes an appeal. In the period that follows, the words of command are heard. The crystallization of the national consciousness will both disrupt literary styles and themes, and also create a completely new public.[143]

The clear style that calls its readers to action, Fanon continues, "may be properly called a literature of combat. . . . It is a literature of combat because it assumes responsibility, and because it is the will to liberty expressed in

---

142. Winston S. Churchill, "The Scaffolding of Rhetoric," in Randolph S. Churchill, companion volume, pt. 2, to *Youth: 1874–1900*, vol. 1 of *Winston S. Churchill* (London: Heinemann, 1967), 820–21.

143. Frantz Fanon, "On National Culture," in *The Wretched of the Earth*, trans. Constance Farrington (London: MacGibbon and Kee, 1965), 192–93. Radical art, too, like radical rhetoric, must be noncathartic—as Carolyn Fowler writes, "One goes away from the theater, the sculpture, the painting, the novel or poem not drained of emotion and at peace, but troubled, and with no place to hide" (*Black Art and Black Aesthetics: A Bibliography* [Atlanta, Ga.: First World, 1976], xxiv).

terms of time and space." To make readers into a public, do not encourage them to express their anger and resentment at past outrages—rather, show them what they can do together and thus open up for them the possibility of a collective future.

Both the art of clarification and the art of defending our existing relations from alteration make use of ethos, in that each seeks the appropriate mode of presenting the speaker's character. The art of clarification aims to make the speaker transparent to the contents of the speech, while the defensive art presents the speaker as one with the community and the opposing speaker, if any, as alien. Both of these arts ought to be concealed: to be transparent to things, your art, like everything else peculiar about you, must be unnoticed.[144] To reweave the bonds of community, you must keep out of the foreground of your audience's attention whatever distinguishes you as an individual from the community.

Although it is not possible to conceal eloquence, it is possible that one's reputation as a great persuader of men will go unnoticed in the light of one's reputation as a great doer of deeds. Eisenhower, who had in the 1930s written speeches for one of the great self-promoters of the twentieth century, Douglas MacArthur, left Washington for good in January 1961 with the reputation of being a bumbling old man who spoke confusedly. Yet as far as we can tell, virtually every expression of his career, uttered in public or in private, was calculated for effect.[145] Eisenhower's is the only administration since Coolidge's whose achievements were untarnished by major scandals or disasters. We must learn to look for the art of rhetoric in the communications that work, that produce action or enforce restraint, rather than in the ornamentation that at best makes people feel but cannot mobilize them to act. Not only will we be in a better position to see the opportunities the world offers and grasp them in the manner of an Eisenhower, but we will have a better understanding of the fundamental possibilities of political action.

144. See Cicero, *Orator* 61.208–9.
145. See, for example, Stephen E. Ambrose, *Eisenhower: Soldier and President* (New York: Simon and Schuster, 1990), 65, and Fred Greenstein, *The Presidential Difference: Leadership Style from FDR to Clinton, with a New Afterword on George W. Bush* (Princeton: Princeton University Press, 2001), 48, 49, and compare to Cicero, *Orator* xlii, 146.

POSTSCRIPT:
HOW TO BEGIN TO ANALYZE A SPEECH

We can analyze any effort at communication as a conglomerate of efforts to communicate something and get us to change our direction accordingly, "assaulting the resistance of inertia," and efforts to preserve a relation from the threat of communication, thereby keeping things going in the direction they are already going.[1] As David Mamet says of the dramatist, the speaker's task is to create order out of disorder, that is to say, order out of disordered circumstances.[2] When things are in disarray, you show what will produce order by showing the things to be in disarray. When people are in disarray because someone is speaking without being heeded, you bring them back into order by showing who is worthy of attention and who isn't: the rhetoric of exclusion, we would call it, which is frequently practiced nowadays by labeling something someone has said as exclusionary.

To understand an effort to communicate something we must understand what is being communicated. We must understand what is requested of the listener, what is the QED, as Eisenhower put it.[3] We also need to understand what the speaker offers as justifications of the request: our judgment is of actions, but it is judgment of actions as they are oriented toward things. As I argued in chapter 3, things have to be shown: to change someone's direction you need to present things more clearly, that is to say, picture them more vividly, more concretely, in greater detail.

We also need to understand what reasons the audience has for accepting the justifications given by the speaker as correct. Here character, in its

---

1. The phrase is from Edward L. Bernays, *Propaganda* (New York: Liveright, 1928), 106–7, but with a somewhat different meaning.

2. Cf. David Mamet, *On Directing Film* (New York: Viking, 1991), 28.

3. Arthur Larson, *Eisenhower: The President Nobody Knew* (New York: Charles Scribner's Sons, 1968), 146–47; James C. Humes, *White House Ghostwriter: Five Presidents and Other Political Adventures* (Washington, D.C.: Regnery, 1997), 37.

central sense of reliability, is crucial. It is by one's record of actions that one proves that one knows what has happened and what is likely to happen, that one demonstrates that one shares the interests of the audience in the manifold possible future outcomes, and that one has a proper sense of what counts as a desirable outcome.

When the speaker speaks so as to preserve or develop an existing relationship, to understand the speech we need to determine what the relationship is, and how the speech seeks to deepen the grooves already worn. To the end of deepening his or her relationship with the audience, the speaker presents himself or herself as trustworthy while disparaging alternative speakers or advisors as mistaken or otherwise unworthy of reliance.

If the speech is complex, we must repeat the analysis recursively until we have got down to the basic units of the speech. These basic units are the actions of narrowest scope that are presented for the judgment of the audience, as when Edward Everett, in that other Gettysburg address, delineated the meaning of the Union cause and the valor of the Union soldiers who fought there through a lengthy account of the specific actions that made up that battle and the units that carried them out.[4] We can then see how these units or unities (to echo the old term of neo-Aristotelian theater criticism) are connected by the speaker in order to urge us to change or maintain course the way the speaker advises.

Let us look at the Israeli Army chief-of-staff Moshe Dayan's short 1956 eulogy of Ro'i (Roy) Rotenberg.[5] Ro'i Rotenberg was born in Tel Aviv to American parents but had grown up on the moshav Kfar Yehezkel in the Jezreel Valley and had been a well-known youth leader in the Labor Zionist youth movement in Tel Aviv. After his army service, Ro'i helped create and lead the settlement of Nahal Oz on the border with the Gaza Strip. Dayan tells us in his book *Living with the Bible* that he had come in April 1956 (Dayan was at the time chief of the General Staff) to Nahal Oz for a kibbutz-style wedding of four couples simultaneously:

> While the kibbutz members were putting the finishing touches to their preparations and receiving their guests, Ro'i rode away on his horse

4. Edward Everett, "Gettysburg Oration," reprinted in Garry Wills, *Lincoln at Gettysburg: The Words the Remade America* (New York: Simon and Schuster, 1992), 213–47.

5. My treatment of Dayan's eulogy builds in part on a seminar paper by my student Emily Scharfman ("Biblicism: A Compelling Ideology for the New Jewish State"). On the context of the speech, see Moshe Dayan, *Living with the Bible* (New York: William Morrow, 1978), 160–69.

to drive off a group of Arabs who had crossed the border [and] were pasturing their flocks in the kibbutz fields and cutting their crops. When Ro'i reached them, he was shot dead, and his body was dragged across the border. His corpse, mutilated, was later handed over to the U.N. soldiers, who delivered it to us for burial.[6]

Dayan delivered the eulogy for Ro'i, and it was broadcast simultaneously on nationwide radio:

> Yesterday, at sunrise, Ro'i was murdered. The quiet of the spring morning blinded him, and he did not see those waiting in ambush to take his life along the line of the irrigation ditch.
>
> Do not today besmirch the murderers with accusations. Who are we that we should bewail their mighty hatred of us? For eight years they sit in the refugee camps in Gaza, and opposite their gaze we appropriate for ourselves as our own portion the land and villages in which they and their fathers dwelled.
>
> Not from the Arabs in Gaza, but from ourselves shall we require the blood of Ro'i. How did we close our eyes so as not to look straight at our fate, so as not to see the goal of our generation in its full measure of cruelty? Did we forget that this group of young men and women, which dwells in Nahal Oz, bear on their shoulders the heavy gates of Gaza, gates on the other side of which are crowded together hundreds of thousands of eyes and hands that pray for our weakness, that it may come, so that they can rip us to shreds—have we forgotten this?
>
> This we know: that in order that the hope to destroy us should die we have to be armed and ready, morning and night. We are a generation of settlement, and without a steel helmet and the barrel of the cannon we cannot plant a tree and build a house. Our children will not live if we do not dig shelters, and without a barbed wire fence and a machine gun we cannot pave a road and channel water. The millions of Jews who were destroyed because they did not have a land look at us from the ashes of Israelite history and command us to take possession of and establish a land for our nation.
>
> But on the other side of the boundary ditch a sea of hatred and longing for revenge rises to flood tide, looks for the day when the tranquility shall confuse our steps, the day when we listen to the ambassadorial

---

6. Dayan, *Living with the Bible*, 162.

messengers of villainous hypocrisy that tell us to put down our weapons. To us the blood of Ro'i screams from his torn body. Even though we have sworn a thousand times that our blood will not be spilled in vain—yesterday we were again seduced; we listened, and we believed.

Our reckoning with ourselves we shall make today. Do not shrink back from seeing the enmity that follows along with and fills the lives of hundreds of thousands of Arabs who dwell around us watching for the moment when their hand can seek our blood. Let us not turn our gaze lest our hand weaken. This is the decree upon our generation. This is the alternative we live—to be ready and armed, strong and firm, or to let the sword fall from our clenched hand, cutting short our lives.

Ro'i Rotenberg, the blond, snub-nosed youth, who left the city of Tel-Aviv to build his house in the gates of Gaza to be a wall for us. Ro'i, the light in his heart blinded his eyes—he did not see the glint of the knife. The siren song of peace deafened his ears, and he did not hear the sound of murder waiting in ambush. The gates of Gaza were too heavy for his shoulders, and they buried him.[7]

Dayan's speech has as its master image the story of Samson from the biblical Book of Judges. Samson, gifted by God with extraordinary strength, warred against the Philistines/Palestinians in Gaza; Samson lifted and carried the gates of Gaza on his back. Blinded by his trust in his Philistine wife, Delilah, Samson was betrayed to the Philistines, and his eyes were put out. The Philistines put the captive Samson on show, bound in the Temple of Dagon in Gaza. Samson, though enchained, prayed to God, recovered his strength, and pulled down the temple on the heads of the Philistines. Dayan relies on his audience's familiarity with the Bible: Samson is not even named.[8]

Ro'i was no Samson, though he took upon himself Samson's task of guarding Israel from the depredations of those who dwelled in Gaza. Ro'i had not the strength of Samson, and Ro'i's death was not part of an act of revenge against the Philistines, nor will Ro'i's death, it would seem, lead to such revenge.

---

7. In *Speeches for All Occasions* [in Hebrew], ed. Tamar Brush (Tel Aviv: Yediot Aharonot and Open University Press, 1993), 103 (translation mine). Dayan, *Living with the Bible*, gives his own translation; his is less literal and thus, I think, less powerful on its own. The English version is, however, better attuned to the rhetorical purposes of the English book within which it is placed.

8. Scharfman, "Biblicism."

Most important, Ro'i's blindness, the blindness that led to his death, was not peculiar to him, as was Samson's—the members of Dayan's audience are blind themselves. Ro'i failed to see things as they are: he failed to see the Arabs waiting to ambush him and kill him, and so he perished. Ro'i was blinded by the light in his heart, a light we all share in some sense. Ro'i's blindness is a blindness to which we Jews all are tempted, Dayan claims, and so we need a Dayan to make us see things as they are, to see the Arabs and their passions and intentions as they are.

The crucial question in the speech is the question of peace versus war, which Dayan reduces to the question of Arab intentions. We have access to these intentions through the accounts of Arab and Jewish actions offered by specific speakers. We assess these accounts by assessing the character of the speaker, and we assess the character of the speakers by reference to the actions that they have performed in the past.

We assess actions in the light of their orientation to things. Dayan's action in the speech is to give us his assessment of Arab intentions. He assesses Arab intentions by pointing to things: to the mutilated body of Ro'i Rotenberg, to the displaced Arab masses seething with hatred for the Israelis from beyond barbed-wire fences, to the ambushers hiding behind the next furrow. Dayan invites us to judge the intentions of the Arabs based on their actions and argues that these intentions are understandable given the consequences of the Israelis' actions.

The fundamental paradox of the speech is that it is not a call for revenge, the traditional and obvious thing to do when a Jew (in Dayan's lexicon, an "Israeli," ישראלי) is murdered by Gentiles:

לא מהערבים אשר בעזה, כי מעצמינו נכקש את דמו של רועי.

Not from the Arabs in Gaza, but from ourselves shall we require the blood of Ro'i.

The purpose of Dayan's speech is to persuade his audience to close its ears to other speeches, to the voices of peace. Those voices tell us nothing true, and so we should listen to nothing they have to say.

In Dayan's short speech all of the five concepts are represented: character appears inasmuch as the credibility of Dayan, chief of the Israeli General Staff, is intended to make us accept his analysis of the Arabs' intentions. Action appears: settlement by the Jews, the murder, Ro'i's mistakes, the mistake in listening to the voice of peace. Dayan shows us these actions by presenting us with sights that, no matter how unpleasant, the mind's eye looks at unblinkingly: the refugees, the body, the fenced-in and armed settlements, all vividly depicted. These are the sights to which Ro'i, but more important we ourselves, were blind: one might almost say that in the land of the blind, the one-eyed Dayan is king.[9]

Dayan counsels us on to whom to listen and to whom to shut our ears. The voices of peace should not be accorded a hearing, Dayan argues, because they ignore the most salient fact: the teeming mass of dispossessed Arab refugees whose hunger for recompense and revenge cannot be satisfied but at best only dulled by time. The young pioneer, Ro'i Rotenberg, fell to marauders from Gaza because he was blinded by the hopes inspired in him by political leaders who held out false expectations of peace.

In this speech we see both art and its limitations. The first step in giving this speech effectively is to be Moshe Dayan, one-eyed veteran of WWII, Palmah officer, hero of the 1948 War of Independence, chief of the General Staff, all traits that Aristotle dismisses in the *Rhetoric* as extratechnical. We see the importance of pointing, of *enargeia*, of letting the facts—the displacement or expulsion of the Arabs, Ro'i's murder, the filthy, teeming refugee camps—speak for themselves.

If Dayan's speech is manipulative, it is so in the way it turns our gaze forcibly toward those things from which we would rather look away. This is an invisible manipulation, because it takes place outside of our field of vision, and we cannot see the manipulating hand in the events themselves.

9. Scharfman, "Biblicism."

Aristotle. *The Art of Rhetoric*. Edited and translated by J. H. Freese. Cambridge, Mass.: Harvard University Press, 1926.

———. *On Rhetoric: A Theory of Civic Discourse*. Translated by George A. Kennedy. Oxford: Oxford University Press, 1991.

Baskerville, Barnet. *The People's Voice: The Orator in American Society*. Lexington: University Press of Kentucky, 1979.

Baumlin, James S., and Tita French Baumlin, eds. *Ethos: New Essays in Rhetorical and Critical Theory*. Dallas: Southern Methodist University Press, 1994.

Bernays, Edward L. *Crystallizing Public Opinion*. New York: Boni and Liveright, 1923.

———. *Propaganda*. New York: Liveright, 1928.

———. *Public Relations*. Norman: University of Oklahoma Press, 1952.

Bessette, Joseph M. *The Mild Voice of Reason: Deliberative Democracy and American National Government*. Chicago: University of Chicago Press, 1994.

Black, Edwin. *Rhetorical Criticism: A Study in Method*. New York: Macmillan, 1965.

———. *Rhetorical Questions: Studies of Public Discourse*. Chicago: University of Chicago Press, 1992.

Blair, Carole, and Davis W. Houck. "Richard Nixon and the Personalization of Crisis." In *The Modern Presidency and Crisis Rhetoric*, edited by Amos Kiewe. New York: Praeger, 1993.

Booth, Wayne. *The Rhetoric of Fiction*. Chicago: University of Chicago Press, 1961.

Churchill, Winston S. "The Scaffolding of Rhetoric." In Randolph S. Churchill, companion volume, pt. 2, to *Youth: 1874–1900*, vol. 1 of *Winston S. Churchill*. London: Heinemann, 1967.

Conley, Thomas. *Rhetoric in the European Tradition*. Chicago: University of Chicago Press, 1994.

Coolidge, Calvin. *Foundations of the Republic*. 1926. Reprint, Freeport, N.Y.: Books for Libraries Press, 1968.

———. *The Price of Freedom: Speeches and Addresses*. New York: Charles Scribner's Sons, 1924.

Della Femina, Jerry. *From Those Wonderful Folks Who Gave You Pearl Harbor: Frontline Dispatches from the Advertising War*. Edited by Charles Sopkin. New York: Pocket Books, 1971.

Diderot, Denis. "The Paradox of the Actor." In *Selected Writings on Art and Literature*, translated by Geoffrey Bremmer, 98–158. London: Penguin, 1994.

Farrell, Thomas B. *Norms of Rhetorical Culture*. New Haven: Yale University Press, 1993.

Fenno, Richard F., Jr. *Home Style: House Members in Their Districts*. 1978. Reprint, with a new foreword by John R. Hibbing, New York: Longman, 2003.

———. *The Presidential Odyssey of John Glenn*. Washington, D.C.: Congressional Quarterly Press, 1990.

————. *Senators on the Campaign Trail: The Politics of Representation*. Norman: University of Oklahoma Press, 1996.

Fuller, Steve. *Philosophy, Rhetoric, and the End of Knowledge: A New Beginning for Science and Technology Studies*. 2nd ed. Mahwah, N.J.: Lawrence Erlbaum, 2004.

————. *Philosophy, Rhetoric, and the End of Knowledge: The Coming of Science and Technology Studies*. Madison: University of Wisconsin Press, 1993.

————. *Science*. Buckingham, U.K.: Open University Press, 1997.

————. *Social Epistemology*. Bloomington: Indiana University Press, 1988.

————. *Thomas Kuhn: A Philosophical History for Our Times*. Chicago: University of Chicago Press, 2000.

Garsten, Bryan. *Saving Persuasion: A Defense of Rhetoric and Judgment*. Cambridge, Mass.: Harvard University Press, 2006.

Garver, Eugene. *Aristotle's* Rhetoric: *An Art of Character*. Chicago: University of Chicago Press, 1994.

————. *For the Sake of Argument: Practical Reason, Character, and the Ethics of Belief*. Chicago: University of Chicago Press, 2004.

Gelderman, Carol. *All the President's Words*. New York: Walker, 1997.

Greenstein, Fred I. *The Hidden-Hand Presidency: Eisenhower as Leader*. New York: Basic Books, 1982.

Habermas, Jürgen. *Knowledge and Human Interests*. Translated by Jeremy J. Shapiro. Boston: Beacon Press, 1971.

————. *The Structural Transformation of the Public Sphere: An Inquiry into a Category of Bourgeois Society*. Translated by Thomas Burger and Frederick Lawrence. Cambridge, Mass.: MIT Press, 1989.

————. *Theory of Communicative Action*. 2 vols. Translated by Thomas McCarthy. Boston: Beacon Press, 1984–89.

Hart, Roderick P. *Campaign Talk: Why Elections Are Good for Us*. Princeton: Princeton University Press, 2000.

————. *Modern Rhetorical Criticism*. 3rd ed. Boston: Pearson/Allyn and Bacon, 2005.

————. *Seducing America: How Television Charms the Modern Voter*. Rev. ed. Thousand Oaks, Calif.: Sage, 1999.

————. *Verbal Style and the Presidency: A Computer-Based Analysis*. Orlando, Fla.: Academic Press, 1984.

Hauser, Gerard. *Vernacular Voices: The Rhetoric of Publics and Public Spheres*. Columbia: University of South Carolina Press, 1999.

Hermogenes. *On Issues*. Translated by Malcolm Heath. Oxford: Oxford University Press, 1995.

Hyde, Michael J., ed. *The Ethos of Rhetoric*. Columbia: University of South Carolina Press, 2004.

Jamieson, Kathleen Hall. *Eloquence in an Electronic Age*. Oxford: Oxford University Press, 1988.

————. *Packaging the Presidency*. 3rd ed. New York: Oxford University Press, 1996.

Johnson, Dennis W. *No Place for Amateurs*. London: Routledge, 2001.

Katz, Elihu, and Paul Lazarfeld. *Personal Influence*. Glencoe, Ill.: The Free Press, 1955.

Kennedy, George A. "The Rhetoric of Advocacy in Greece and Rome." *American Journal of Philology* 89, no. 4 (1968): 419–36.

Kerferd, G. B. "Meaning and Reference: Gorgias and the Relation Between Language and Reality." In *The Sophistic Movement: Papers Read at the First International*

Symposium on the Sophistic Movement Organized by the Greek Philosophical Society, 27–29 September 1982. Athens: Athenian Library of Philosophy, 1984.

Latour, Bruno. *The Pasteurization of France.* Translated by Alan Sheridan and John Law. Cambridge, Mass.: Harvard University Press, 1988.

———. *Science in Action: How to Follow Scientists and Engineers Through Society.* Cambridge, Mass.: Harvard University Press, 1987.

Latour, Bruno, and Steve Woolgar. *Laboratory Life: The Construction of Scientific Facts.* 1979. Reprint, with a new postscript and index, Princeton: Princeton University Press, 1986.

Leff, Michael, and Gerald Mohrmann. "Lincoln at Cooper Union: A Rhetorical Analysis of the Text." *Quarterly Journal of Speech* 60, no. 3 (1974): 346–58.

Lippmann, Walter. *The Phantom Public.* 1925. Reprint, with a new introduction by Wilfred M. McClay, New Brunswick, N.J.: Transaction, 1993.

———. *Public Opinion.* 1922. Reprint, New York: The Free Press, 1965.

Mamet, David. *David Mamet in Conversation.* Edited by Leslie Kane. Ann Arbor: University of Michigan Press, 2001.

———. *On Directing Film.* New York: Viking, 1991.

Mansfield, Harvey C., Jr. *Statesmanship and Party Politics: A Study of Burke and Bolingbroke.* Chicago: University of Chicago Press, 1965.

McGee, Michael Calvin. "'Not Men, but Measures': The Origins and Import of an Ideological Principle." *Quarterly Journal of Speech* 64, no. 2 (1978): 141–54.

———. *Rhetoric in Postmodern America: Conversations with Michael Calvin McGee.* Edited by Carol Corbin. New York: Guilford Press, 1998.

McGinniss, Joe. *The Selling of the President, 1968.* 1969. Reprint, New York: Penguin, 1988.

McKeon, Richard A. "Character and the Arts and Disciplines." *Ethics* 78, no. 2 (1968): 109–23.

McPherson, Harry. *A Political Education.* Boston: Little, Brown, 1972.

Medhurst, Martin J., ed. *Beyond the Rhetorical Presidency.* College Station: Texas A&M University Press, 1996.

Noelle-Neumann, Elisabeth. *Spiral of Silence: Public Opinion, Our Social Skin.* 2nd ed. Chicago: University of Chicago Press, 1993.

Noonan, Peggy. *On Speaking Well.* New York: HarperCollins, 1999.

———. *What I Saw at the Revolution.* New York: Random House, 1990.

Ober, Josiah. "Classical Athenian Democracy and Democracy Today." In *Athenian Legacies,* 27–42. Princeton: Princeton University Press, 2005.

———. *Mass and Elite in Democratic Athens: Rhetoric, Ideology, and the Power of the People.* Princeton: Princeton University Press, 1989.

Orwell, George. *The Collected Essays, Journalism, and Letters of George Orwell.* 4 vols. Edited by Sonia Orwell. 1968. Reprint, London: Penguin, 1970.

Perelman, Chaïm, and Lucie Olbrechts-Tyteca. *The New Rhetoric.* Translated by John Wilkinson and Purcell Weaver. Notre Dame, Ind.: University of Notre Dame Press, 1969.

Popkin, Samuel. *The Reasoning Voter: Communication and Persuasion in Presidential Campaigns.* Chicago: University of Chicago Press, 1994.

Quintilian. *Institutio oratoria* 4 vols. Translated by H. E. Butler. Cambridge, Mass.: Harvard University Press, 1920–22.

———. *The Orator's Education* 5 vols. Edited and translated by Donald A. Russell. Cambridge, Mass.: Harvard University Press, 2001.

Ritter, Kurt, and Martin J. Medhurst, eds. *Presidential Speechwriting: From the New Deal to the Reagan Revolution and Beyond.* College Station: Texas A&M University Press, 2003.

Sabl, Andrew. *Ruling Passions: Political Offices and Democratic Ethics.* Princeton: Princeton University Press, 2002.

Safire, William. *Before the Fall: An Inside View of the Pre-Watergate White House.* New York: Belmont Tower Books, 1975.

Schwartz, Tony. *The Responsive Chord.* New York: Doubleday, 1973.

Segal, Charles. "Gorgias and the Psychology of the Logos." *Harvard Studies in Classical Philology* 66 (1962): 99–155.

Shamir, Jacob, and Michal Shamir. *The Anatomy of Public Opinion.* Ann Arbor: University of Michigan Press, 2000.

Shapin, Steven. *A Social History of Truth: Science and Civility in Seventeenth-Century England.* Chicago: University of Chicago Press, 1994.

Smith, Adam. *Lectures on Rhetoric and Belles Lettres.* Edited by J. C. Bryce. Oxford: Oxford University Press, 1985.

Sugarman, Joseph. *Advertising Secrets of the Written Word.* Las Vegas: DelStar, 1998.

Sullivan, Luke. *Hey, Whipple, Squeeze This! A Guide to Creating Great Ads.* New York: John Wiley, 1998.

Thomas, Francis-Noël, and Mark Turner. *Clear and Simple as the Truth: Writing Classic Prose.* Princeton: Princeton University Press, 1994.

Waldman, Michael. *POTUS Speaks: Finding the Words That Defined the Clinton Presidency.* New York: Simon and Schuster, 2000.

Wardy, Robert. *The Birth of Rhetoric: Gorgias, Plato, and Their Successors.* London: Routledge, 1996.

Webster, Daniel. "A Discourse in Commemoration of the Lives and Services of John Adams and Thomas Jefferson." In *Webster's Great Speeches.* Boston: Little, Brown, 1879.

Wells, Susan. *Sweet Reason: Rhetoric and the Discourses of Modernity.* Chicago: University of Chicago Press, 1996.

Williams, Joseph. *Style: Ten Lessons in Clarity and Grace.* 6th ed. New York: Longman, 2000.

Wills, Garry. *Cincinnatus: George Washington and the Enlightenment.* Garden City, N.Y.: Doubleday, 1984.

———. *Nixon Agonistes: The Crisis of the Self-Made Man.* 1970. Reprint, New York: New American Library, 1979.

Yunis, Harvey. *Taming Democracy: Models of Political Rhetoric in Classical Athens.* Ithaca, N.Y.: Cornell University Press, 1996.